THE GAITSKELLITES

THE GAITSKELLITES

REVISIONISM IN THE
BRITISH LABOUR PARTY
1951–64

STEPHEN HASELER

MACMILLAN

© Stephen Haseler 1969

First published 1969 by
MACMILLAN AND CO LTD
Little Essex Street London WC2
and also at Bombay Calcutta and Madras
Macmillan South Africa (Publishers) Pty Ltd Johannesburg
The Macmillan Company of Australia Pty Ltd Melbourne
The Macmillan Company of Canada Ltd Toronto
Gill and Macmillan Ltd Dublin

Printed in Great Britain by
RICHARD CLAY (THE CHAUCER PRESS) LTD
Bungay, Suffolk

Contents

List of Illustrations		vii
List of Tables		viii
Preface		ix
Chronology of Dates		xi
List of Abbreviations		xiv
1	Left, Right and Centre	1

PART ONE: 1951–7

2	'Bevanism' and the Rise of Gaitskell	19
3	Labour and the 'Shopping-List'	43
4	The Emergence of the 'New Thinkers'	61
5	The Success of the 'New Thinkers'	99
6	The Spectre of Ernest Bevin	112

PART TWO: 1957–64

7	Revisionist Leadership	141
8	The Clause IV Debate	158
9	The Alliance and the Bomb	178
10	The Campaign for Democratic Socialism	209
11	The Modern, Revisionist Labour Party	237
Appendix I	The Constitution of the Labour Party	254
Appendix II	An Amplification of Labour's Aims	266
Bibliography		269
Index		279

List of Illustrations

PLATES

Between pages 128 and 129

Trade Union bosses
  George Brown talks to Sam Watson – *Central Press*
  Tom Williamson and Frank Cousins – *Keystone*
  Ernest Bevin – *U.P.I.*

The rise of Hugh Gaitskell
  With Bessie Braddock – *Keystone*
  With Herbert Morrison – *U.P.I.*
  Elected Leader 1955 – *Keystone*

John Strachey – *Stuart Heydinger*
Roy Jenkins – *Camera Press*
Anthony Crosland – *Camera Press*
The Labour Party of the early fifties – *Keystone*
The Labour Party of the late fifties – *U.P.I.*

The 1959 General Election
  Gaitskell and his wife leave Transport House for an election tour of Essex – *Keystone*
  Gaitskell concedes defeat at the press conference – *Keystone*

Gaitskell in trouble
  Listening to Richard Crossman – *Keystone*
  Hitting back at hecklers – *Keystone*

Gaitskell mends his fences with the Left, 1962 – *Keystone*
Clement Attlee and Harold Wilson on the eve of the 1964 election campaign – *Keystone*

CARTOONS

'Brother Hugh, Brother Hugh, you've written that sinful word again . . . !' by Vicky   *page* 160
'. . . and may I say to Hon. Members opposite me. . . .' by Vicky   *page* 180

   *

List of Tables

1   Chart of Unions' Voting Record 1945–57   30
2   Shadow Cabinet Election Results 1951–5   37
3   Probable Breakdown of Treasurership Votes 1954   39
4   NEC Proposals 1952–61   174
5   Common Market Division   229

Preface

Labour has now been in office for four and a half years. Its very existence as a Government belies the dire predictions of the fifties that it had lost its impetus to govern. The political success of the Conservatives under Churchill, Eden and Macmillan and Labour's own internal wrangling seemed, at one time, to point to political oblivion; but the Party successfully resisted the suicidal tendencies that have plagued it since its inception.

Labour's will to live was strengthened by roots which reached deep into the fabric of British political life. Its tradition of social-democratic reform based upon working-class aspirations was temporarily threatened by extremist ideology more at home with continental political philosophy than with the moderate traditions of the British voter.

Labour was rescued from the threat of extremism by the very forces that brought it into existence – the trade unions. But the trade union Right needed an intellectual justification for its stand against the Left. The Gaitskellite revisionists provided it and in so doing reasserted majority, moderate opinion.

This is the story of the thirteen years in which Labour fought for its survival.

As a doctoral student of politics at the London School of Economics and Political Science I decided to use the opportunity provided by my thesis to explore the characteristics of the Labour Right, the core of the Movement. So much public attention has been riveted upon the dilemmas of the Labour Left by journalists and scholars that the layman may be forgiven for believing that the Left-wing represents more than a minor faction of the Party as a whole. At certain periods the Left has played a crucial role in Labour's development, but normally the Party is governed and controlled by the Right. To understand the contemporary Labour Party one must first understand its Right-wing and particularly its intellectuals, the Gaitskellites.

As well as those who granted me formal interviews I wish to thank all those in the Labour Movement, too numerous to mention, whose time and consideration have enabled me to understand more clearly certain aspects of this subject. I also wish to thank the officers of the British Library of Political and Economic Science for permission to examine and reproduce extracts from the private diaries of Hugh Dalton.

Above all, I wish to express my gratitude to my two PhD Supervisors, Professor Richard Pear, who saw much of the early work in draft form, and Dr Bernard Donoughue, whose own interest and involvement in the subject has been of invaluable assistance to me. My thanks, too, to Miss Norma Percy, Research Assistant to John Mackintosh, MP, for her help with details on the Common Market dispute.

London, 1968   STEPHEN HASELER

Chronology of Dates

1951 March   Bevin leaves Foreign Office. Morrison becomes Foreign Secretary.

       April   Bevan, Wilson and Freeman resign from the Government over rearmament programme.

       October   General Election. Conservatives elected with a majority of 26 seats over Labour.

1952 March   57 Labour MPs defy Shadow Cabinet by voting against Conservative Government's defence statement.

       October   Morrison and Dalton lose their seats on NEC to Wilson and Crossman. Annual Conference decides upon a 'shopping-list' for future public ownership. 'Bevanites' wound up as a formal group following PLP resolution.

       PUBLICATIONS: *New Fabian Essays*; *Socialism: a new statement of principles*; *Facing the Facts* (NEC).

1953 February   *Tribune* 'Brains Trust' to continue as 'Bevanites' resist attempt to close it down.

       October   Annual Conference passes fundamentalist document *Challenge to Britain*. Bevan elected to Shadow Cabinet in ninth place.

1954 April   Bevan resigns from Shadow Cabinet over Labour's attitude to SEATO.

       October   Gaitskell defeats Bevan for Party Treasurer at Annual Conference. German rearmament accepted at Annual Conference by small margin.

1955 May   General Election: Conservatives elected with a majority of 67 over Labour.

       December   Attlee retires from Leadership. Gaitskell elected Leader over Bevan and Morrison.

       PUBLICATION: *Forward with Labour* (manifesto for the General Election).

1956 February   Griffiths elected Deputy Leader over Bevan.
     October   Bevan defeats Brown for Party Treasurership at
                Annual Conference.
     PUBLICATIONS: Crosland's *Future of Socialism*; Strachey's
                Contemporary Capitalism; and Socialist Union's
                Twentieth Century Socialism.

1957 October   Revisionist document *Industry and Society* passed at
                Annual Conference. At same Conference, rejection
                of unilateral nuclear disarmament by 5,055,000
                votes. Bevan supports Gaitskell on the bomb.
     PUBLICATIONS: *Industry and Society* (NEC); *Public Enterprise*
                (NEC).

1958 October   Rejection of unilateral nuclear disarmament at
                Annual Conference by 4,721,000 votes.
     PUBLICATION: *The Arms Race: a programme for World Dis-
                armament* (NEC/TUC).

1959 July   'Non-nuclear club' proposal adopted by NEC.
     October   General Election. Conservatives elected with a
                majority of 107 over Labour. Jay calls for a new
                name for the Party and for a break with the trade
                unions.
     November   Gaitskell asks for an amplification of Clause IV at
                the 'post-mortem' Conference.
     PUBLICATIONS: *The Next Step* (TUC/NEC); *Britain Belongs
                to You!* (manifesto for the General Election).

1960 March   Gaitskell's 'amplification of aims' passed by NEC.
     May   AEU oppose proposed change in Party aims.
     June   TGWU oppose proposed change in Party aims.
     July   NUM and NUR oppose proposed change in Party
                aims. NEC decide not to proceed with a change in
                Party aims. Death of Aneurin Bevan.
     October   Defeat of official defence policy at Party Con-
                ference.
     November   Gaitskell defeats Wilson for Leader in PLP ballot.
                CDS officially launched.
     PUBLICATION: *Labour in the Sixties* (NEC).

1961 February   New defence policy, *Policy for Peace*, published by
                NEC/TUC/PLP.

1961 October   *Policy for Peace* passed and unilateralism rejected at
                Annual Conference. Also, resolution demanding
                removal of American Polaris bases passed.
     November   Gaitskell re-elected as Leader unopposed.
     PUBLICATIONS: *Policy for Peace* (NEC); *Signposts for the
                Sixties* (NEC).

1962 October   Gaitskell makes anti-Common-Market speech to
                Annual Conference.
     PUBLICATION: *Labour and the Common Market* (NEC).

1963 January   Death of Hugh Gaitskell.
     February   Harold Wilson elected Leader.
     October   Wilson makes his 'science speech' to Party Con-
                ference.
     PUBLICATION: *Labour and the Scientific Revolution* (NEC).

1964 October   General Election. Labour win with overall majority
                of 4.
     PUBLICATION: *Let's Go with Labour for the New Britain* (NEC)
     (manifesto for the General Election).

List of Abbreviations

ADM	Annual Delegate Meeting of the USDAW
ASW	Amalgamated Society of Woodworkers
BDC	Biennial Delegate Conference of the TGWU
BISKTA	British Iron, Steel and Kindred Trades' Association
ILP	Independent Labour Party
LPACR	*Labour Party Annual Conference Report*
NEC	National Executive Committee of the Labour Party
NUAW	National Union of Agricultural Workers
NUGMW	National Union of General and Municipal Workers
NUM	National Union of Mineworkers
NUR	National Union of Railwaymen
PLP	Parliamentary Labour Party
TGWU	Transport and General Workers' Union
TSSA	Transport Salaried Staffs Association
USDAW	Union of Shop, Distributive and Allied Workers
UTFWA	United Textile Factory Workers' Association

CHAPTER ONE
Left, Right and Centre

Professor G. D. H. Cole has described socialism as a 'broad human movement on behalf of the bottom dog'. British Labour's distinctive brand of social democracy fits this definition well; born of the need to improve working-class conditions, it has shunned systematised dogma and instead tapped the wells of instinctive human reactions to poverty and injustice. This has been both its strength and its weakness. The lack of a coherent ideology has appealed to the traditional British mistrust of abstract notions, and although Labour's idealistic element has inspired many of its middle-class leaders, the Party's success electorally has depended upon its historical identification with working-class interests. Sidney and Beatrice Webb helped, but it was the trade unions that made Labour a major party of state. Ernest Bevin, not Methodism or Marxism, is Labour's heritage.

The leadership of the Party, however, has traditionally been middle-class. In an attempt to articulate what was at root a social phenomenon – the rise of organised Labour – the Party's intellectuals have constructed elaborate theories and engaged in fratricidal ideological debate. Socialism, in the form of Clause IV of the Party Constitution, was grafted on to the Party in 1918 and, ever since, the historical purpose of representing the less fortunate, although going on apace, has been obscured in an endless debate about the meaning and definition of this term.

Unlike the Conservatives, Labour became obsessed with defining itself and this process came to a head following the defeat of 1951. The post-war search for identity and role started, however, while the Party was in office and the exigencies of government soon appeared to limit its ability to shape the present according to moulds laid down by pre-war socialist aspirations. As early as 1946 certain sections of the Party were already becoming disillusioned at the lack of traditional socialist content in policy and the battle-lines for the fifties began to form.

A certain minimal agreement existed throughout the period of government. The social policy of the post-war years was seen by all wings of the Party as a unifying factor which differentiated it from the Conservatives as did the increase of state power generally. The end of Empire, as witnessed by the independence of India, Burma and Ceylon, and a marginal internationalism in the form of a British commitment to the United Nations provided a solid bedrock of unity upon which all sections of the Party could rely. But this liberal radicalism was only an agreed minimum programme – all else was debatable.

The nationalisation of some of the basic industries (Coal and Civil Aviation, 1946; Railways, Road Haulage and Electricity Supply, 1947; Gas, 1948) also provoked little internal dissension, but was hardly a revolutionary exercise based upon socialist doctrine. It was not even intended as such. The 1945 manifesto proves the point, for most of the industries scheduled for nationalisation were justified upon the technical grounds of efficiency and integration. Although they voted against most of the nationalisation measures, the Conservatives were half-hearted in their condemnation and, for the most part, restricted their criticism to minor points. This, therefore, was hardly the barricades.

Steel nationalisation was another matter. It represented the break-off point between those who supported public ownership as a technical exercise and those who held to it as an article of faith. The implementation of this particular manifesto pledge was one of the few major successes for the Left of the Party. It remained a success in that it became a permanent feature of the Party's programme right through until the Nationalisation Act of 1966. The Right of the Party accepted the Steel proposal, albeit reluctantly, as a necessary gesture to the Left, but initiated a campaign to remove public ownership from the list of Party shibboleths. The history of the campaign forms a large part of this work.

Although important as an issue of the fifties, public ownership was not the primary cause of the internal divisiveness during the period of office. After all the Government faithfully carried out all the promises made at the election and the change involved was seen at the time as a momentous break with the past. To the Left the nationalisation measures of 1945–51, although inadequate, were at least a precondition of further socialist advance. On the other hand, the foreign and defence policies of His Majesty's Labour Government contained no such precondition. It was over this area of policy that the first dramatic upheavals of the Party took place. In a sense the post-war split started and ended on the question of foreign and defence policy. It was not until 1961, and Gaitskell's victory at Blackpool, that the issue was finally resolved.

In the field of foreign policy the third Labour Government was overtaken by events. It was born into a world in which Britain's power was restricted and Soviet influence in Europe grew apace. To cope with this situation Britain's Labour Government was placed in the unenviable position of having to rely upon American power and, in the immediate post-war years, to court it. The difficulty of implementing socialist dogma in this sort of situation, and in a field in which power to act is anyway of necessity limited, was an early lesson for the Party Leadership. Others in the Party were slow to learn – some never did. Consequently the resentment against Ernest Bevin's foreign policy was a major source of Party disillusionment.

Bevin did more than simply pursue a traditional 'national-interest' foreign policy. He injected an ideological element. But it was not a socialist ideology; instead it consisted of a bitter and determined anti-communism. As the countries of Eastern Europe fell consecutively into the Soviet orbit, Bevin's already strongly felt anti-communism, conceived while General Secretary of the Transport and General Workers' Union, was progressively strengthened. The Government, the Parliamentary Party and, surprisingly, the Annual Conference in turn supported his policies if not his attitudes. Labour took Britain into NATO and by the end of its period of office undertook the most ambitious and costly rearmament programme in peacetime.

All this effectively destroyed the traditional socialist concept of neutrality between Western capitalism and Soviet communism and made a mockery of the view held in Conservative circles that Labour's hostility to American capitalism would affect relations between the two nations. The majority of Labour went along with all this and in the process isolated the extreme Left. It was only when the Government's rearmament programme necessitated certain incursions into the free Health Service that the revolt reached serious proportions. Even then the Parliamentary Party remained loyal.

Overriding the specific issues of public ownership and foreign policy was the larger question of the role and direction of the Party. Was it, in effect, a party of power or of protest? In a sense the question was academic. It had been answered by the experience of the post-war years. As to its future, that became a subject which absorbed the Party for most of the fifties and beyond. It was during the life of the Labour Government, however, that the factions which were to carry the debate forward began to emerge in a coherent form.

The Left was the first to become a cohesive force. It existed in 'embryo' form following the formation of the 'Keep Left' group early in the post-war Parliament and it maintained a constant barrage of criticism of Ernest Bevin's foreign policy. The forum for this criticism was limited primarily to Parliamentary Labour Party meetings, but it widened, on occasion, to the Press and public platform. On one occasion it actually spread to the floor of the House of Commons when in March 1947, 80 Labour backbenchers signed an amendment asking the House to reject the Government's Conscription Bill which provided for an eighteen-month period of conscription. Subsequently, 72 Labour MPs voted against the bill on the floor of the House of Commons and the Government finally gave in and reduced the conscription period from eighteen to twelve months. This early example of the Left's flexing its muscles on the floor of the Commons was never repeated during the lifetime of the post-war Parliament. The general direction of government policy remained unchanged and the Left responded with a series of ineffectual revolts. It was only when Aneurin Bevan's resignation from the Government in 1951 provided the Left with a Leader that it became a coherent

and organised force within the Party. The era of 'The Bevanites', however, only obscured what in the long term remained
a diversified and fractured Left.

The Left wing of the Party is difficult to define in any precise
form. It is, and has been, an amalgam of groups and viewpoints. Marxists of one form or another (Communists, Trotsky-
ites, and even Maoists) have played a significant, though
minority, role within left-wing Labour politics. As a philosophical foundation of left-wing thought Marxism has, however, been mixed up with other systems – Christian socialism,
anarchism, syndicalism, pacifism, to name but a few. The 'Left'
frequently referred to in the text below is based upon a combination of all those viewpoints. Owing to the fact that none of
these political attitudes are held either consistently or strongly
enough the orthodox Left is often faced with a fundamental
dilemma regarding the role of political revolution. The Left-
wing of the Party contains 'a good many people who, while
also rejecting revolutions, would like to see the Party do the
sort of thing that can normally be done only by revolutions'.[1]
Most elements of the Left tend to resolve this uneasy conflict in
favour of the 'democratic method' based upon constitutional
proprieties. Indeed, certain members of the Left, particularly
Michael Foot, have some of the symptoms of old-fashioned
'Whiggery' in their attitude towards the sanctity of both
Parliament in general and the floor of the House of Commons
in particular. The Labour Left, more 'constitutional' than
'revolutionary', has carried on the debate within the framework of parliamentary democracy even though the occasional
resolution at Party Conference has been in conflict with this
principle. Except for a brief period in the thirties the fundamentalism of the Left has not been concerned with a challenge
to existing political arrangements even though it may be implied as a precondition to the achievement of its policy aims.
Rather they have sought to change society through the existing
institutions. This 'constitutionalism' has been its primary
weakness in dealing with the Right wing of the Party, which,
within a parliamentary context, has had a logic and a con-
sistency which the Left has lacked. The 'dice were loaded'

1. Editorial in *The Political Quarterly* (Oct–Dec 1964) p. 371.

from the start as the battle was fought on the Right wing's home ground.

The strength of the Right in Labour politics, especially in the 1945–51 period, lay in its appeal to loyalty and Party unity. The moderate leadership of the Party continually tapped the fund of loyalty which existed for it among the large group of trade union MPs. The traditions of solidarity, learnt painfully in the collective-bargaining process of industrial relations, spilled over into the political arena and the political Leadership of the Party became its beneficiaries. Unity was a sacred cow and splitting the Party became the greatest crime in the book; a crime of which many on the Right considered the Left to be guilty. This strident and often authoritarian victimisation of the Left, a permanent feature of the early fifties, was absent during the immediate post-war years. The Government had a comfortable majority, Party unity was guaranteed on all but minor issues and the Left was leaderless. The continual pin-pricks of the 'Keep Left' group annoyed some right-wing MPs but not to the point where the withdrawal of the whip was demanded. The Right, therefore, had little need to combat what, at that time, was a minor protest movement on the Left of the Party. It also controlled the Party apparatus through its large majorities in the Parliamentary Party, the National Executive Committee and the Annual Conference of the Party.

The resignation of Bevan, Wilson and Freeman from the Government in the spring of 1951 changed everything. The Right saw the Party as coming under attack from within and its unity threatened. In response to this danger a powerful informal alliance of trade union leaders (Deakin, Lawther and Williamson), together with many trade union and other right-wing MPs and right-wing members of the Cabinet (and later the 'Shadow Cabinet'), made it their business to ensure the defeat of the 'Bevanites' and what they considered to be a threat to the very existence of the Party.

The Right's response to the growing left-wing challenge in the final months of the Labour Government was uninspiring. It relied for its justification largely upon an appeal to unthinking loyalty and little else. It was left to a numerically small group of right-wing intellectuals in the Parliamentary Party and later in the 'Shadow Cabinet', themselves often distrusted by the trade union Right, to put the positive intellectual case against the aims and methods of the Left-wing. This group (the principal subject of this book) came to be known as the 're-visionists'.

To define the revisionists simply as right-wing intellectuals, as those who gave articulate justifications for the policies and direction of the Labour Leadership, is inadequate. They were certainly 'intellectuals' in the sense that they presented logical and theoretical backing for their views. They were also 'Right-wing' in that they supported the moderate policies of the Leadership and rejected the attacks made on these policies from the Left. They were, however, more than this. The 'revisionists' differed from other right-wing sections of the Party in that they tended to be less stagnant and conservative in their approach and were often radical in their prescriptions. Also, of course, they were predominantly middle class.

Labour Party revisionism was more than a body of men. It was also a body of doctrine. Professor Samuel Beer uses the term 'revisionism' not simply to describe a group of right-wing politicians but to indicate that, as he put it, 'It consisted of a body of doctrine – fairly coherent doctrine'.[1] He rejects the view that revisionism lacked the ideological and doctrinal element of the political thought of other groups in the Party; 'on the contrary, they sought to construct a new theoretical analysis and prescription . . . they too believed that Labour was united by an idea'.[2] Dr Ralph Miliband also uses revision-ism as a useful category to which 'the new leader (Gaitskell) was ideologically and politically committed'.[3] Revisionism was more than a grouping of practical and moderate politicians; it contained an ideology. Even so, some of its distin-guished proponents, particularly those who wielded consider-able political power, reacted (often violently) against such a

---

1. S. H. Beer, *Modern British Politics* (1965) p. 238. In his description of revi-sionist ideology Beer suggests that it 'attacked Socialist ideology at its heart – the doctrine of fellowship' (p. 238). This view does not take account of the fact that one of the central doctrines of the Socialist Union group (a leading revisionist body) was this very idea of fellowship. This is further discussed in Chapter Four.
2. Ibid. p. 236.   3. R. Miliband, *Parliamentary Socialism* (1961) p. 332.

proposition. They considered much of Labour's then current
ideological preoccupation irrelevant to the needs of the mid-
twentieth century but, in effectively destroying it, elevated a
new body of thinking to a system of doctrine.

Revisionism, as doctrine, was not new. The history of
socialism is also the history of revisionism. Marxist revisionism
contained so many elements that an exact precursor of the mid-
twentieth-century British Labour revisionists is hard to find. In
a sense Eduard Bernstein, the German philosopher, started it
all. David Childs, a recent scholar, correctly points out that
'Bernstein's view shows that much of today's "rethinking" is
not really so new at all'.[1] There is a direct link between Bernstein's rejection of Marxism in the nineteenth century, the
Fabians' social engineering of the early twentieth century and
Evan Durbin's economics of the 1930s. Durbin, Gaitskell and
Dalton were already beginning to grope towards a revisionism
tailored to fit British Labour when the war interrupted their
efforts. Durbin and Gaitskell entered Parliament in 1945 with
Durbin already established as a major political theoretician.[2]
His tragic and premature death in a 1948 swimming accident
robbed the Labour Party of an important political as well as
intellectual element. It also deprived Gaitskell of a friend and
stimulating intellectual companion whose political influence
on the future Leader of the Labour Party was to be considerable
and enduring.[3]

The war and the subsequent landslide Labour victory interrupted the progress of Labour revisionism. The experience of
1945–51 also brought nearer the day when a reappraisal
became necessary and although Gaitskell and Dalton were in
the Government, a small group of young back-bench MPs,
notably Crosland, Jenkins, Mayhew and later Healey, con-

1. D. H. Childs, 'The Development of Socialist Thought in the SPD 1945–58.'
(Unpublished PhD thesis, London Univ. 1961.)
2. See particularly E. F. M. Durbin, *The Politics of Democratic Socialism* (1940).
3. Gaitskell wrote an introduction to the above work in which he described the
views of the young group of socialist intellectuals who gathered about himself and
Durbin in the thirties: 'The most fundamental ideal of those who shared this outlook was social justice – but it was an ideal inspired in no way by class hatred.
They were equally devoted to democracy and personal freedom. They believed in
tolerance and they understood the need for compromise. They were for the
rational and the practical, and suspicious of large general ideas.' (ibid.)

tinued yet again the process of questioning traditional socialist ideology. Following the defeat of the Labour Government in 1951 this group was strengthened and led by Gaitskell, now fresh from the constraints of office. Their influence on the Movement in the early years following the 1951 defeat was so marked and their attitude so distinctive that Aneurin Bevan singled them out as 'would-be socialist revisionists. These are people who want to substitute novel remedies for the struggle for power in the state.'[1] Even before the defeat of Labour in 1951 the revisionists were using as an instrument the new right-wing periodical *Socialist Commentary* in order to combat the prolific attacks made upon the Leadership by the Bevanite newspaper, *Tribune*. This exchange intensified following Bevan's resignation.

Caught in the middle of the political crossfire and attempting to hold the ring and reconcile the warring factions was the Prime Minister, Clement Attlee, and a growing yet still small grouping, the centralists. The Centre did not exist in any real form until the late 1950s although the attitudes which produced it were present earlier on. It tended to abdicate from the ideological debate and concentrated instead upon finding formulae (often contradictory in nature) behind which the Party could unite. Harold Wilson was to lead this group in the late fifties, and the manner of his resignation from the Government in 1951 and his subsequent actions already bore the hallmark of his bridge-building political mentality. Although they both resigned over the rearmament programme Wilson's motivation was less ideological than Bevan's. He thought the country could simply not afford its then current defence expenditure whereas Bevan resigned upon an issue of principle and made his dissatisfaction with the Government's overall programme ostentatiously public. Wilson's final break with Bevan came in 1954 when he joined the 'Shadow Cabinet' following Bevan's resignation from it over Labour's acquiescence in the Conservative Government's decision to enter the South-East Asia Treaty Organisation.

While Wilson and a few of his close parliamentary friends were feeling their way towards centralism, Attlee was putting

1. A. Bevan, 'The Fatuity of Coalition' in *Tribune* (13–26 Jun 1952) p. 2.

it into practice. There was never a need for a centralist group
while the Prime Minister and Leader of the Party did its job
for them. Having held together a group of talented and rum-
bustuous politicians for six years, Attlee's skills as a party
manager were second to none. He rarely gave a lead politically
and often seemed uninterested in aims. The unity of the Party
was his primary consideration and he was loath to alienate
sections of it for fear that this unity would snap. His reluctance to disband the 'Bevanites' as an organised group in
1952[1] and his opposition to withdrawing the whip from Bevan
in 1954 confirmed the loyalists' suspicion of him. Arthur
Deakin, the General Secretary of the Transport and General
Workers' Union, openly rebuked Attlee at the 1953 Biennial
Conference of his Union.

> While I was making my speech (at the 1952 Labour Party Con-
> ference) Clem Attlee was on the platform and I looked at him
> and I almost said – perhaps I ought to have done – it should not
> be my job to raise this question. It should be the responsibility
> of the Leader of the party to challenge the antics of these people
> (the 'Bevanites').

This right-wing frustration with Attlee as Leader only rarely
emerged into the open and the Left never overtly called for his
resignation either. The power struggle that was developing
contained itself within levels lower than the Leadership but
nevertheless placed considerable strains upon the institutional
structure of the Party.

These power struggles, a permanent feature of political life
under Attlee's conciliatory party management and Gaitskell's
more positive leadership, were reconciled within the imperfect
structure of Labour's institutional framework, the Annual
Conference, the National Executive Committee and the Parliamentary Labour Party. The ultimate inability of the Party
to reconcile its differing conceptions of socialism and to de-
personalise its power struggles was not a failure of the structure,
however, but rather of the coalition nature of the Party.
Nevertheless, many disputes were both aggravated and in-

---

1. Attlee's call for an end to a 'party within a party' and his sponsoring of a
PLP resolution banning unofficial groups in 1952 was in response to overwhelming
Right and Centre pressure. The motion was carried by 188 votes to 51.

tensified by the diffusion of power centres and by uncertainty as to ultimate sovereignty.

This uncertainty has produced a running debate within the Party concerning the location of authority. It resolves itself essentially into a conflict between those who see the Party as a parliamentary force and those who see it as a broader 'Movement' whose parliamentary wing is secondary and responsible to the 'Government' of the Party, the Annual Conference. The Party Constitution is vague on this point as it states that 'the work of the Party shall be under the direction and control of the Party Conference'. It is not explicit as to whether this means the Party 'in the country' or the Party in Parliament. All sections agree that the mass Party organisation, and its officers, are responsible to the Annual Conference but whether or not this includes the Parliamentary Labour Party (hereafter termed PLP) remains in dispute. Both Labour Party literature and traditional teaching stress that 'The Parliamentary Party carries through its duties within the framework of a policy laid down by the Annual Party Conference to which it reports each year'.[1] The PLP certainly reports to the Annual Conference but only in the sense that its report is voted upon. Conference has no power to determine either its officers, its political strategy or indeed its policies.

When the Party is in government there is no question of the Conference's dictating policy to the Cabinet or to the PLP but in opposition the situation remains confused. Clement Attlee's own conception of the role of the Conference when in opposition illustrates the distinction between legal myth and political reality, an understanding of which is a prerequisite for any student of Labour politics. In 1937 Attlee said that

> The Labour Conference lays down the policy of the Party and issues instructions which must be carried out by the Executive, the affiliated organisations and its representatives in Parliament. . . . The Labour Party Conference is in fact a Parliament of the movement.[2]

This indeed was the accepted legal myth. Attlee's Leadership

1. *The Rise of the Labour Party* (issued by the Party in 1948).
2. C. R. Attlee, *The Labour Party in Perspective* (1937) p. 93.

and Premiership questioned it and Gaitskell's Leadership destroyed it.

If the Annual Conference of the Party is the 'Parliament of the movement', as Attlee suggested, then it is an unrepresentative Parliament. The composition of the Annual Conference is threefold: the constituency and central parties, the trade unions and the socialist and co-operative societies. The latter are unimportant in terms of both membership and votes at the Conference, whereas the trade unions 'represent' a total membership that has varied from 3,038,697 in 1945 to 6,582,549 in 1957, its highest post-war figure. The constituency parties represent on average rather less than one-sixth of the total membership that the trade unions bring into the Party and consequently have voting power commensurate to their strength. The unions, therefore, control the Annual Conference both in terms of policy and of power.

The method whereby many of the larger unions arrive at policy decisions and mandate their delegates has caused considerable controversy. In many cases the unions have a reasonably democratic structure but the low attendance at local branch meetings lessens the representative nature of many of the decisions taken. Also, a small majority at the mandating conference of the union will cause the whole 'bloc' of that union's vote to be cast in favour of the decision taken. A union, by its very nature, represents its active members rather than its large 'sleeping' membership. Although the Left and the Communists benefit from this system disproportionately to their real strength, the block vote of the unions has remained a source of right-wing domination. This inbuilt moderate majority at Annual Conference, although often not reflective of the constituency parties' views, more often than not reflects the feelings of Labour's voters and in so doing saves the Party from the electoral handicap of extremism.

Even so, Annual Conference week is a trying time for the Leadership as it provides a national platform for the Party's fundamentalist wing and public exposure to dissensions and revolts. It is a time for affirmation of faith rather than detailed debate and in such an atmosphere the moderate sections of the Party are automatically at a disadvantage. Nevertheless the

Annual Party Conference serves a supreme purpose: it gives the mass movement the semblance, if not the reality, of power. As such it acts as a 'lightning conductor' and 'safety valve' for extremism.

The Annual Conference elects the National Executive Committee (henceforth termed NEC), which 'shall, subject to the control and directions of the Party Conference, be the Administrative Authority of the Party'.[1] In practice the NEC's responsibility is more than organisational and disciplinary. It possesses an important policy formation and initiation function carried out by its many sub-committees. It is an important power centre, when the Party is in opposition, in between Annual Conferences. It is composed of 28 members, including two *ex officio* members, the Leader and the Deputy Leader of the PLP, and the Treasurer of the Party. The rest of the NEC is divided into four sections: the trade union section elected by trade unions only and comprising 12 members; the socialist, co-operative and professional organisations' sections elected by the whole Conference and comprising 1 member; the constituency organisations' section elected by the constituency parties only and comprising 7 members; and the women's section elected by the whole Conference and comprising 5 members.

The trade unions, who elect their own 12 members directly, control the NEC by virtue of their majority in the whole Conference as the Treasurer, the co-operative member and the 5 women's members cannot be elected without their consent. In effect, therefore, the unions elect 19 of the 28 members of the NEC and, although the individual unions cannot always control their representatives, the NEC is predominantly right wing in character.

Whereas the Conference meets yearly and the NEC monthly, the PLP is continually in being, albeit in an informal manner during parliamentary recess. It is not only its permanent nature that makes the PLP the primary power centre in the Party but also the character of the Labour Party itself. Labour is a parliamentary force committed to the constitutional method and very aware of the dangers inherent in extra-parliamentary

1. See p. 260, Clause VIII (1).

mass-movements. It is this parliamentary 'ethos' rather than the theoretical organisational structure of the Party that ensures PLP dominance. The Party Constitution may hint at PLP subservience to the Annual Conference but in practice this remains another myth. It is the PLP which elects the Leader of the Labour Party, not the Annual Conference, and it is PLP elements which take the lion's-share of decisions regarding manifesto policy and programmes.[1]

The constitutional propriety involved in the independence of the PLP is well understood by the trade union group of MPs. They may act as a cohesive force within the PLP but their loyalty to the parliamentary Leadership transcends their obligations to their unions even though their seats in Parliament may be owed to trade union sponsorship.

This *de facto* supremacy of the PLP over the other power centres in the Party does not lessen the importance of the Annual Conference and the NEC in terms of maintaining party unity. The divergence of the PLP and Annual Conference on questions of policy and leadership when the Party is in opposition can be politically damaging for the Party as a whole and a debate is never resolved until they both come into line with one another. For instance, although in 1960 Gaitskell successfully defended his leadership against Wilson's challenge in the PLP, it was not until the Blackpool Conference and the defeat of unilateralism that his victory was complete and the leadership problem was resolved. Both Attlee and Wilson, as Leaders, have been conscious of the need to keep the power centres of the Party united and in part this explains their similar styles of leadership. Both are party managers.

While Attlee remained Leader the contending policy factions, denied ultimate supremacy, set out their views and staked their claims upon the Labour Party. As with the Left, the revisionists became a 'party within a party' although not so ostentatiously as to vote against the Party or abstain on the floor of the House of Commons. Indeed they had little need of doing so as the Leadership pursued rightist, if not revisionist,

1. The Labour Party Constitution states that 'no proposal shall be included in the Party Programme unless it has been adopted by the Party Conference by a majority of not less than two-thirds of the votes recorded on a card vote'.

policies. Unlike the traditional loyalists in the trade unions, the revisionists were less concerned with discipline than with setting out policy objectives and attempting to rid the Party of what they considered to be dangerous and out-of-date shibboleths.

Revisionists were not unconcerned about their power base however. They knew that they could rely upon the trade unions to maintain the rightist Leadership in power, although not to establish the radical and imaginative leadership that they thought necessary in order to modernise the Party. Hugh Gaitskell's emergence as a major political figure provided this leadership. It served as a focal point for future political action. His election to the Leadership in 1955 was a watershed in Labour Party history, as the revisionists, who previously had been an articulate but small group, became the predominant influence in the Party.

The story of the early 1950s (Part One of this book) is the story of their claim to power. The late fifties and early sixties (Part Two) is the story of their achievement of power and the painful and divisive process of preparing Labour for its electoral victory in 1964.

Part One: 1951-7

CHAPTER TWO

'Bevanism' and the Rise of Gaitskell

The early years of the Labour Party in opposition saw the polarisation of political thinking and the emergence of factionalism. During this period 'Bevanism', as it came to be called, became a major force in both the Parliamentary Party and in the Movement. This new force not only attempted to change the domestic and foreign policies of the Party but also it attempted to control its decision-making centres, and even the central Leadership itself. The right-wing and moderate sections of the Party saw this as a direct threat not only to their own positions but also to the Party as such, and they were quick to respond to the challenge. The leaders of the large trade unions and the bulk of the PLP had, by 1955, restored their authority and also had bolstered this success by ensuring that Hugh Gaitskell (the major revisionist figure in the Party) succeeded Clement Attlee as Leader. The struggle between the 'Bevanites' and the right-wing establishment of the Party is important not only in illustrating the power structure of the Party and the Movement, but also in that it serves to show the firm base of right-wing and moderate opinion that launched the revisionism of Gaitskell.

THE ANTECEDENTS OF 'BEVANISM'

Most of the Left's antipathy to the Labour Government's handling of affairs from 1945 to 1950 manifested itself in ineffectual revolts, which, although they gained a considerable amount of publicity, had no real effect upon official policy. The first major rebellion against the new Government occurred on

18 November 1946 when 53 Labour MPs placed an amend-ment to the address on the order paper of the House of Com-mons, asking for a 'Socialist alternative'[1] to what they con-sidered the otherwise inevitable conflict between American capitalism and Soviet communism. This was the beginning of a continuing battle by left-wing MPs against the foreign policy of Ernest Bevin which raged not only in Parliament but also in the Press and at Party Conferences. A further round in this battle occurred the following year over the conscription plans of the Government – and this met with some success.[2] How-ever, the dissatisfaction with the Government was sporadic, isolated and lacking in coherence. This was changed somewhat by the publication, on 2 May 1947, of *Keep Left*, a pamphlet concerned mainly with a critical analysis of the foreign affairs and defence policies of the Government. It made particular reference to what it called the fallacy of collective security against the Soviet Union, a policy that was a cornerstone of Ernest Bevin's approach to foreign affairs. *Keep Left* was writ-ten by Richard Crossman, Michael Foot and Ian Mikardo, all of whom were later to become leading members of the 'Bevanite' group, and was signed by a further 12 MPs.[3] In 1950 a sequel to this pamphlet entitled *Keeping Left*[4] was pub-lished, but was less neutralist than the previous contribution as it accepted, albeit reluctantly, the American alliance. Its tone was fairly mild on the question of public ownership, although it advocated a much more extensive 'shopping-list' of industries to be nationalised than did official policy.

Although embarrassing for the Leadership these incidents offered little challenge to orthodox control. They did serve, however, to provide a focus for left-wing disenchantment which Bevan's resignation turned into a political force. Indeed

1. *Hansard* (18 Nov 1946) col. 526.

2. Seventy-two Labour MPs voted against a Government bill (in March 1947) to introduce an 18-month conscription period. The Government later reduced the period to 12 months. For more details see J. M. Burns, 'The Parliamentary Labor Party of Great Britain', in *American Political Science Review* (Dec 1950) pp. 865ff.

3. They were: G. Bing, D. Bruce, H. Davies, L. Hale, F. Lee, B. W. Levy, R. W. G. Mackay, E. L. Mallalieu, E. R. Millington, S. Swingler, G. Wigg and W. Wyatt.

4. Signed by: R. Acland, D. Bruce, B. Castle, R. Crossman, H. Davies, L. Hale, T. Horabin, M. Lipton, I. Mikardo, S. Swingler, G. Wigg, T. Williams.

it was only with Bevan's leadership that what Miliband has called 'a fairly loose group of MPs without any hard centre'[1] became a well-disciplined and organised faction within the Party.

BEVANISM

The motives behind Bevan's resignation from the Government in the spring of 1951 are complex. It has been suggested that following the appointments of Gaitskell as Chancellor of the Exchequer and Morrison as Foreign Secretary, Bevan considered that his chances of reaching one of the three major positions in the Government were slim and as a result he resigned in a fit of pique.[2] A more likely explanation however is that Bevan realised that his ability to influence policy had lessened and felt that by resigning he would be free to organise opposition to official Party policy. Although he resigned on a technicality – Gaitskell's imposition of charges for teeth and spectacles – Bevan later broadened the issue to the growing expenditure on rearmament.[3]

Therefore even before the 1951 election a major 'party within a party' had emerged although Bevan and the other resigning ministers, Wilson and Freeman, continued to vote with the Government simply in order to keep it in being.

By March 1952 the full effects of the new faction were being felt. The new Conservative Government's 'statement on defence' provided the rejuvenated Left with a chance to show the strength of its support in the PLP. On 5 March 1952 the House debated the Government's defence statement and the official Opposition placed an amendment to it that read: 'That this House approves the "Statement on Defence, 1952" but

1. R. Miliband, *Parliamentary Socialism*, p. 296.

2. See L. Hunter, *The Road to Brighton Pier* (1959) pp. 32ff. This is not a particularly academic work, but it does throw some light, in private conversations between various leaders of the Party and the author, on Bevan's possible motives during his resignation.

3. It is significant, however, that he had defended the Government's increased rearmament programme, in February of the same year, in a debate in the House of Commons on an Opposition no-confidence motion. See *Hansard* (15 Feb 1951) cols 728-40.

has no confidence in the capacity of Her Majesty's present advisers to carry it out'.[1] The PLP was advised by the Whip's office to vote for the Opposition amendment but to abstain on the government motion. This tactic led to a major set-back when it became obvious that 57 Labour MPs had not abstained on the government motion but had actually voted against it. An interesting sidelight on this challenge to the official Party Leadership can be found in the division-lists. Those MPs defying the whips were not all 'Bevanites'. The hard core of left-wing MPs were on this occasion joined by pacifists and certain 'moderate Left' elements.[2]

The result of this vote was to set in train a public controversy regarding the new 'Bevanite' force that had hitherto been simmering below the surface. The *Daily Herald*, a newspaper loyal to the Leadership which had maintained a silence on the 'Bevanites' for some months, published a vitriolic attack on the left-wing minority[3] and *Tribune*, whose editors at the time were Miss Jennie Lee (the wife of Aneurin Bevan) and Michael Foot, replied by suggesting that the revolt was necessary in order to expose what it called the 'sham-fighting' that was developing between the two front benches.[4]

Another major success for the 'Bevanites' occurred at the Party Conference in the autumn when both Herbert Morrison and Hugh Dalton lost their seats on the constituency section of the NEC to Wilson and Crossman, leaving James Griffiths as the only non-'Bevanite' left on the constituency section. This development caused considerable alarm in the moderate sections of the Party and particularly among the right-wing trade union leaders. The growing publicity given to what Attlee referred to as a 'party within a party'[5] and its consequent

1. *Hansard* (5 Mar 1951) col. 552.

2. For example, pacifists voting against the Government included G. Thomas (MP for Cardiff) and R. Acland (MP for Gravesend). Others included D. Donnelly, C. R. Bence, H. Wilson and W. Padley. For the full list see *The Times* (7 Mar 1952) p. 6, col. a.

3. I.e. 'We must tell Mr Bevan and his supporters that they have set out on a course which will harm the country and imperil the future of the Labour Movement.' *Daily Herald* (6 Mar 1952) p. 6.

4. *Tribune* (7–20 Mar 1952) p. 1.

5. Attlee's week-end speech (London, 11 Oct 1952). This speech is reported in part in *The Times* (13 Oct 1952) p. 2, col. 5.

embarrassment to the Leadership increased the already existing pressure on Attlee to take action.

On 23 October Attlee submitted to a PLP meeting a resolution which stated:

> This Parliamentary Labour Party accepts and endorses the statement of the leader of the Party and calls for the immediate abandonment of all group organisations within the Party other than those officially recognised; it further calls upon all members to refrain from making attacks on one another, either in the House, the Press, or on the Platform.[1]

Of the 239 MPs who recorded their vote at the meeting 188 supported the resolution and 51 opposed it, most of them 'Bevanites'.

The passage of this resolution put an end to Bevanism as a formal, organised parliamentary force although the group and its leader continued to operate both inside and outside the House in an attempt to change Party policy. Bevan contested the deputy leadership election in 1952 and the Left continued to press for increased representation on the NEC and the parliamentary committee of the PLP. It was not until 1954, when the Leadership had narrowly defeated the Left on German rearmament (and Bevan had resigned from the Shadow Cabinet and failed to be re-elected to the NEC by way of the Party Treasurership) that the Left began to lose the ground they had gained in 1952. With the election of Gaitskell as Leader and the desertion of the Left by Wilson,[2] Bevan finally came to terms with the right-wing leadership and the period of intense polarisation ended. Two major factors contributed to the decline of Bevanism: one was the inbuilt right-wing strength in the PLP and the other was the role of the trade unions, and particularly the trade union leadership, as a 'rightist', if not revisionist, force in the Movement.

THE ROLE OF THE TRADE UNIONS

The Labour Leadership could always rely upon the votes of the major trade unions in order to force major political

---

1. *The Times* (24 Oct 1952) p. 8, col. g.
2. Wilson joined the Parliamentary Committee of the PLP in Bevan's place, and against his will, after the latter's resignation in 1954.

decisions through Conference or the NEC. Indeed, it was not until 1960 that the Leadership's grip upon Conference and the NEC failed; and on this occasion it was because of the defection to the opposite side of the Transport and General Workers' Union.[1]

This record of support for official policy was built up during the period of the post-war Labour Government when the majority of unions faithfully backed Bevin's anti-Soviet Greek policy in addition to supporting NATO and the Marshall Plan.[2] In 1950 another attempt by the Left to persuade Conference to reject the increasingly rigid foreign policy of the Government failed at the hands of the major unions.[3] In 1951 however, at the Trades Union Congress, the Government came near to defeat, managing a majority of only 503,000.[4]

Even so, for such a controversial issue the pro-Leadership forces had done exceedingly well. They performed even better at the Labour Party Conference of 1952, when, in a show of strength with the 'Bevanites', a coalition of the Transport and General Workers' Union, the National Union of Mineworkers and the National Union of General and Municipal Workers defeated even a moderately worded proposal calling for a rejection of the rearmament programme on economic rather than moral grounds. The voting was 3,644,000 to 2,288,000, a decisive majority for the Right. Similar victories were attained in 1953 on the numerous proposals for increased nationalisation, and in 1954 on the question of German rearmament.[5]

1. Gaitskell failed to carry the NEC on the issue of Clause IV of the Party Constitution and the Conference on the question of defence policy.

2. An amendment to the Marshall Plan moved at Party Conference in 1948 was defeated by 4,097,000 to 224,000 votes. *LPACR 1948*, p. 200. This formed part of a wide-ranging amendment, moved by Zilliacus, the main burden of which was to call for an end to British dependence on the United States. *LPACR 1948*, pp. 185–6.

3. A mild motion demanding a series of initiatives in order to stop the increasing danger of war was defeated at Party Conference by a huge majority. *LPACR 1950*, pp. 141–50.

4. This was a motion in support of the Health Service Charges imposed by the Government. *TUC Report 1951*, pp. 501–5. In 1950 the TUC had come even nearer to opposing the Government when a resolution opposing the wage-freeze was lost by only 222,000 votes. *TUC Report 1950*, pp. 467–73.

5. The 'Platform' was saved in this debate by the narrow margin of 248,000 votes, and this was only because the Amalgamated Society of Woodworkers' delegation defied their mandate. For further details see M. Harrison, *Trade Unions and the Labour Party Since 1945* (1960) pp. 228–9.

This reservoir of support for official policy in most of the major unions was the product of an innate conservatism coupled with a concern for the unity of the Party. Also a fund of goodwill and an identity of interest existed between some of the key post-war trade union leaders and the then Foreign Secretary of His Majesty's Government, Ernest Bevin. The influence that this former General Secretary of the TGWU exerted on some of the most powerful union leaders is illustrated by Sir William Lawther, the President of the NUM and a member of the TUC General Council for many years:

> During the war when he was bombed out we[1] used to go and see him in the Strand Palace Hotel. Any night we could pop in there and sort things out with him. And when he became Foreign Secretary and moved into Carlton Terrace we still nipped off to chat with Ernie.[2]

There is little doubt that Bevin's influence on many top trade union leaders conditioned their attitude to foreign policy, and this influence continued for many years after his death. Moreover there were certain right-wing attitudes inherent in British trade unionism, irrespective of the influence of Ernest Bevin, which ensured that, in the political arena, the trade unions would follow a moderate and responsible leadership. One of these attitudes was a revulsion against the methods and policies of the Communists with whom they often naïvely identified the social-democratic Left.

The union with the longest history of anti-Communist activity, and also the most moderate politically, was the NUGMW. As early as 1928 Communists were barred from holding office in the union. Furthermore, during the Second World War the union retained its suspicion of the aims and methods of British Communists and consequently was out of sympathy with majority opinion in the Labour Movement.[3] In 1942 the NUGMW Annual Congress defeated a resolution which asked the Government to raise the ban on the *Daily Worker*, and Jack Cooper, later to become General Secretary,

1. 'We' refers to Lawther and Arthur Deakin, General Secretary of the TGWU.
2. Quoted in 'When Cripps Made it Work', by Nicholas Tomalin and David Levitt, in *Sunday Times* (24 Jul 1966) p. 32.
3. See H. A. Clegg, *General Union in a Changing Society* (Oxford, 1964) p. 155, for a more detailed account.

argued the case again in 1945, referring to Communist pressure in the branches of the union as 'rarely of an industrial character'.

This suspicion of communism, and consequent action against it, occurred much later in the TGWU. The union banned Communists from holding office as late as 1949.[1] However, from 1945 to 1947 the Biennial Delegate Conference of the Union, its governing body, along with most other leading unions, repeatedly rejected the 'progressive unity' pleas for Communist Party affiliation to the Labour Party. Arthur Deakin, the General Secretary, was a leading member of the anti-Communist pressure group in the trade union movement. One reason for Deakin's often obsessive suspicion of communism and Communists lay in his experience in inter-war organised labour. His views were confirmed and hardened throughout his active participation in the World Federation of Trade Unions up to 1949 when the TUC, largely under his instigation, withdrew because of growing Communist domination. Deakin's anti-communism also resulted from his suspicion that political motives dominated industrial aims in a dedicated Communist and that this was unhealthy for organised labour. He once said, 'I must emphasise that a Communist is a Communist first and a Trade Unionist second'.[2] Although he was an active and loyal supporter of the Labour Party, in Deakin's list of priorities politics always took second place to industrial affairs and the betterment of the living standards of his members.

Deakin's hatred and suspicion of communism was shared by other notable trade union leaders: for example, Thomas Williamson (NUGMW), William Lawther[3] and Sam Watson (NUM) and Tom O'Brien (National Association of Theatrical and Kine Employees). It was a commonly held belief among many of them that the Left in general, and the 'Bevanites' in particular, were playing into Communist hands by splitting the

1. The initiative for this move came, not from the General Secretary, but from the branches.

2. *Report on XV BDC 1953* (Southsea); *TGWU Record* (Aug 1953) p. 70.

3. William Lawther once went as far as describing Bevan as 'a man with his feet in Moscow and his eyes on 10 Downing Street'. *The Times* (8 Oct 1952) p. 4.

Party. It is possible, however, to over-emphasise anti-communism as a foundation for 'rightism' in the trade union movement. A more fundamental concern of the right-wing trade union leaders was the question of loyalty both to the Party as a whole and the Leadership of the Party in particular.

Solidarity and unity were the first principles of organised industrial labour, and trade union leaders often transferred this concept to the political arena. Indeed there was no greater 'crime' than to be divisive, and this Bevanism had become. It resulted in a concerted union campaign against 'factionalism' in the Party and appeals for unity were coupled with threats of discipline. Williamson summed up the feelings of many of his colleagues:

> A disgruntled group of ambitious individuals have been organising within the party, and have succeeded in forming a recalcitrant faction which now seriously threatens to undermine the unity and stability of the movement. This organisation has been at work for some two years or more ... its methods have been directed towards the undermining of the leadership, and its ultimate objective the usurpation of power. . . . The Trade Union movement cannot stand aside and ignore what is taking place.[1]

Deakin had earlier taken the advantage of his 'fraternal delegacy' to the Party Conference of 1952 to attack the 'Bevanites' for disregarding 'those principles and *loyalties* to which our movement has held so strongly throughout the whole course of its existence'.[2]

Another important factor in post-war British trade unionism was a moderation in policy formulation and a suspicion of radical and adventurous commitments. The leading trade unionists were practical men who believed that when the Party committed itself to a course of action its policies should be well thought out and the necessary ground-work completed. This was the objection that Williamson made to the inclusion of Sugar and Cement in the Party 'shopping-list' for nationalisation in the 1950 election. In 1952 after a further commitment had been made to extend public ownership he wrote an

1. T. Williamson, 'Disloyalty within the Labour Party' in *NUGMW Journal*, vol. 15, no. 11 (Nov 1952) p. 336.
2. *LPACR 1952*, p. 127. (Italics mine.)

articulate and well-argued article for his union journal in which
he attacked 'shibboleths and slogans' and advocated greater
study before extra commitments were entered into.[1]

Therefore, it was an amalgam of a revulsion against communism, natural conservatism and an overriding concern for
loyalty and unity that placed the major unions firmly on the
right wing of the Party during the 'Bevanite' challenge.
However, the 'rightist' unionists were not simply concerned
with affirming their position. Deakin, for instance, continually
reminded the Movement that the unions financed the Party and
supported by this foundation of power he demanded action.
He brought pressure to bear, not always successfully, on his
fellow trade unionists both inside and outside Parliament in an
attempt to wind-up the 'Bevanite' group in 1952 and to expel
Bevan from the Party in 1954. It is a measure of the limitation
of his influence on the union's voting behaviour on the NEC
that he could not persuade a majority to vote in favour of the
expulsion.[2] A major obstacle for Deakin on this occasion was
Attlee's rigid neutrality in the matter. The Leader's inaction
during this period together with his general lack of resolve
against Bevan, persuaded Deakin that a more resolutely right-
wing Leader was needed.

THE 'TRIUMVIRATE'

Deakin alone was not powerful enough to influence policy or
power in the Party. The strength of 'rightism' in the Movement
in this period before Gaitskell became Leader was based upon
a coalition of the NUGMW, NUM and the TGWU. These
three unions provided a hard core of support for official policy
and ensured about two and a third million votes as a foundation upon which to add the other union votes and the constituency votes.[3] Table 1 shows that these three unions failed

1. T. Williamson, 'Social Ownership and Control', in *NUGMW Journal* (Dec
1952) p. 368.
2. E.g. he could not persuade his own Assistant General Secretary, J. Tiffin, to
vote for the expulsion of Bevan in 1954.
3. If 1953 is taken as an average year the votes of the various sections of the Party
are as follows: Constituency and Central Parties, 1,004,685. Trade Unions,
5,056,912. Socialist and Co-operative Societies, 32,225. This information is taken
from *Report of NEC to 53rd Annual Conference of Labour Party, 1954.* For an analysis

to act in unison on a major issue on only one occasion. From the table below the solidarity of the TGWU/NUM/ NUGMW axis is apparent, and by 1955 the Amalgamated Engineering Union seemed to be joining the group. This concerted action had its roots planted much earlier than the period of polarisation in the Party and the 'Bevanite' years simply hardened and invigorated a process that had been under way during the period of Labour Government. This process started with the wage-freeze policy of Stafford Cripps. The economic committee of the TUC, which dealt with the problems arising from the Cripps policy, brought together in alliance the leaders of the general unions (Williamson and Deakin), Lawther and Bowman (of the Mineworkers) and Chester (of the Boot-workers). It was these unions, under the direction and control of their leaders, that managed to keep the wages policy of the Government existent for two years despite substantial opposition from within the trades union movement. This apprenticeship in concerted action later matured into an understanding with regard to the political wing of their activities. No formal machinery was ever set up for consultation between the leaders of the three unions, but there is little doubt that many informal meetings, which had important repercussions on both Party policy and power structure, took place. Reports of these meetings began circulating as early as the 1951 Labour Party Conference after Barbara Castle had succeeded in forcing Emanuel Shinwell off the constituency section of the NEC.[1] There is little doubt, however, that at the Margate Party Conference of 1953 a number of important union leaders were intimately involved in a series of private meetings in an attempt to return Morrison to the NEC.[2] This group, slightly expanded by the addition of Sir Lincoln Evans (Steelworkers) and Jack Tanner (AEU), continued to apply concerted pressure on behalf of Gaitskell for the office of Treasurer of the Party in

of the importance of the NUM/NUGMW/TGWU votes see Chapter Eight on Clause IV and K. Hindell and P. Williams, 'Scarborough and Blackpool', in *Political Quarterly* (Jul–Sep 1962) pp. 306ff.

1. At the Party Conference of 1951, Robert Willis (General Secretary of the London Society of Compositors) denied reports of a meeting. *LPACR 1951*, p. 125.

2. See Lord Williamson, 'Winning the Trade Unions', in *Hugh Gaitskell 1906–1963*, ed. Rodgers (1964) pp. 106–7.

Table 1. Chart of Unions' Voting Record 1945–57[1]

ISSUE	TGWU	NUGMW	NUM	AEU	NUR	USDAW[2]
Pre-Bevanite Period						
1945 Communist Party affiliation to Labour Party	F	F	A	A	A	A
1947 Conscription and a reduction in military commitments abroad	F	F	F	F	F	A
1948 Marshall Plan	F	F	F	F	F	F
1948 Expulsion of Zilliacus and Solly	F	F	F	F	F	A
1949 No confidence in Bevin's foreign policy	F	F	F	F	F	A
Bevanite Period						
1952 Rearmament programme	F	F	F	A	A	A
1953 Extensive nationalisation[3]	F	F	F	?	?	A
1954 German rearmament	F	F	F	A	A	A
1954 Proscription of *Socialist Outlook*[4]	F	F	F	A	F	A
1954 Gaitskell for Treasurer	F	F	F	F	A	F
1955 Unilateralism	F	F	F	F	A	F
1955 Gaitskell for Treasurer	F	F	F	F	A	F
1957 *Industry and Society*	F	F	F	F	A	F

1. Sources: Trade union annual conference reports; *Labour Party Annual Conference Reports*; Harrison, *Trade Unions and the Labour Party Since 1945*. Chart references: F equals a pro-Leadership position, A equals an anti-Leadership position.

2. USDAW did not exist as a union until 1946. It emerged from an amalgamation of the National Union of Distributive and Allied Workers and the National Amalgamated Union of Shop Assistants, Warehousemen and Clerks.

3. There was no single motion on this subject. Instead, a batch of motions was presented to the 1953 Conference advocating nationalisation of individual industries.

4. ANEC decision was taken earlier in the year that persons associated with or supporting *Socialist Outlook* would be ineligible for membership of the Labour Party. Conference was asked to uphold this decision.

1954.[1] This increasingly significant role of the 'triumvirate', and its allies in the less right-wing unions, was nurtured by regular meetings at the TUC General Council and at its various committees and sub-committees.

The members of the 'triumvirate' had little difficulty in persuading the sovereign bodies of their unions to adopt and confirm their political positions. There is little evidence to uphold the view that these leaders were acting against the wishes of either their large dormant membership or their small but active officer corps.

The least secure and consistent union of the three was the NUM. Lawther and Watson[2] often had difficulty in controlling the Scottish and Welsh areas which had a history of industrial militancy and political radicalism. Also, the difficulties of moderate leadership were increased when Arthur Horner, a Communist Party member, became General Secretary.[3] Bevan seized on the relatively insecure base from which the NUM leaders worked after he had been defeated for Treasurer in 1954: 'We are not going to be bullied, we are not going to be intimidated by individual trade union leaders (just a handful of them) . . . I say to Ernest Jones, "In the votes you gave this week you did not represent the miners of Britain".'[4] Nevertheless, despite Bevan's contention that the miners' leaders were not representing rank-and-file opinion, the Annual Conference of Delegates, which is the major decision-making body of the union, at no time supported a 'Bevanite' view. It can also be argued that because the NUM, unlike the other 'big 6' unions, decided on nomination for the NEC at conference rather than executive level their vote on the Treasurership issue in 1954 more accurately reflected 'grass-roots' opinion than did that of the other unions.

Deakin had a far easier time in persuading the TGWU to

1. Information on this was presented to this writer by Lord Williamson in an interview in the House of Lords, 4 Aug 1966.

2. Sam Watson was the NUM's representative on the NEC of the Labour Party.

3. For an account of Horner's battles with Lawther and Watson, see A. Horner, *Incorrigible Rebel* (1960).

4. Reported at a *Tribune* meeting. *The Times* (4 Oct 1954) p. 5, col. c. Ernest Jones had succeeded Will Lawther as President of the Miners' Union.

accept right-wing policies than had Watson and Lawther with the Miners. He was aided in this by the fact that the TGWU had a Biennial Conference and he was not therefore subjected to annual pressures as were the other union executives. Nevertheless, there was genuine respect at 'grass-roots' level for Deakin himself and for the political position he adopted. We have already seen how the initiative to ban Communists from holding office in the union came from the branches and not the Executive; in his long term of office there was only one attempt to reprimand the General Secretary for his actions. This occurred at the Biennial Delegate Conference (BDC) of the Union in 1953 when a motion was proposed 'that this Conference dissociates itself from the utterances of the General Secretary at the Labour Party (1952) Conference and in his speech at Bristol on 28 February 1953'.[1] These two speeches had been among the most controversial of his career. He had threatened, as his opponents read it, to withdraw financial support from the Party unless the 'Bevanites' were disciplined. In his speech opposing the above motion he openly criticised Attlee for his lack of resolution in dealing with Bevan's disloyalty. It is a measure of Deakin's control over his Conference that this motion, critical of his leadership, was overwhelmingly defeated with only 6 delegates out of 700 voting for its acceptance.[2]

The NUGMW has been the most moderate and right-wing orientated of the 'inner three', and it has also had a record of non-militancy in industrial problems.[3] Martin Harrison, the foremost scholar in this field, has no reservations in saying that this reflects 'grass-roots' opinion. NUGMW leaders when they vote on policy at the Party Conference 'are faithfully reflecting Congress which, until 1959,[4] had not adopted one resolution deviating from Party policy since 1945'.[5] The most spectacular example of the NUGMW's 'safeness' as a union took place in

1. BDC Report, *Transport and General Workers Record* (Aug 1953) p. 76.
2. *TGWU Record* (Aug 1953). *Report on XV BDC*, p. 76.
3. For more details on this see Clegg, *General Union in a Changing Society*, pp. 193ff.
4. Here he is referring to the decision of the NUGMW Congress to vote in favour of unilateral disarmament by 150 to 126 votes. This was later reversed by a 'recall' conference.
5. Harrison, *Trade Unions and the Labour Party*, p. 152.

1954 on the issue of German rearmament. At a time when even those elements in the Party who supported official policy were accepting *regretfully* the necessity for German rearmament, the NUGMW Congress went on record decidedly and unequivocably in favour of it. By the huge margin of 237 to 78 the Congress passed a motion stating that 'it is *imperative* that Germany should make a contribution to the armed forces of the West'.[1] The German rearmament issue was the nearest that the Party Leadership came to being defeated in the fifties. Even so the NUGMW remained stubbornly and overwhelmingly loyal.

Outside the NUM/TGWU/NUGMW axis some of the other 'big 6' unions contained elements of 'rightism'. The AEU fluctuated considerably in its political attitudes from 1945 to 1955 and the large Communist element on its sovereign body[2] combined with the left-wing Socialists to commit the union on many occasions against the Government and Leadership. By 1955 the moderate leadership of William Carron, Jack Tanner and Ben Gardner[3] had steered the union into less troubled waters. It voted against unilateralism (1955) and in favour of *Industry and Society*, the moderate policy statement on public ownership (1957). Even so the AEU could never automatically be counted upon as a 'loyalist' union. The two other big unions, USDAW[4] and the NUR, have also had fluctuating records although they remained consistently 'Bevanite' in the early fifties. The Right therefore could never rely upon the 'big 6' as a block vote, but as long as the inner core of the 'triumvirate' remained firm they could usually expect to carry the day at Party Conference.

The 'triumvirate' was important not only because it provided a secure base for Ernest Bevin's foreign policy and Morrison's policy of consolidation at home, but also because it

---

1. *NUGMW Journal* (Jul 1954) p. 204. (Italics mine.)

2. On average a Communist or 'fellow-travelling' motion can gain between 10 and 19 votes on the National Committee of 58 members.

3. President, Past-President and General Secretary respectively.

4. USDAW voted against unilateralism in 1955 and in favour of *Industry and Society* (1957). Later it was to come very much under the personal influence of its President, Walter Padley, a Centralist in party terms but also a dedicated anti-Communist.

became the launching-pad for Gaitskell's rise to power in the
Party.

THE RISE OF GAITSKELL

It was inevitable that the Right-wing and moderate elements
would succeed in electing the Party Leader from amongst their
own ranks. The power-structure of the Party was inherently
anti-Left and therefore Bevan's candidature was never realistic, at least as an attempt to grasp the Leadership.

Although the PLP is the final arbiter in the election of a
Leader, success with Conference and the NEC can be of vital
importance to a candidate. As far as the Party Conference is
concerned, we have seen how the union votes had always
rubber-stamped rightist policies. The unions' control over the
NEC[1] has been, theoretically at least, as complete as it has
been over Conference. During the 1950s NEC membership
varied between 27 and 28 members (it was enlarged after 1953
when the Deputy Leader was made a member) and in practice
19 out of the 28 are dependent upon trade union support. This
is perhaps as it should be, since, after all, the unions not only
dominate Conference in terms of delegates but also hold the
purse strings. As the NEC takes vital decisions about finance
and the employment of personnel it is reasonable that the largest
shareholder should be adequately represented on the Board of
Directors.

Union control of the NEC was therefore reasonably guaranteed although the leaders of the big unions did not always have
it all their own way. There remained pockets of resistance. For
instance, in the early fifties the union leaders found it fairly
difficult to control the voting behaviour of their own representatives on the NEC in a 'month-to-month'[2] manner.[3] The
women members also acted.

1. For a complete history of the composition of the NEC see R. T. McKenzie,
British Political Parties, 2nd (revised) ed. (1964) pp. 516ff.
2. The NEC meets once a month.
3. Deakin was unable to influence enough trade union and women's section
support on the NEC for the expulsion of Bevan in 1954.

fairly independently of union policy.[1] This did not mean that
the average NEC was rebellious and left-wing.[2] In fact throughout this period the NEC reflected right-wing strength in the
movement, for on no occasion did the combined 'Bevanite'
and left-wing grouping (even including the emerging centralist,
Wilson) reach above 8 of the 28 members.

Right-wing domination of the Parliamentary Committee of
the PLP (hereafter referred to as the 'Shadow Cabinet') was
even more marked than of the NEC. The 'Bevanites' at no
time had more than one of their number on the Shadow
Cabinet – in 1952 and 1953 it was Bevan himself – and as
Table 2 shows most of the leading right-wingers in the PLP
were elected with unfailing regularity.

The Leader of the Party (in this respect, technically the
Chairman of the PLP), the Deputy Leader (Deputy Chairman)
and the Chief Whip also sat on the Shadow Cabinet as elected
officers.

With both the major power centres in the Movement so
solidly right-wing, both Morrison and Gaitskell could expect
to be in strong positions from which to launch themselves into
the Leadership when Attlee resigned. Morrison had been a
leading figure in both the PLP and the Movement as a whole
since 1929 but Gaitskell's rise in the post-war years was, by
comparison, meteoric.

Gaitskell owed his strength in the PLP at this time to his governmental experience from 1945 to 1951. In May 1946, after a

1. There is good evidence to suggest, however, that Mrs Eirene White lost her
seat on the women's section of the NEC because of certain trade union leaders'
antipathy to her conciliatory position regarding 'Bevanism'. Mrs White withdrew
from the contest in 1952, after it had become apparent that she would not win,
and issued the following statement: 'I have good reason to think that the leaders
of some of the larger unions have decided that a person of my moderate views is
not acceptable to them on the Executive.' This statement appears in Hunter,
Road to Brighton Pier, p. 109.

2. An average year was 1953-4. The following members of NEC were 'rightists':
P. Knight (NUS), W. A. Burke (USDAW), E. G. Gooch (NUAW), H. Earn-
shaw (UTFWA), A. Tiffin (TGWU), S. Watson (NUM), J. Haworth (TSSA),
G. Epingham (ASW), J. Cooper (NUGMW), D. Davies (BISKTA), J. Griffiths
(Constituency), Mrs M. Herbison, A. Bacon, E. Summerskill, J. Mann and
J. Horam (Women's Section), Greenwood (Treasurer), Attlee (Leader of PLP),
Morrison (Deputy Leader of PLP), and A. Skeffington (Co-op. Section) These
total 20 in all.

few months as a back-bench MP, he was appointed Parliamentary Secretary to the Ministry of Fuel and Power and later, following the fuel crisis of 1947, he became the Minister.[1] After the General Election of 1950 he was made Minister of State at the Treasury with special responsibility for economic affairs and carried out much of the work of the Chancellor, Stafford Cripps. His rapid rise was due partly to exceptional intellectual and administrative ability but also to the influence that Hugh Dalton wielded on his behalf. Dalton had first come into contact with Gaitskell when they both worked in the New Fabian Research Bureau in the early 1930s. Later, Gaitskell had been Dalton's personal assistant when he was Minister of Economic Warfare during the Second World War. As a result of his forced resignation from the Chancellorship in 1947 following a Budget 'leak', Dalton concentrated on furthering the careers of young and able politicians. Many of those later to become the leading revisionists of the Party had close associations with Dalton in the early years of the war.[2] Possibly because he was older than the others, Gaitskell appeared as the most likely to succeed in a big way. A token of the faith that Dalton had in him can be seen from this letter written while Gaitskell was still a Minister of State at the Treasury: 'And opportunity is carrying you forward on a great wave, and your future is taking on, more and more, the inevitable shape . . . that we spoke of . . . and that I spoke to the P.M. of . . . before you took your present title'.[3]

One month later, in October 1950, Gaitskell became Chancellor of the Exchequer during the difficult period of the Korean War and the resultant rearmament programme. His policy of imposing charges for teeth and spectacles in his 1951 Budget was unpopular, but it paid political dividends. Gaitskell came to be associated with anti-Bevanism when Bevan chose to resign on the specific issue of the National Health

1. A first-hand account of this period of Gaitskell's career is given by Douglas Jay in 'Civil Servant and Minister', in *Hugh Gaitskell 1906–1963*, ed. Rodgers, pp. 77ff.

2. Particularly Crosland, Jenkins and Healey. See H. Dalton, *High Tide and After* (1962), for numerous examples of Dalton's interest in the future careers of young revisionists.

3. Hugh Dalton to Hugh Gaitskell, 2 Sep 1950 (unpublished Dalton papers).

Service charges. In the public eye Gaitskell and Bevan represented the warring factions of the post-war Labour Party.

Table 2. SHADOW CABINET ELECTION RESULTS 1951–5[1]

	1951[2]	1952	1953	1954	1955
J. Griffiths	*	194	180	170	186
H. Gaitskell	*	179	176	170	184
F. Soskice	*	111	168	164	..
H. Dalton	*	140	159	147	..
J. Ede	*	189	134	125	..
A. Robens	*	148	133	140	148
Dr E. Summerskill	*	130	129	142	133
P. Noel-Baker	*	121	118	125	100
J. Callaghan	*	137	160	124	148
G. Hall	*	113	106	121	..
A. Bevan		108	126	..	118
H. Wilson		..	..	120	147
E. Shinwell	*	124	108	126	..
A. Greenwood	*	..	..	..	91
R. Stokes	*	..	..	..	77
G. Brown		..	..	..	101
G. R. Mitchison		..	..	..	76

Following the defeat of the Party at the General Election of 1951 Gaitskell continued to win high positions in the poll for the Shadow Cabinet. He rose steadily from third place in 1952 to joint first with James Griffiths in 1954. At the same time his main political competitor, Morrison, had had an unsuccessful period as Foreign Secretary and because of his position as Deputy Leader had not been subjected to the annual 'opinion polls' of the Shadow Cabinet elections.[3]

Although Gaitskell's standing was high in the PLP the decisive breakthrough for him came with the aid of the unions. Until 1954 Gaitskell had achieved little success at Party Conference and had been defeated when nominated for a position on the constituency section of the NEC. With the death of Arthur Greenwood in June 1954, a vacancy occurred on the

1. Sources: *The Times*, 14 Nov 1951, 20 Nov 1952, 6 Nov 1953, 19 Nov 1954. Also *NEC Reports*, 1951–5.
2. The voting details were not announced in 1951. Those elected are indicated by an asterisk.
3. However, Morrison had defeated Bevan for the Deputy Leadership of the Party on 22 Oct 1953.

NEC by way of the Treasurership of the Party. This post was elected by the whole Conference and the unions therefore would determine the outcome. It was Gaitskell's newly developed ties with the 'triumvirate' of right-wing trade unions that, with added support from the AEU, ensured him the post.

The contest for the Treasurership, in itself an insignificant position, was the beginning of a fusion between the revisionism of Gaitskell and his associates and the loyalism and moderation of the major trade unions. This alliance controlled the Party for the rest of his lifetime and was only temporarily breached in 1959 and 1960 over Clause IV. Ironically it was Bevanism that forged this partnership for although Gaitskell had a number of leading contacts in the trade union movement who were impressed by his qualities,[1] it was his vitriolic attacks on Bevanism in 1952 which illustrated his identity of interest with the union leaders. Deakin, in particular, was impressed by a statement of Gaitskell's at Stalybridge following the Morecambe Conference of 1952:

> A most disturbing feature of the conference was the number of resolutions and speeches that were Communist-inspired, based not even on the *Tribune* so much as the *Daily Worker* . . . the Communist Party has now adopted a new tactic of infiltration into the Labour Party. I was told by some observers that about one-sixth of the constituency party delegates appear to be Communists or Communist-inspired. This figure may well be too high; but if it should be one-tenth or even one-twentieth it is a most shocking state of affairs to which the NEC should give immediate attention.[2]

Gaitskell's attack on Communist infiltration in the constituency parties, his call for discipline and his isolation of the 'Bevanites' as 'a group of frustrated journalists'[3] was identical with much right-wing trade union sentiment and it warmed the hearts of Deakin, Lawther and Williamson. Gaitskell's 1952 outburst, together with his personal history of articulate anti-Bevanism

1. Sam Watson (NEC representative of the NUM) met Gaitskell through Dalton when he and Dalton were on the NEC during the war. Also, Gaitskell had made many contacts with the unions' leaders when he was Minister of Fuel and Power.
2. *The Times* (6 Oct 1952) p. 6.
3. Ibid.

as Chancellor of the Exchequer, gave him the vital support he needed when the Treasurership of the Party fell vacant.

With the death of Arthur Greenwood, Gaitskell automatically became the candidate of the right-wing trade unions for the post that was to be filled at Party Conference in the autumn. However, it was only after Bevan had announced that he had decided to withdraw from his secure constituency-section seat in order to contest the Treasurership that the vacancy assumed importance. Bevan's action and the announcement of Gaitskell's candidacy served notice on the Party that the battle for this unimportant post was to become a trial of strength in power terms between the Right and the Left of the Movement. Gaitskell, an 'intellectual' and a 'revisionist', quickly became the symbol of the amalgam of forces that were arrayed against Bevan from the Right of the Party. This backing proved too strong for the Left and the result of the ballot was a more than two to one victory for Gaitskell over Bevan (by 4,338,000 votes to 2,032,000).

An analysis of this result further illustrates the inherent strength of the right-wing trade unions when an open vote of the whole Conference is recorded. It has been estimated that the constituency vote, on this occasion, split two to one in favour of Bevan[1] but this did not offset the huge support that Gaitskell received from the unions. Table 3 shows how in the smaller unions too, Gaitskell probably had a majority.

Table 3. PROBABLE BREAKDOWN OF TREASURERSHIP VOTES 1954[2]

	Gaitskell	Bevan
'Big 6' votes	3,010,000	634,000
	(NUGMW, AEU, TGWU, NUM)	(NUR, USDAW)
'Other union' votes	990,000	766,000
Constituency votes	300,000	600,000
Total vote	4,300,000	2,000,000[3]

1. See Harrison, *Trade Unions and the Labour Party*, p. 316.

2. This is a 'probable' estimate because, although the voting pattern of the 'big 6' can be verified (Harrison, and *The Times*), the constituency ratio, and therefore the 'other union' ratio, is less accurate.

3. Both these totals are to the nearest 100,000 for purposes of clarification. In actual fact Gaitskell received 4,338,000; Bevan, 2,032,000.

The importance of this achievement for Gaitskell soon became apparent, as not only did it guarantee him a place on the NEC, but also it enabled him to speak from the platform at Party Conference. This exposed Gaitskell for the first time since 1951 to the limelight of a full national platform. The following Party Conference in 1955 was as near a 'convention', in the American sense, as anything that the Movement has experienced before or since. Gaitskell took advantage of this unique situation by elaborating, in a winding-up speech to a debate on the nationalised industries, his own particular attitude to socialism.[1]

This speech was a breakthrough, in terms of personality, for a political figure who had previously been considered lacking in leadership and charismatic qualities. Therefore by 1955, on the eve of Attlee's retirement, Gaitskell not only had overwhelming support in the parliamentary section of the Party but had added to that a mass backing in the Movement. Gaitskell had succeeded Morrison as the major right-wing figure at Conference and in so doing enlarged the power-base for revisionism. His victory over Morrison for the Leadership was to complete the process.

It was only after he became Treasurer that Gaitskell appeared as a possible contender to succeed Attlee. Indeed, as late as 21 December 1954, Deakin and Gaitskell had agreed actively to support Morrison's candidature.[2] However Attlee continued as Leader for yet another year and during those twelve months a concentrated campaign was launched, mainly by Dalton,[3] to bring younger men into the Leadership of the

1. 'I would like to tell you, if I may, why I am a Socialist and have been for some thirty years. I became a Socialist quite candidly not so much because I was a passionate advocate of public ownership but because I disliked the class structure of our society, because I could not tolerate the indefensible difference of status and income which disfigures our society.

'I hated the insecurity that affected such a large part of our community while others led lives of security and comfort. I became a Socialist because I hated poverty and squalor.' *LPACR 1955*, p. 175.

2. This was at a meeting at the Howard Hotel. See Lord Morrison of Lambeth, *Herbert Morrison: An Autobiography* (1960) p. 292.

3. Dalton resigned from the Shadow Cabinet on 3 June 1955, and in his letter of resignation to Attlee said, 'it is essential in my view, that, from the start of the new Parliament there should be a much younger Shadow Cabinet'. Quoted from the unpublished Dalton Diaries and *The Times* (4 Jun 1955) p. 6 (*continued on p. 41*).

Party. This campaign, coupled with the loss of the General Election in May 1955, tended to add momentum to Gaitskell's candidacy. There is little doubt that Attlee's continuing as Leader until December 1955 helped Gaitskell, particularly in view of the youth campaign. Morrison certainly took this view,[1] a tenable one inasmuch as the age factor does appear to have been decisive in Gaitskell's selection.

On 14 December 1955 Gaitskell became Leader of the Labour Party with 157 votes to Bevan's 70 and Morrison's 40. It was a sea change. The new Leader gave revisionism and the revisionists the important and decisive role which they had hitherto lacked. With Attlee as Leader, revisionism had been only one of the many pressures on the Leadership. Although Attlee's political philosophy was of a mild social-democratic nature and his programmes were moderate at election time, he had been reluctant to take action against Bevanism. He had also seen his role as Leader to be that of a conciliator between the various factions in the Party. Gaitskell was to adopt a very different approach to the method and style of political leadership.

The rise of Gaitskell in the Party was a major factor in the general advance of socialist-revisionism. It seemed inevitable that a moderate would have succeeded Attlee in any case, but not necessarily someone schooled in revisionist political attitudes. Morrison, on the other hand, although remaining within a general right-wing framework, would probably have provided a very different type of leadership. He would have been old-fashioned, concerned more with restricting the influence of the Left in the Party than with widening political horizons through the encouragement of new thinking. Nevertheless Morrison's role as a bulwark against the Left in the early 1950s was highly significant. Without it the advance of revisionism would not have been possible.

Morrison may have been a wet blanket as far as new thinking

Even after the new Shadow Cabinet had been elected – and produced a younger average age – Dalton was still not satisfied with the speed of the process. On 26 June at Skegness he declared that the average age of the newly elected Shadow Cabinet was still 'a bit high' and hoped they would reduce their average age further (sic). *The Times* (27 Jun 1955) p. 2.

1. See Morrison, *Autobiography*, p. 293.

was concerned but his stagnant and conservative approach was nevertheless a bulwark against the Left. It gave the Party time to rest and re-evaluate itself. Morrison's stalwart defence of Labour's traditional moderation, although not exciting, kept the Party wedded to power and saved it from plunging headlong into extremism. While Morrison was in charge of home-policy planning, Labour's manifestos were dull but safe.

In the years following the General Election defeat of 1951 the Left concentrated its guns upon the public-ownership front and achieved a minor success in establishing a 'shopping-list' principle for nationalisation in Labour's future programme. The seeds of this particular controversy were sown in the final years of the Labour Government when most of its major proposals for nationalisation had already been carried out. Morrison, unlike the revisionists, offered nothing new, but fought a rearguard action against growing demands from the Left for a greater commitment to public ownership.

CHAPTER THREE

Labour and the 'Shopping-List'

MORRISON AND 'THE SHOPPING-LIST'

By 1949 most of the proposals for public ownership outlined in Labour's policy document of 1945, *Let Us Face the Future*, had been put into effect.[1] The Party was then faced with the question of how it was to proceed in formulating policy for the next five years. Herbert Morrison was given charge of drafting a policy for the coming election. In this task he worked closely with Michael Young, the Head of the Research Department at Transport House, and also with the TUC, but the style and policy of the resultant document was essentially his. *Labour Believes in Britain*, as the document was called, saw the beginnings, in a mild form, of a split between the Leadership and the Left on the question of public ownership. This discord continued from 1949 until 1953 and centred around a host of policy proposals concerning nationalisation issued by the National Executive Committee. A distinctive feature of the period was a growing concern with the question of how many and what sort of industries should be included in a public-ownership proposal. This approach became known as the 'shopping-list' attitude to public ownership. Morrison, and the right-wing Leadership and unions, tended to favour a shorter 'shopping-list' whereas the Left advocated a vast increase in the number of industries that should be included.

The amount of nationalisation proposed therefore became the criterion whereby Left and Right in the Party could be identified. Terms such as 'consolidation' and 'expansion'

---

1. The Steel Nationalisation Bill went through Parliament in 1949, but the industry remained in private hands because of a delayed vesting-date.

came to be used as synonymous for Right and Left. *Socialist Commentary* illustrated this tendency in its editorial of January 1950:

> Two factions have come into existence, 'the expansionists' – those who want to maximise nationalisation, and 'the consolidationists' . . . without much examination the premise is being accepted that it is the right who are putting the brake on nationalisation and those on the left who want to forge ahead.

But as *Socialist Commentary* suggested, the division in the Party was not really that simple. For instance, although opposed to the 'shopping-list' philosophy Morrison was never in favour of dropping public ownership altogether. Instead he preferred to use another more general method of advancing public ownership. He and many others on the Right preferred a system in which broad criteria were advanced as a justification for public ownership and no specific industries were named. It is sometimes argued that Morrison adopted the 'broad criteria' approach in order to force the Party into accepting less nationalisation. This seems valid when his attitude to socialism is analysed.

Morrison considered that the need to work within the democratic process was more important than all other values including the social and economic ones embodied in socialist doctrine. He was never strictly a revisionist. It is doubtful whether he saw clearly the changed nature of capitalist society and the irrelevance of much of traditional socialist thinking. Morrison's rightism consisted of a rigid adherence to his own particular concept of 'responsible' government which would only advance at the pace dictated by the electorate. He summed up this attitude best in his 1950 speech to Party Conference:

> The art of government is not making general propositions and running them like a steamroller over all the members of the population. We are dealing with human beings. . . . If we seek to build a new society successfully . . . what is desirable is the conscious and willing co-operation of the population. Indeed that is democracy; any other system is not democracy.[1]

This passage shows not only his distrust of theoretical politics

1. *LPACR 1950*, p. 112, col. 1.

but, more important, his kinship with the British democratic and parliamentary tradition. Morrison was a democrat first and a socialist second.

Another aspect of Morrison's political thinking which could point to a genuine reluctance to proceed with major extensions of public ownership was his interpretation of the aims of socialism. In his view the five ultimates of British socialism were: peace, a better standard of living for all the people, full employment, greater equality and social justice, and an active and vigorous democracy.[1] Public ownership would have its part to play in the realisation of these ends, but Morrison remained indifferent to the theoretical proposition that common ownership and the transfer of economic power to the people was a prerequisite of a socialist society. In this respect only can he be identified as a revisionist of the Gaitskell–Crosland school. His lower-middle-class background, his distrust of theoreticians and his ability to emotionally, rather than intellectually, identify with the working class were the major factors that separated him from the 'new thinkers' of the Right. Both Morrison and the revisionists, however, were lumped together by the Left as timid and unexciting moderates and as right-wing 'consolidationists' in the field of public ownership. Morrison was indeed the main proponent of right-wing and moderate thinking during this period as he was intimately involved in the drafting and presenting of Labour policy documents and manifestos. The first of these, already mentioned, was *Labour Believes in Britain*, the policy document for the 1950 election.

LABOUR BELIEVES IN BRITAIN

Labour Believes in Britain was published by the NEC in April 1949 and accepted by Conference in Whitsun of the same year. The list of industries proposed for outright public ownership was naturally smaller than that presented in the 1945 campaign, but included Water, Cement, Sugar, Sugar-Refining, Meat Wholesaling and a fairly radical proposal – the nationalisation of Industrial Assurance. This latter proposal was later

1. *LPACR 1949*, p. 153, col. 2.

watered down to one in which Industrial Assurance was to be mutualised. The document also stated that 'appropriate sections of the Chemical Industry' would be brought under public ownership 'if it should prove necessary in order to assure vital national interests'.[1] Although Steel was retained in the programme it was a hang-over from the principles of 1945 rather than a radical new departure.

That *Labour Believes in Britain* caused little controversy or left-wing resentment is surprising. Not only was the 'shopping-list' fairly short but also a new concept was introduced that later on in the fifties was to lead to heated debate. In the section of the document entitled 'Up with Production' the concept of competitive public enterprise was introduced. Herbert Morrison called this innovation 'a new application of Socialism and of Socialist doctrine'.[2] Nevertheless, criticism of this document did not break out into open party warfare mainly because the impending General Election tended to unite, as always, the previously antagonistic forces. The fact that the embryo Leader of the Left, Aneurin Bevan, was still in the Government and on the NEC reinforced this tendency.

This did not mean that the Left were satisfied with the document. Its own particular 'shopping-list' was far more extensive than anything official. Ian Mikardo, a signatory of the *Keep Left* pamphlet of 1947, called for the nationalisation of the Joint Stock Banks, the Shipbuilding Industry, Aircraft and Aero-Engines and the assembly branch of mass-produced Motor Vehicles.[3] This was an individual contribution but was symptomatic of the 'Keep Left' group's far-reaching attitude. By January 1950 12 MPs produced a pamphlet entitled *Keeping Left* in which they advocated the public ownership of Road Haulage, Steel, Insurance, Cement, Sugar and Cotton. This list was shorter than the Mikardo one of 1948 but was more adventurous than anything official. Both the *Keeping Left* pamphlet and the Mikardo proposals had one significant point in common: the need to change economic power relationships

---

1. *Labour Believes in Britain* (1949) p. 13.
2. *LPACR 1949*, p. 155, col. 1.
3. See I. Mikardo, *The Second Five Years*, Fabian Research Series no. 124 (Apr 1948) pp. 11–15.

by means of common ownership. They differed fundamentally from the official line, which remained firmly on a pragmatic, efficiency basis. Therefore, as early as 1949 two opposing positions about future extensions of public ownership had emerged: the official position which was developing a limited 'shopping-list' attitude based upon efficiency grounds and the nucleus of thinkers around the *Keep Left* group who were pressing for an enlarged 'shopping-list' based upon economic-control arguments.

With the very small majority after 1950 none of the measures outlined in the 1949 policy document was implemented by the Government save for the Steel commitment. The question of Steel nationalisation had been a major issue in the Party from the moment Labour assumed office in 1945. Officially the Party remained committed to it and this pledge was re-iterated in *Labour Believes in Britain*. Nevertheless, Morrison always had reservations regarding the suitability of outright Steel nationalisation. In 1946 he is thought to have approached Sir Andrew Duncan of the Iron and Steel Federation with a compromise plan which would not have involved total nationalisation.[1] Also in 1950 he supported in Cabinet George Strauss's contention that the vesting-date for nationalisation should be postponed by six months because of the possibility of having to legislate on the Schuman Plan for a European Iron and Coal Community. This view was rejected by Attlee and a majority of the Cabinet.[2] Steel nationalisation went ahead.

A major set-back for the Left in the 1950–1 Parliament was the retreat on Industrial Assurance. This was possibly one of the most radical measures proposed by the Party since 1945 and its inclusion in the 1949 policy document was a severe set-back for Herbert Morrison. At a meeting on 23 March 1949 the NEC rejected a Morrison proposal to omit a declaration in favour of the public ownership of Industrial Assurance and substitute a promise of an enquiry following the election with an open-ended option to reorganise Industrial Assurance in a way in keeping with the report. This proposal gained the support

1. See *Age of Austerity*, ed. Sissons and French (1963) p. 304.
2. Unpublished Dalton Diaries.

of only four members of the NEC and one union delegate.[1] Nevertheless, following the election this NEC proposal, together with other public-ownership proposals, save Steel, was not implemented. The Cabinet became almost totally preoccupied with the balance-of-payments situation, the strength of sterling and the maintenance of its slender parliamentary majority. The whole issue of public ownership was shelved; however, a policy statement had to be drawn up with a view to the coming election and the problem of future public ownership had to be dealt with in it.

LABOUR AND THE NEW SOCIETY

The new policy statement, *Labour and the New Society*, produced by the NEC in August 1950 and accepted by Conference in October, was novel. For the first time since the war no specific candidates for nationalisation, save the hardy perennial Iron and Steel, were proposed. The pledges in the 1949 document, Cement, Sugar and Industrial Assurance, were dropped and the whole question of future public ownership was dealt with in a new and radically different way. Three broad criteria were laid down which would govern the tests that were to be applied in determining the industries suitable for public ownership. First, it was argued that public ownership 'is a means of controlling the basic industries and services on which the economic life and welfare of the community depend'.[2] Secondly, public ownership would be suitable where an industry was inefficient and the private owners lacked the will or capacity to make improvements. Thirdly, public ownership would be a method that safeguarded the public from exploitation by private monopolies. Also, the new document enlarged upon a theme already present in Party thinking – namely the the alternative methods of public ownership to nationalisation.[3] Six main methods of approach were adopted, the most important being municipal enterprise, competitive public enterprise and co-operative enterprise.

1. The four were: Morrison, Dalton, Alice Bacon and Burke (of USDAW). Unpublished Dalton Diaries (Mar 1949).
2. *Labour and the New Society* (1950) p. 20.   3. Ibid. pp. 20–1.

In terms of socialist rhetoric *Labour and the New Society* was fairly acceptable to the Left as the following passage, attuned to fundamentalist thinking, illustrates:

> Big businessmen, aristocratic landowners, bankers and merchants directed the economic life of the nation . . . the whole nation was imperilled by private control of the economy. . . . Therefore the public must be supreme . . . public ownership is the most effective way of public control because it makes industry directly accountable to the people.[1]

Despite these fundamentalist sentiments two points emerged from this document that illustrate the victory for Morrison inherent in it. First, an emphasis was placed upon public control through investment decisions, location of industry decisions, the Monopolies Commission and the Development Councils, all of which meant a decreasing role for public ownership. Secondly, the line of contention within the Party had been drawn on the issue of the 'shopping-list' and no matter how rhetorically fundamentalist and revivalist the document sounded, especially with broad criteria for public ownership spelt out, the lack of any new candidates was a major set-back for the Left. The Left's immediate reaction to what was virtually a *fait accompli* carried through by Morrison was strangely non-belligerent.[2] This can be explained partly by the fact that Bevan spoke in support of the new policy document on behalf of the NEC at Party Conference and also because the political scene was at that stage dominated by the international situation in Korea. Also, the impending General Election tended to mute overt criticism. As always, Labour papered over the cracks just in time.

Immediately following the loss of the election in the autumn of 1951 a challenge to the pragmatism that had captured the Party was launched. The campaign culminated at the Morecambe Conference of 1952. It is important, however, to understand the situation that nurtured the need for this challenge. During the period of the Labour Government three

---

1. Ibid. pp. 18–19.
2. Dalton in his unpublished diary (3 Aug 1950) noted with surprise the ease with which the policy document was passed through the NEC.

important policy documents regarding public ownership had
been presented to, and were accepted by, the Party. They progressively contained less specific proposals for outright nationalisation and elevated the concept of control over that of
ownership. Indeed, if Labour had won the 1951 election it
would have been pledged to nationalise absolutely nothing at all.
Also, every major document relating to public ownership in
these years had been largely composed by Morrison, the prime
mover of consolidationist philosophy. The revolt against this
trend that started after the election was to result in the rebirth
of the 'shopping-list' philosophy and the removal of Morrison
from the NEC of the party and ultimately from the central
leadership itself.

THE RISE AND FALL OF THE 'SHOPPING-LIST' PRINCIPLE

Following the election of 1951 basic agreement was reached in
the Party to re-nationalise the two industries, Steel and Road
Haulage, that the returned Conservative Government had
proposed to de-nationalise. Even Arthur Deakin, the right-wing
General Secretary of the TGWU, moved a resolution at the
1952 Party Conference calling on the Party to re-nationalise
Road Haulage when returned to power and 'on such terms as
will prevent private owners from profiting at the expense of
the nation'.[1] There was also unanimity on the need to re-
nationalise Steel. This, however, was where agreement stopped.
The major issue of how Labour was to proceed with further
public ownership emerged.

   In August 1952 the NEC published what it called an
'interim statement' mainly concerned with guidelines for
future home policy. Six months previously the NEC had
decided to appoint a number of sub-committees to review
important fields of policy and had set in motion the preparation
of a series of discussion pamphlets that would help the Movement in coming to a decision on future policy. It was in order
to 'assist the Conference to make its contribution to the formulation of policy'[2] that *Facing the Facts* – as the August publication was entitled – was published. *Facing the Facts* spoke in

1. *LPACR 1952*, p. 70, col. 2.   2. *Facing the Facts* (Aug 1952) p. 1.

general terms about future public-ownership proposals in very much the same vein as had *Labour and the New Society* and could be considered a moderate, indelibly Morrisonian document. Technically the passing of this document by Conference meant that the Movement had consented to proceed upon general lines by laying down broad criteria for further advances in public ownership. However, as so often happens at Labour Conferences, this was negated by a vital resolution (this time from the Islington North Constituency Labour Party, moved by Wilfred Fienburgh MP), which called upon the NEC 'to draw up a *list* of the key and major industries to be taken into public ownership during the five-year programme'.[1] The NEC accepted this resolution in the spirit in which Fienburgh moved it when he said: 'We have not given them a "tied hand and foot" sort of resolution. We have tried to light here a searchlight pointing the way ahead. Now they must chart the course for us.'[2]

Conference carried this resolution and thereby put certain members of the NEC in a difficult position. The Islington proposal was a direct repudiation of those in the Party who wanted an end to 'list-making'.[3] Indeed in his speech summing up the public-ownership debate, Morrison, after accepting the Islington resolution, said:

> But there are two ways of doing it [nationalisation]: there is the making of a short list of the industries you are going to socialize, in which case you have fettered yourself as to what you can do. You have fettered yourself because what will be relevant in this matter in the circumstances obtaining when the time for action comes is more important than to set out a list of industries which you are going to nationalize.[4]

Yet, according to a logical interpretation of Morrison's position, by its decision to call for a 'shopping-list' the Party had prepared the way for 'fettering' itself on public ownership. The 1952 Conference therefore was a defeat for the Right wing, and a double defeat for Morrison as he also lost his seat on the NEC.

1. *LPACR 1952*, p. 91, col. 2. (Italics mine.)
2. Ibid. p. 92, col. 2.
3. Others supporting the Morrison position at the 1952 Conference were Austen Albu, George Brown, Roy Jenkins and Hugh Gaitskell.
4. *LPACR 1952*, p. 111, col. 2.

Although the Party was technically facing both ways after passing both the NEC document and the Islington motion, it was in reality now committed to drawing up a list of industries for public ownership. From October until June of 1953 the central issue became which of the industries still in private ownership should be taken over. The debate centred around Land, Industrial Assurance, Shipbuilding and Chemicals.

Many in the Party were disappointed that Land nationalisation was not included in the programme in 1945. A new attempt was made to commit the Party to it in 1952 by way of a resolution moved by the Broxtowe Constituency Labour Party. However, the NEC managed to persuade Conference to remit the resolution to the executive[1] by the persuasive argument that the Agricultural Workers' Union did not think it appropriate at that time. Nevertheless, in the ensuing months *Tribune* carried a series of articles on the subject of Land nationalisation. Reginald Paget, not normally considered a left-wing member of Parliament, pressed for a scheme whereby local authorities would take over all rented houses and the State would buy up farms and form them into groups for greater production.[2] Another idea put forward was a system of land taxation and rating; this would compel the owners to pay a tax on the value of each piece of land whether they used it or not.[3] This plan was put forward by Richard Stokes MP, a former Lord Privy Seal, who opposed outright nationalisation on the grounds that compensation payments would be far too expensive. No proposal for the nationalisation of land appeared in the final policy document *Challenge to Britain* although vague hints regarding possible areas of increased public ownership were implicit in the statement.[4]

On the issue of the nationalisation of Industrial Assurance the Leadership had beaten a steady retreat since the time when it was included in the programme of 1949. By 1950 national-

1. This is a method whereby instead of accepting or opposing the motion the NEC asks that it should be 'left on the table' to be considered later.

2. See R. Paget, 'The Case for Land Nationalisation', in *Tribune* (12 Dec 1952).

3. See R. Stokes, 'Why Pay Out £20,000 Million?', in *Tribune* (19 Dec 1952).

4. See the section 'More From Our Land', in *Challenge to Britain* (Jun 1953).

isation had been replaced by mutualisation and by 1951 no proposal at all was made! With the formulation of policy after 1951 the issue came to light again and it was revealed that the Fabian Society, in a report that was never published, had in 1948 urged on the NEC that 'all industrial and ordinary life assurance should be nationalised'.[1] The Society had also proposed that the General Insurance business should ultimately be nationalised, but not immediately because of the dangers inherent in disturbing its earnings of foreign currency. Therefore the Party had retreated yet again on a major issue of nationalisation. *Challenge to Britain* offered no comfort to those who wanted Assurance included in the list. The statement simply advocated yet another enquiry into the Industrial Assurance business and neglected to make any specific proposals.

Another inter-party campaign was instigated in favour of including the Chemical Industry in the proposals. This met with rather more success than Land or Industrial Assurance. The document went so far as to say that in order to establish control over investment and to stop dangers of private monopoly power 'a substantial degree of public ownership is required'.[2]

Challenge to Britain was published in June 1953 and was the culmination of all thinking in the Party since it left office. It introduced a list of industries that were either to be nationalised outright or were to be taken partially into public ownership. The list for outright nationalisation was much smaller than the 1945 proposals and included Iron and Steel, Road Haulage, Water and Sugar. It also proposed the municipalisation of all rented accommodation. However, in the sphere of partial public ownership the list was the largest ever produced by the Party. Referring to the engineering industry it said, 'the next Labour Government will, where necessary, take particular sections of the industry into public ownership'.[3] This was a huge advance for the Left, particularly when the definition of engineering used by *Challenge to Britain* is studied.

1. See Hugh Jenkins, *Tribune* (2 Jan 1953) p. 3.
2. *Challenge to Britain*, p. 10. The text of this document is also published in *LPACR 1953*, pp. 61ff.
3. For a full list of the nationalisation proposals see the resolution moved by the Amalgamated Union of Foundry Workers, *LPACR 1953*, p. 108.

Engineering was taken to include: Motor Cars, Machine Tools, Aircraft, Shipbuilding, Farm Tractors and Agricultural Machinery. More specifically the document when referring to Machine Tools said, 'Labour will acquire in the public interest a number of the key . . . firms.' As far as Aircraft were concerned the policy was laid down that 'the next Labour Government will . . . take powers to acquire any firm which falls down on its job'.

Therefore, by 1953, the experiments in 'broad criteria' arguments had been replaced by the 'shopping-list' principle. These new direct proposals, however, were not as firm as the 1945 crop had been. The lack of commitment to *outright* nationalisation led to a number of resolutions at the 1953 Conference aimed at changing the situation. The Left, scared of future retreats by the Leadership, wanted *specific* and *definite* commitments, but amendments calling for the outright nationalisation of Machine Tools, Mining Machinery, Aircraft, Electrical Equipment, Shipbuilding, Radio Manufacture, Textiles and Motor Vehicles were all lost by three to four million votes and one calling for the nationalisation of Armaments was lost by about two million votes.[1] Amendments calling for joint marketing policies for the nationalised industries and an integrated policy for Public Transport were carried, and were later incorporated into a revised *Challenge to Britain* published in December 1953.

Therefore, although amendments that advocated *outright* nationalisation were lost quite substantially, the official Party document contained many more pledges than the 1949 or 1950 documents. *Challenge to Britain* together with the 'Bevanite' successes on the NEC provided a high-water mark for the expansionist views of the Left. Although the major power centre of the Movement – the unions – voted for the document at the Party Conference of 1953 many union leaders were far from satisfied with certain aspects of it. For instance the TGWU only agreed to support the Labour Party's proposals with reservations about even the partial-nationalisation plans for the Chemical Industry. There was also a conflict of opinion within that

1. For a full list of the nationalisation proposals, see the resolution moved by the Amalgamated Union of Foundry Workers, *LPACR 1953*, p. 108.

union about the proposals for the Aircraft and Machine-tool industries.[1]

Some of the fears of the more moderate trade unionists were alleviated by the time the next election was fought since the manifesto for the 1955 election, *Forward with Labour*, omitted the plans about Aircraft and Mining Machinery. The manifesto was understandably more moderate than the 1953 document although it did promise some major additions to the public sphere:

> Public ownership of the steel and road haulage industries is essential to the nation's needs and we shall re-nationalize them.
> We shall bring sections of the chemical and machine tool industries into public ownership. Where necessary we shall start new public enterprise.

By 1955, therefore, the possibility implicit in *Challenge to Britain* of an extension of public ownership to a whole range of industries was nullified. With the exception of Machine Tools none of the other engineering industries was threatened with either total or partial public ownership. Also, if 1955 is taken as a watershed, a whole series of proposals that had been included in official Party programmes since the war had been dropped. No mention was made of Land nationalisation (that had been in the programme in 1945), of Sugar (1949), of Meat Wholesaling and Fruit Wholesaling (1949), of Cement (1949) or of Industrial Assurance (1949).

By 1955 the Party was yet again committed to a moderate programme and the flood-gates that 1953 could have opened remained firmly closed.

Here is a good example of how the exigencies of electoral politics supersede even declared Party policy. *Challenge to Britain* was diluted by the Leadership in its formulation of the manifesto of 1955 and Conference decisions were simply and blatantly flouted. Yet the pressures on the Left not to revolt over the deletion of certain aspects of *Challenge to Britain* were, as usual, considerable as the General Election was only a few weeks away when *Forward with Labour* was published. Morrison's

---

1. TGWU Biennial Conference (Southsea, 14 Jul 1952), reported in the *TGWU Record* (Aug 1953). See especially pp. 72–3.

influence on the election manifesto was, not surprisingly, considerable.

The Left, with the victory of 1953 tucked under their belts, were cheated of their ultimate goal – a Socialist election manifesto. Perhaps extensive nationalisation was too much to ask of a major party of state in the mid-fifties, but the Left had very good grounds for resentment over the obvious and calculated about-face of the Leadership. It was yet another victory for Herbert Morrison and the moderates. 'Consolidate what we have' was the motto. More old-fashioned nationalisation was probably not appropriate for the British economy and would certainly lose votes, but the lack of adventure in Labour's proposals was stultifying the Party and frustrating its true radicals; on the Right as well as the Left.

What was desperately needed, many thought, was a responsible yet invigorating approach to the nation's problems. New forms and enterprises needed to be pioneered outside the strait-jacket of traditional thinking. Although revisionism was yet to be coherently expressed some of its ingredients were already present.

SOME REVISIONIST TRENDS

The sterile Right–Left debate over nationalisation of the early 1950s was not without its compensations. Out of this reappraisal came some novel ideas.

A significant breakthrough had been made by 1953 in the attitude the Party adopted towards other forms of public ownership than nationalisation. *Let Us Face the Future* had been far too busy with outright nationalisation to include any other methods of public ownership but by 1949, and *Labour Believes in Britain*, the principle of competitive public enterprise had become tentatively established. A whole section of the 1949 document was devoted to this very topic and the new scheme was justified in a refreshingly non-doctrinaire fashion: 'But unless there is economic necessity, there is no reason for always socialising whole industries. For private and public enterprise to fairly compete with each other can be good for both.'[1] In

1. *Labour Believes in Britain*, p. 12.

the 1949 document this idea was to be applied to the Chemical Industry. By 1950, however, the principle of alternative methods of public ownership was firmly laid down and these alternative methods actually enumerated. A feature to be found in both the 1949 and the 1950 policy statements was that these new ideas regarding public ownership were never – with the exception of Chemicals in 1949 – applied to any specific industry. However by 1953 the idea, for instance, of competitive publicly-owned firms had become wedded to certain practical proposals. For example, Labour was to acquire certain key Machine-tool firms. 1953 saw yet another idea in this field emerge, for *Challenge to Britain* contained a general and specific undertaking to obtain for the State a 'controlling interest in existing enterprises'. This idea was to be applied to vital firms in the Mining Machinery Industry. In this new proposal for State share-buying the germ of the idea that was to create so much controversy in *Industry and Society* (in 1957) was born. In 1953, however, the idea was hardly noticed save for one speech at the Conference directly concerned with Mining Machinery – it was thought of as 'a Tory method of taking power dressed up'.[1]

Another important trend in official thinking about future public ownership was the growing awareness of the importance of separating ownership from control. For the major sectors of the economy public control (as opposed to ownership) would suffice. *Labour and the New Society* was something of a breakthrough in this direction, as it produced a long list of the methods whereby the Government would control the private sphere. Twelve spheres of governmental control were listed, the most important ones being: investment decisions, foreign exchange, location of industry, monopoly and restrictive practices and development areas by means of development councils.[2] *Facing the Facts* and *Challenge to Britain* continued this trend and underlined the prime importance of government controls in order to ensure full employment. The latter document dealt at length with the various financial and fiscal controls that a future Labour Government would use in order to ensure that the

1. H. Blair, *LPACR 1953*, p. 8.
2. For a fuller account see *Labour and the New Society*, pp. 23ff.

*

private sector continued to play its full role in the economy.

Implicit in this emphasis on *control* as opposed to *ownership* was an acceptance, at least for the foreseeable future, of the mixed economy. The Party was obviously not going to transform all private enterprise into public concerns overnight but it could have taken a less positive attitude to existing private ownership. Nevertheless, in the 1950 document the merits of private enterprise were mentioned and its future virtually guaranteed by the statement that 'private enterprise has a proper place in the economy. Indeed we shall aid and encourage its efficiency and enterprise.'[1] *Facing the Facts* also stressed the need to maintain a private sector and to give assistance to it in order that it might become more efficient. Significantly however *Challenge to Britain* made no bold statement regarding the continuation of the private sphere, but this remained implicit rather than explicit.

Another interesting trend in the early fifties was the growing critical faculty towards the existing nationalised industries. All sections of the Party agreed that mistakes had been made during the 1945 to 1951 Parliament, but whereas the Left were wary of making too overt criticisms of the existing system, for fear of adding to arguments that advocated less nationalisation in the future, the moderate wing of the Party had no such inhibitions.

Three major areas of criticism emerged from the thinking of the early fifties. First, nationalisation was criticised for over-centralisation and for an absence of devolution of responsibility. *Socialist Commentary*, in a series of articles comprising a symposium on nationalisation, dealt with this question but came to the conclusion that:

> Just as in private large-scale industry, for example I.C.I., a phase of centralisation was followed by efficient decentralisation, there is no reason to doubt that nationalised industry will emerge from its present difficulties, which are probably unavoidable in a period of mass reorganisation.[2]

Deakin, on the other hand, did not take so optimistic a view in his 14 July speech at the TGWU Biennial Conference. He

1. *Labour and the New Society*, p. 23.
2. 'Thoughts on Nationalisation', *Socialist Commentary* (Feb 1952) p. 42.

simply contented himself with saying, in a rather sweeping manner, that the centralising policies of the nationalised industries had led to the top decision-making levels becoming too remote and that 'none of the members were satisfied with the degree of success so far achieved in nationalisation'.[1]

This remoteness of workers from the boards of the nationalised industries was openly admitted by both Left and Right although few suggestions for improvements, save the predictable yearnings of the far-Left for British-style 'soviets', were proffered. An interesting contribution to this re-thinking was made by Ernest Davies MP in a policy-discussion pamphlet published in 1952. He pointed out that nationalisation had helped industrial democracy in two major ways: first by the appointment of trade union officials to boards, and secondly through joint consultation. Problems, however, had appeared in the former case because of the question of divided loyalty, and in dealing with the latter case he had some critical analysis to apply to the existing system:

> Although comprehensive joint consultative machinery has been established in all the nationalised industries, the machine frequently creaks . . . there are too many cases where the management regard consultative committees as an unnecessary nuisance. On the other hand, the workers have sometimes failed to make use of these committees.[2]

Gaitskell was also writing at this time on the problem of the organisation of the existing nationalised industries. His Fabian Tract, *Socialism and Nationalisation*, although published in 1956, was mostly written in 1953.[3] In this work he dealt with the argument that nationalisation means a transfer of power from irresponsible private owners to the workers. On the whole Gaitskell was sympathetic to the nationalised industries, but he readily admitted that in private as well as public industry the power 'of employers over workers is nowadays severely limited by the trade unions'.[4]

1. *TGWU Record* (Aug 1953) p. 70.
2. E. Davies, *Problems of Public Ownership* (a Labour Party publication, Aug 1952) p. 23.
3. See the Foreword to Fabian Tract No. 300, H. Gaitskell, *Socialism and Nationalisation* (1956).
4. Ibid.

Another aspect of the nationalised industries that worried those in the Labour Movement who concerned themselves with these matters was the question of finance. One of the most interesting ideas in this field was produced by Ernest Davies, who believed that 'the nationalised sector of industry should be regarded as a whole, instead of as a number of separate industries'. This would make it possible, he argued, for the profitable socialised industries to subsidise the less profitable ones and for a financial pool in the nationalised sector to be created.

This critical faculty with regard to nationalisation and the existing nationalised industries did not find its way into official Party documents, which continued to praise, without reservations, the achievements of the nationalised sector. Nevertheless, the writings of Davies, *Socialist Commentary* and Gaitskell provided a not insignificant starting-point from which the Party could reappraise, in a less doctrinaire fashion, the relevance of nationalisation as a future method of State ownership.

Although public ownership remained the central specific problem of official policy, a whole new philosophy of British socialism was emerging at a lower level. A largely unconnected group of intellectuals was already groping its way towards new horizons. New thinking was becoming fashionable again although little notice was taken of it by the Leaders of the Party until after the General Election defeat of 1955.

This fresh approach to social-democracy did not surface into full public limelight until after Gaitskell became Leader. Nevertheless, within the confines of the Labour Party a new and vital reappraisal of modern British Socialism went on uninterrupted by either the orthodoxy of the old-fashioned Right or the narrow, constricting dogma of the Left.

CHAPTER FOUR

The Emergence of the 'New Thinkers'

By the Labour Party Conference of 1952 a body of opinion had grown up within the Party which felt that a reappraisal of the relevance of democratic socialism to the economic, political and social problems facing the nation was needed. This group also tried to define the philosophical base upon which some of its practical policy proposals were founded, and because many of its views were moderate and 'revisionist' in nature this reappraisal was considered by many as a justification and intellectual rationalisation of the right-wing social democratic position. Testimony to this was the attack made on the new thinkers by Aneurin Bevan, who had himself in 1952 attempted a similar analysis of Socialism's future in his book *In Place of Fear*,[1] on 13 June 1952:

> The second danger to which we shall be exposed comes from what may be called the Fresh Thinkers. . . . Perhaps a better term would be Socialist Revisionists. These are people who want to substitute novel remedies for the struggle for power in the state. They suggest that an extension of public ownership is an old-fashioned and outmoded idea.[2]

Bevan was accurate in ascribing to the 'new thinkers' a philosophy and policy that was in conflict with the Marxist and quasi-Marxist Left. An example of the Left's suspicion of the new thinking that was emerging can be seen in the columns of *Tribune*. In 1951 and 1952 its editorials and articles continued to talk in terms of a 'new Labour élite'[3] or the

1. A. Bevan, *In Place of Fear* (1952).
2. A. Bevan, 'The Fatuity of Coalition', *Tribune* (13–26 June 1952) p. 1.
3. See T. Balogh, *Tribune* (7 Mar 1952) p. 7.

'synthetic radicals of the Movement'[1] when referring to thinkers on the Right of the Party.

This new bout of writing was primarily the responsibility of supporters of the Party Leadership and those who would generally be regarded as non-Marxist and non-Utopian thinkers. Two major groups emerge among these new thinkers that serve to prove this point. *Socialist Commentary* and Socialist Union provided one rallying-point for this re-appraisal of socialist thinking and, equally significantly, so did the Fabian Society through its publication *New Fabian Essays*. There was a certain amount of overlapping. Some writers served in both groups, but, at least formally, their work was not co-ordinated. Nevertheless a similarity of approach to the questions facing the Movement was adopted by both groups. *The Times* thought that 'the fact that two separate groups in the socialist movement should have provided a restatement of socialism which so closely follows the same line of thought is significant'.[2] Also, on particularly contentious policies the two groups would tend to agree, and this further identified them as Right-wing in sympathy. Frank Pakenham said of them: 'But on this subject [of nationalisation] Socialist Union is surely much closer to *New Fabian Essays* edited by Dick Crossman, a Bevanite, than is either to the position of *Tribune*.'[3]

Although a good case could be made out that both *Socialist Commentary* and Socialist Union were staffed almost entirely by those who would support the Leadership on most major issues, the case of *New Fabian Essays* was more complex.

NEW FABIAN ESSAYS

New Fabian Essays originated before the fall of the Labour Government. They were initiated in 1949 by G. D. H. Cole who, as Chairman of the Fabian Society, gathered together a group of Fabians for a week-end at Buscot Park in July of that year. This was the first of a series of conferences at which papers were presented on particular problems. Professor Cole resigned

1. Ibid.
2. Editorial in *The Times* (27 Jun 1952).
3. F. Pakenham, *Tribune* (8 Aug 1952) p. 8.

from the group in 1950 because of 'a basic disagreement on policy',[1] but an important by-product of his resignation was that a unity of approach could be established within the group.[2] This unity carried itself through into the actual Essays. Five of the contributors (Anthony Crosland, Roy Jenkins, Austen Albu, Denis Healey and John Strachey) were already associated through their writings in *Socialist Commentary* with revisionist attitudes. Ian Mikardo, whose views were well to the left of the others, contented himself with an analysis of 'Trade Unions in a Full Employment Economy', a subject that offered little chance for him to take issue with the other essayists. Margaret Cole, in her essay 'Education and Social Democracy', dealt with one of the major topics that the previous Labour Government had largely ignored and indeed simply by writing about it broke new ground.[3]

The most interesting of the non-revisionist essayists was R. H. S. Crossman. Crossman was a 'Bevanite'. He had attacked many of the policies of the Labour Government in its later years and had called for a greater socialist content in future proposals. He was also in the future to become one of the small group of Labour politicians who, with Wilson, formed the 'centralist' group during the years of the Leadership of Hugh Gaitskell. He was therefore not, in the strict sense, a revisionist, but his essay in 1952 accepted many of the revisionist assumptions. It fell to Crossman, as editor, to spell out the reasons for the publication of this new set of essays. He felt

1. *New Fabian Essays*, ed. Crossman (1952) p. 12.
2. The following is the list of the members of the group, out of whose discussions *New Fabian Essays* sprang: Austen Albu (co-author with N. Hewett of *The Anatomy of Private Industry*), Dr N. Barou (author of *British Trade Unions*), Ritchie Calder (Science Editor of *News Chronicle*), Donald Chapman MP (General Secretary of the Fabian Society), Hugh Clegg (Fellow of Nuffield College), Professor G. D. H. Cole, Margaret Cole, C. A. R. Crosland MP, R. H. S. Crossman MP, Lord Farringdon (Chairman of the Fabian Colonial Bureau), Allan Flanders (Lecturer in Industrial Relations at Oxford), R. J. Goodman (Director, PEP), H. D. Hughes (Principal of Ruskin College, Oxford), Roy Jenkins MP, Ian Mikardo MP, John Parker MP, Harold Wilson MP, G. D. N. Worswick (Fellow of Magdalen College, Oxford), Michael Young (Research Adviser to the Labour Party).
At a later stage John Strachey and Denis Healey (International Secretary of the Labour Party) joined the group.
3. *New Fabian Essays*, pp. 91–120.

that the Labour Party, having completed its social programme, had lost most of its momentum and therefore needed a return to first principles. This led him to cast doubt upon the advantages of a wholly empirical approach to politics and to press for more philosophy: 'Philosophy begins where pragmatism fails.'[1] In this connection Crossman praised Evan Durbin and his work *The Politics of Democratic Socialism* as a valuable guide to a philosophical base for socialism. However he was worried by the general absence of philosophical thinking in the Party as a whole and noted that only one important book had been published on socialist philosophy since the war.[2] Crossman displayed in his essay several revisionist approaches, the most important of which was his awareness of the new 'managerial revolution'. His message on this point was essentially libertarian. He suggested that socialists must guard against the increase of privilege and totalitarian control that the managerial society could lead to. In this he had the agreement of the Party Leader, who used the term 'managerial autocracy'[3] when referring to the trend Crossman attempted to illustrate.

Anthony Crosland, in his essay entitled 'The Transition from Capitalism', elaborated Crossman's thesis: 'The power previously wielded by the owners of property has now largely, though not entirely, passed to the class of managers – working directors, managing directors and the higher grades of salaried executives.'[4] In their view of the transition of capitalism, Crosland and Crossman came to the same analytical conclusions, for Crossman in an earlier work had stated that 'the first Copernican revolution is to recognise that Property no longer equals Power, and the wealthy are a relatively impotent class in the country'.[5] Crosland was much more ruthless as to the

1. R. H. S. Crossman, 'Towards a Philosophy of Socialism', *New Fabian Essays*, p. 6.

2. He was referring to *Restatement of Liberty* by P. C. Gordon Walker MP (1951).

3. Attlee, Introduction to *New Fabian Essays*. Crossman further warned against increasing autocracy – not only in the managerial field, but also in the political parties – in R. H. S. Crossman, *Socialism and the New Despotism*, Fabian Tract No. 298 (1956).

4. *New Fabian Essays*, p. 38.

5. R. H. S. Crossman, *Socialist Values in a Changing Civilisation*, Fabian Tract No. 286 (1951) p. 11.

conclusions that should be drawn from this analysis. He listed certain lines of policy which in the future ought to be dismissed as contributing to the essence of 'good socialism': first, the continued extension of free social services; secondly, more and more nationalisation of whole industries; thirdly, the continued proliferation of controls; and, fourthly, further redistribution of income by direct taxation. 'It is in other directions', he advocated, 'that the Left must look for its new inspiration . . . the ownership of wealth . . . the educational system . . . the crucial problem of the psychology of industrial relations'.[1]

Austen Albu rounded off this thesis with a brilliant analysis of the new 'managerial autocracy' and suggested certain reforms, some of which he had called for in his earlier works,[2] such as greater worker participation on management boards.

John Strachey, in his essay 'Tasks and Achievements of British Labour', pursued two main themes. First, that the experience of the recent Labour Government had rekindled rather than dampened his faith in the parliamentary system and in the success of 'Fabian tactics'. Secondly, that because of Keynesian fiscal measures, supplemented by physical controls, the State had now in its power all the tools that were needed to enable it to do what it wanted.

Roy Jenkins wrote on the question of equality[3] and warned against over-emphasising 'equality of opportunity'. This concept, he argued, should be considered a useful weapon but it should never be a substitute for ensuring equality both of reward and esteem.

Finally, *New Fabian Essays* served to launch Denis Healey as a major contributor to the growing 'power-political' school of thinking in the Party on foreign and defence policy. In his essay, 'Power Politics and the Labour Party', Healey argued for a strong British commitment to the United States through NATO and also implicitly rejected the concept of a 'socialist

1. *New Fabian Essays*, p. 65.
2. See A. Albu, *Management in Transition*, Fabian Society Research Series no. 68 (1942). Also Albu and Hewett, *The Anatomy of Private Industry*, Fabian Society Research Series No. 145 (1951).
3. Jenkins, 'Equality', in *New Fabian Essays*, ed. Crossman.

foreign policy'.[1] Healey was to develop these themes at much greater length in the later fifties.[2]

These extracts from *New Fabian Essays* have, of necessity, been sketchy because the ideas and themes involved are treated in much greater detail in other parts of this work. Nevertheless it is interesting to see some of the general points that emerge from these Essays in the form of views held in common by the majority of the essayists. All except one of the contributors to the Essays were Members of Parliament, or as Balogh preferred to call them 'parliamentary representatives of the movement'.[3] They were therefore, not unnaturally, very much concerned with making socialism appeal to the electorate and consequently with the 'relevance' of the Party's thinking to what they considered to be the deep-rooted changes in society that had occurred since the theorising of Laski and Cripps.[4] In the thirties emphasis had been placed upon the attainment of socialism by extra-parliamentary means – not because it was desirable but because it was unavoidable if certain ends were to be achieved. The authors of these new essays seemed quite content with the parliamentary method and indeed, in Strachey's case, positively enthusiastic about it. This view stemmed from another general line of thinking that the Essays portrayed: namely that economic society itself had changed considerably since before the war. There was a particular awareness of the new managerial role that had developed in decision-making, but none of the 'revisionist' thinkers put forward any constructive views on how the undesirable effects of this new structure could be minimised. Some of them simply contented themselves with vague denunciations of the autocracy involved, while others did not even feel that the new system provided any new problems.

1. His understanding of a 'Socialist Foreign Policy' was that it is a method of conducting British foreign relations according to socialist principles without reference to either (a) British national interests or (b) balance-of-power considerations.
2. E.g. see D. Healey's pamphlet, *Neutralism* (1955).
3. See T. Balogh, 'Fabians at Sea', in *Tribune* (30 May 1952) p. 6.
4. E.g. see H. J. Laski, *The State and the New Social Order*, Fabian Tract No. 200 (1922); Laski, *Socialism and Freedom*, Fabian Tract No. 216 (1925); Laski, *The State in Theory and Practice* (1936); R. S. Cripps, *Can Socialism Come by Constitutional Methods?* (1933); Cripps, *Why This Socialism?* (1934); Cripps, *The Struggle for Peace* (1936).

Another trend that emerges from all the essays is the belief that constructive political action is more than simply the erection of ideal political goals. It should also consist of an understanding of the complexities of political practice and action. This led to a distrust of utopian solutions but not to an outright rejection of the need to redefine absolute ideals. Indeed, the major point that emerges from an analysis of most of the contributions, and that isolated them from the 'Bevanite' wing of the Party, was the absolute conviction that a redefinition of socialism was necessary. In a leading article on 26 June 1952 *The Times* suggested that the publication of these essays had left the 'Bevanites' alone in their belief that no re-definition of socialism was necessary. This was perhaps extreme but the Left were decidedly loath to question their basic assumptions. They still held to the view that the fundamental tenets of socialism – public ownership and an economic interpretation of all political and social phenomena – remained valid. *New Fabian Essays* was an important weapon in the revisionist attack on this entrenched position.

The reception given to *New Fabian Essays* by the Labour Movement was predictable. It was no real surprise that the left-wing thinkers in the Party were not impressed by its new analysis. It was called 'an obvious failure . . . to contribute new thought or new spirit to the flagging cause of social democracy'.[1]

Socialist Commentary, although basically sympathetic, allowed a book review by Andrew Filson[2] which provided a fundamental and deserved criticism of the essays: 'And yet we need more than logic to shape the new society and make it rich in human values. We need a vision and warmth lacking in these essays. . . .' But this did not detract from the general support which the Right and the Leadership gave to this new contribution to socialist thinking; indeed, Clement Attlee wrote a preface which welcomed its views. Attlee's support for *New Fabian Essays* was also extended, in even more positive form, to the other major revisionist grouping of the time – *Socialist Commentary* and Socialist Union.

1. See T. Balogh, *Tribune* (30 May 1952) p. 6.
2. Andrew Filson was General Secretary of the Fabian Society from 1947 to 1949.

'SOCIALIST COMMENTARY' AND SOCIALIST UNION

Socialist Commentary was the mother periodical out of which Socialist Union was born and the views and attitudes of the two organisations[1] were naturally similar. *Socialist Commentary* was founded in 1942 by a small group of German Socialist refugees from Nazism. They were particularly influenced by the ideas of a German philosopher by the name of Leonard Nelson[2] and they based their approach to socialism upon ethical, rather than scientific, foundations.[3] They were originally called the Socialist Vanguard group and their publications in *Socialist Commentary* during the war years often bore this name. *Socialist Commentary* was run by an editorial committee which by the early 1950s consisted of 12 members. The key figure, and indeed lynch-pin of the periodical, was Rita Hinden, but the members of the committee had final say on policy, articles and editorials. In the early 1950s, when *Socialist Commentary* was beginning to be noticed in the Party as an identifiable revisionist periodical, the membership of the editorial committee remained surprisingly constant,[4] but was joined by Lucjan Blit in February of 1951. By early 1952 the editorial board had acquired two parliamentarians, Fred Mulley and Kenneth Younger, who had been Minister of State at the Foreign Office in the 1950–1 Labour Government. Both these MPs were articulate moderates and reinforced *Socialist Commentary*'s revisionist image.

Parliamentary support for *Socialist Commentary* was further enhanced by an organisation set up in 1953 called Friends of Socialist Commentary. This group was launched to promote the periodical's growth and through it Hugh Gaitskell came into close and intimate contact with *Socialist Commentary*. Gaitskell became Treasurer of the Friends of Socialist Commentary in 1953

1. *Socialist Commentary* was not 'organisational' in the sense that Socialist Union was. It was purely a periodical and did not hold meetings and summer schools, etc.
2. Nelson's main works still await translation into English. See Mary Saran, 'Leonard Nelson (1881–1927)', *Socialist Commentary* (Oct 1947) p. 14.
3. Background information regarding *Socialist Commentary* and Socialist Union was given to this student in a series of interviews with Dr Rita Hinden, editor of *Socialist Commentary* (28 Feb, 12 and 19 Mar 1964).
4. They were: Emmeline Lohen, Allan Flanders, Walter Fliess, Jack Gray, G. F. Green, Rita Hinden, Frank Horrabin, W. Arthur Lewis, Joe Madin, Mary Saran and G. D. N. Worswick.

and remained so until 1955 when he was elected Leader of the Party. He brought considerable financial aid to the periodical through his contacts with the unions[1] and even after his resignation from the Treasurership, he maintained strong ties with the journal. For instance, there was a standing arrangement whereby Gaitskell spoke at *Socialist Commentary*'s Annual Conference tea-party.[2] This close political alliance between *Socialist Commentary* and Gaitskell was based upon an agreed political philosophy,[3] which overcame later differences on the issue of Britain's entry into the Common Market. As well as Gaitskell, two other MPs, Francis Noel-Baker and Alfred Robens, were closely associated with the Friends of Socialist Commentary group in the early fifties.

Socialist Commentary had established itself on the Right of the Party by the early fifties because of its 'consolidation' with regard to public ownership and its general support for the foreign policy of Ernest Bevin during the period of Labour Government. The major strand of Bevin's foreign policy that *Socialist Commentary* supported, and elaborated on after his death, was the commitment of Britain to the North Atlantic Treaty Organisation and particularly to the Anglo-American Alliance. Although in the early years after the war the editorials of the journal called for a foreign policy independent of both the U.S.A. and the U.S.S.R.,[4] by the time that NATO was set up[5] the periodical was a firm and resolute champion of the alliance. Indeed, the seeds of this view can be seen in an editorial entitled 'Controversy on Foreign Policy' published as early as December 1946: 'a much greater ideological affinity ties us to the U.S.A., and this affinity is not affected by the sharp divergencies between the economic policies of the two

1. Interview with Dr Hinden.
2. At the 1962 meeting, however, Gaitskell and Dr Hinden debated from different viewpoints on the issue of the Common Market.
3. Gaitskell and *Socialist Commentary* did disagree, however, on the emphasis to be given to equality in the priorities of socialist philosophy. Gaitskell was too rigidly egalitarian for some members of the editorial board.
4. See editorial 'Britain and the Big Two', in *Socialist Commentary* (Mar 1946). Also editorial 'After the Moscow Conference', in *Socialist Commentary* (May 1947).
5. For *Socialist Commentary*'s endorsement of the British Government's signing of the NATO Pact, see editorial 'The Atlantic Pact', in *Socialist Commentary* (Mar 1949).

countries '. The support for NATO and the close ties with the United States of America was a noticeable feature of *Socialist Commentary* in the early fifties,[1] but even more pronounced was its insistence that Britain should, if possible, avoid public differences with United States foreign policy. On one occasion it advocated that disagreements within the alliance, even over the Korean situation, should be settled by secret diplomacy.[2] Even the Tories would have balked at this idea, and so, in fact, did *Socialist Commentary* when it got down to cases. Its vivid generalisations about geopolitics could not be sustained on all occasions. For instance, like the official Leadership of the Labour Party, it found itself openly disagreeing with certain aspects of American foreign policy, especially in the Far East. American policy towards certain military operations in Korea, towards Chiang Kai-shek and towards Communist China's diplomatic status came under criticism, but on the broad policy of containment of communism through the alliance *Socialist Commentary* stood firm. This was a very different position from that taken by other left-wing journals, particularly the *New Statesman and Nation* and *Tribune*, although *Tribune*, surprisingly, supported British membership of NATO.

When compared with these two left-wing periodicals, *Socialist Commentary*'s position in the Movement on foreign policy was isolated and extreme. It was extreme in the sense that it positively welcomed British membership of NATO with a dedication that touched on moral fervour. It seems that underlying its fierce support for the legacy of Bevin's policy was a negative factor, a hatred by its editorial committee, and its foreign-policy contributors in particular, of communist expansion. The East European social-democratic influence in the journal was important in injecting a bitter cynicism towards both Russian foreign-policy objectives and indigenous Communist Party ambitions in post-war Europe.[3] As early as 1945 *Socialist Commentary* was opposed to the idea of the proposed fusion of the Communist and Social-Democratic Parties in France, on the grounds of their incompatibility and differences over

1. As an example, see editorial 'Uncle Sam', in *Socialist Commentary* (Apr 1952).
2. Editorial 'For Better or for Worse', in *Socialist Commentary* (Jan 1951) p. 3.
3. Hinden interview.

fundamental democratic principles.[1] Unlike other left-wing periodicals,[2] *Socialist Commentary* took a very anti-Communist line over the Hungarian and Czechoslovakian crises of 1947 and 1948.[3] During the 1951 debate over rearmament this anti-Communist position of *Social Commentary*, by factors inherent in its own logic, led the periodical into a staunch defence of the Gaitskell budget which allowed for defence expenditure of £4,700 million over three years compared with an original estimate of £3,600 million.[4]

Although *Socialist Commentary* supported the right-wing Leadership of the Party on the main foreign policy issue of the period, it agreed with the Left on what were, at that time, subsidiary issues. For instance, a good deal of suspicion of German remilitarisation found its way into the pages of the periodical in 1950 and 1951,[5] and although it supported German rearmament in the crisis of 1954,[6] it did so with much less enthusiasm than it had given to the American alliance. To East Europeans, German militarism still posed a very great psychological threat.

Tough though they may have been on cold-war questions, thoroughgoing radical positions were taken up on the problems of colonisation (with particular reference to Africa) and on aid to underdeveloped countries, a speciality of the Editor, Rita Hinden. A bridge to the Left was built by *Socialist Commentary*'s positive attitude to the concept of eventual world government, the United Nations and to China's admittance to that body.[7]

On other internationalist issues, however, *Socialist Commentary* tended more to the Right. One such was the question of British participation in European integration movements.

1. See editorial 'French Working Class Unity', in *Socialist Commentary* (Sep 1945).
2. See D. Healey, 'A Chance for Hungary's Socialists', in *Tribune* (14 Feb 1942) p. 5.
3. See editorial 'The Lessons of Czechoslovakia', in *Socialist Commentary* (Apr 1948).
4. See editorial 'One Way Only', in *Socialist Commentary* (Aug 1951).
5. See W. Fliess, 'Rearmament of Germany — Now or Later', in *Socialist Commentary* (Mar 1951) p. 52.
K. Younger, 'Germany and Western Defence', in *Socialist Commentary* (May 1952) p. 97.
6. See editorial 'Look Before You Leap', in *Socialist Commentary* (Oct 1954).
7. See editorial 'UNO and China', in *Socialist Commentary* (Feb 1951).

Socialist Commentary was much disheartened by both the Labour and Conservative Governments' lukewarm attitude to such ventures as the Schuman Plan and the European Army. Dr Hinden, particularly, was very much in favour of Britain becoming part of an integrated Europe and she was in the fore-front of the campaign in 1962 to take Britain into the European Economic Community. In the early fifties the enthusiasm in the periodical for closer integration stopped short of British association in a federal Europe;[1] nevertheless *Socialist Commentary* remained the foremost British left-wing periodical in favour of much closer European ties.

The major difference in the field of foreign affairs between *Socialist Commentary* and the other left-wing periodicals did not lie in any one issue, or group of specific issues. Rather, it was based upon a difference of outlook about the underlying assumptions that had to be made when constructing a foreign policy. Fundamental to *Socialist Commentary*'s position was an awareness of the anarchial nature of international politics and also the irrelevance of an ideological approach to it. Therefore, the journal dismissed as unattainable a distinctive socialist foreign policy:

> Even if all this were done [support for UNO, support for freedom and rights of native peoples in South Africa, struggle against Imperialism, to abolish the state of anarchy in international relations and to abolish inequalities between nations] we still could not claim that our foreign policy was distinctly socialist. On every item there would be others who would be wholly with us. . . . What we would have, then, would not be that unique socialist foreign policy for which so many of our comrades are looking in vain, but a foreign policy for socialists to pursue.[2]

Here was a categoric denial of the relevance of doctrinaire socialism to international affairs in an anarchical world. The revisionism of *Socialist Commentary* was complete. Month after month its pages were filled with elaborations and variations upon this theme by young revisionist writers, particularly Kenneth Younger MP and Denis Healey. The latter had been International Secretary of the Labour Party at Transport

---

1. See editorial 'Europe Asks Why', in *Socialist Commentary* (Jan 1952).
2. Editorial 'A Socialist Foreign Policy', in *Socialist Commentary* (Oct 1952).

House during the period of the Labour Government, and after a brief post-war violent left-wing flirtation he became, under the tutelage of Ernest Bevin, a leading international expert.[1] In addition to his articles in *Socialist Commentary*,[2] in 1951 he edited a critique of the methods whereby Communist Parties came to power in Eastern Europe.[3] In the following year his important contribution to *New Fabian Essays* was published. These works, together with his pamphlet of 1955,[4] which argued in the most extreme form for almost total reliance by Britain on the United States and talked of the immorality of neutralism, established Healey as a major intellectual force behind Labour's commitment to collective security. It was no coincidence therefore that he remained a regular contributor to *Socialist Commentary*, or that the Left considered him the *éminence grise* among intellectual 'cold-warriors'.

The other strand of political thinking that *Socialist Commentary* emphasised during the early post-defeat years was a 'consolidationist' attitude to nationalisation. This concept has been dealt with earlier but *Socialist Commentary*'s contribution to its development was very significant. Before the end of the Labour Government the journal ran a number of symposia on certain aspects of the Party's election manifesto, the most important of which was one on Industrial Assurance,[5] and the preface to this collection of articles was written by James Griffiths, the then Minister for National Insurance. A more important symposium was published between the months of January and April of 1952, and this dealt with the future of nationalisation[6] and provided an analysis as a framework for the Party Conference of that year. These were fairly objective and also highly academic exercises for a political journal whose aim was persuasion rather than analysis. The editorials of the period

1. *Cards on the Table*, the NEC's official foreign policy answer to *Keep Left*, was drafted by Healey.
2. See 'Britain and Europe', in *Socialist Commentary* (May 1951) p. 114; 'The Defence of Western Europe', ibid. (Oct 1951) p. 234; and 'Working with the U.S.', ibid. (Feb 1954) p. 41.
3. See D. Healey (ed.) *The Curtain Falls* (1951).
4. Healey, *Neutralism* (1955).
5. W. Ewant, P. W. Anton, A. A. Best, J. Thompson, 'Industrial Assurance', in *Socialist Commentary* (Feb 1950) p. 43.
6. 'Thoughts on Nationalisation', in *Socialist Commentary* (Jan–Apr 1956).

came down very decidedly in favour of a consolidationist, 'leave-things-as-they-are' policy. Also, it was *Socialist Commentary* that published some of the earliest writings of Crosland on the subject of public ownership,[1] and it was in these articles that part of the basic framework was laid for later attacks on the fundamentalists.

Although it devoted a large amount of space to the problems of nationalisation, *Socialist Commentary* tended to regard the issue as basically irrelevant to the continuation of a social-democratic economic system. One of the first principles of *Socialist Commentary*'s socialism was co-operation and participation.[2] Because of this, the periodical specialised in the problems involved in achieving industrial democracy, considered far more important than nationalisation. Fred Mulley wrote an article dealing with the problems of joint consultation as early as June 1949, and this was followed by articles on allied topics by Alan McCulloch, Alfred Robens, J. Roper, H. A. Turner and Austen Albu,[3] who, like Healey, was elaborating his views in *Socialist Commentary* and *New Fabian Essays* concurrently.

Underlying *Socialist Commentary*'s moderation at home and power-politics abroad was a desire to offer an alternative philosophical position to the Labour Movement than that of the Marxist and Left social-democratic school. The most important single contribution to this end was the publication of a new contribution to socialist thought by R. H. Tawney[4] entitled 'British Socialism Today'. Many of the ideas that had already taken root in his earlier books, *The Acquisitive Society* and *Equality*, were embodied in his *Socialist Commentary* article. He listed four bases for British socialism: first, that the impulse behind the Movement has been, and should continue to be,

---

1. C. A. R. Crosland, 'Function of Public Enterprise', in *Socialist Commentary* (Feb 1950) p. 28; 'Monopoly Legislation', ibid. (Jan 1951) p. 4.

2. This was articulated at greater length later by Socialist Union publications.

3. A. Albu, 'Proposals for Industrial Reform', in *Socialist Commentary* (Sep 1952); E. McCulloch, 'Workshop Representation', ibid. (Aug 1951); A. Robens, 'The Human Factor in Industry', ibid. (Jul 1952); J. Roper, 'Joint Consultation', ibid. (Feb 1951); H. A. Turner, 'Is Joint Consultation Enough?', ibid. (Jun 1952).

4. R. H. Tawney, 'British Socialism Today', in *Socialist Commentary* (Jun 1952) p. 124.

ethical rather than scientific and economic; secondly, that institutions, including the State, should exist for men and not vice versa; thirdly, that the Labour Movement has always placed socialism in a democratic framework (and a rigid framework at that – embodying the four freedoms of speech, writing, worship and meeting); and lastly a non-doctrinaire approach to political problems. The last of these four points he explained thus:

> Finally, the structure of the movement has been of a piece with its premises. Unlike some of the continental versions of socialism, it was not formed into doctrinal moulds prepared when the Industrial Revolution was still young, by political theorists and men of letters. It developed as the product of a fusion between the experience of an already vigorous trade unionism and the work of organisations and individuals, like the Fabian Society and the Webbs. . . .[1]

Tawney was undoubtedly the catalyst for the large number of editorials (surprisingly large for a political affairs journal) which appeared in *Socialist Commentary*, attempting to analyse the theoretical and philosophical position of the Labour Movement in the social-democratic spectrum.[2] This task was later to be left to Socialist Union, as by 1951 *Socialist Commentary* had abdicated from philosophy and instead was concentrating its guns on political developments. It took up a very definite position in the rhetorical and vitriolic battle that was developing in the Party.

Socialist Commentary was as committed and as consistent as *Tribune* in its attitude to the 1951 Budget, the subsequent resignations, the year-long controversy over national rearmament, and the rebellion of the 57 Labour MPs after the defence debate of 1952. It was during this period of polarisation within the Party that the periodical began to adopt a specific anti-'Bevanite' posture and attacked 'factionalism' within the Party. It criticised Bevan's book *In Place of Fear*,[3] his resignation from the Government[4] and the 'Bevanite' group of Members

1. Tawney, ibid. p. 124.
2. For examples see *Socialist Commentary* editorials for Sep 1949, p. 204; Nov 1949, p. 252; May 1951, p. 97; Jun 1951, p. 125; Aug 1952, p. 169; and Jun 1954, p. 141.
3. 'One Way Only', p. 173.   4. *Socialist Commentary* (Apr 1952) p. 82.

of Parliament, which it branded as disruptive and dangerous: '... there is one danger not to be lost sight of for a moment. It is the danger of an organised faction at work, which is bound in the end to poison party life.'[1] Attacks like this continued in its editorials during the period of 'Bevanite' success in 1951 and early 1952. Socialist Union's first publication, *Socialism: A New Statement of Principles*, was seen as a further round in the battle.

Socialist Union was set up immediately after the fall of the Labour Government in 1951. Its aim was to 'think out afresh the meaning of socialism in the modern world'.[2] Although it had no formal membership it did hold public meetings and week-end schools, but it was not set up as an organisational faction, to achieve certain political ends at constituency and trade union level, as was the Campaign for Democratic Socialism in the early 1960s.

There were as many as fifty people concerned with drafting, presenting and approving the various publications of the group,[3] and the method of formulation and subsequent publication of views was purely a collective affair, as its first publication stated:

> One of the distinctive features of Socialist Union is that its publications present views which its members broadly hold in common. Drafts are of course written by individuals, but they are first discussed in committee, then submitted for comment to meetings of all the members, and revised until a substantial measure of agreement has been found.[4]

Its fifty members divided themselves from the outset into policy groups, each with a specialised topic; the principles group, the foreign policy group, the education group,[5] the

---

1. 'Militancy for What?', in *Socialist Commentary* (May 1952) p. 93.
2. *Socialism: A New Statement of Principles* (*Socialist Commentary* publication, 1952) p. 64.   3. Interviews with Rita Hinden (editor of *Socialist Commentary*).
4. *Socialism: A New Statement of Principles*, p. 64.
5. It is interesting to see that a specialised group considered education separately. Very little thought was given to future education policy by the Labour movement at this time, and although the group did not publish the results of its work, its treatment of education separately from the social services illustrates the importance, in terms of policy-making, that it was afforded.
Much later, in September 1959, *Socialist Commentary* carried out a group study

economic group and the social services group. The first publication, *Socialism: A New Statement of Principles*, was drafted by the principles group, and, like all the others, was presented to the full membership for approval. This booklet received wide publicity in the national as well as in the Labour press because its thoroughgoing attack on Marxist concepts was seen as a direct confrontation to the 'Bevanites' and as a further round in the Left–Right struggle. However, the importance of this document was precisely the opposite. Although it contained the first principles upon which many of the arguments in *Socialist Commentary* editorials of 1949 to 1952 were based, it was a positive attempt to give some philosophical backing to contemporary socialism rather than to contribute to Party in-fighting. It did take issue with the Left; not on the level of petty party abuse, but rather on broad matters of attitude, principle and philosophy.

The importance of this booklet in revisionist thought rests upon its direct and unyielding challenge to Marxist dogma. It insisted upon an ethical approach to socialism and a rejection of economic collectivism.[1] It was humanitarian rather than Christian in its ethical approach; three main ethical foundations for its socialism, those of freedom, equality and fellowship, supported its political, economic and social structures. Although it often sounded slightly naïve, its philosophy was warmer and less modish and technological than, for instance, that of the Fabians.

The booklet was also valuable in its timing. At a period of growing controversy, disillusionment and muddle in the Movement, it proffered a steady hand. It provided a philosophical basis for the Leadership's moderate and increasingly revisionist position. So often in the past, and particularly in the Morrison era, the Leadership's policies were justified by the exigencies, realities and electoral possibilities of the time. These arguments

---

of the problems of higher education, which made certain recommendations. Among those participating were: John Vaizey (Oxford), Prof. W. J. M. Mackenzie (Manchester), Michael Stewart (MP) and Robin Marris (Cambridge).

1. As a quote at the beginning of *Socialism: A New Statement of Principles* said: 'We should take to socialism because it is ethically right, otherwise we shall stop short at collectivism.' (Robert Blatchford.)

were often arraigned by the Left on the loftier theoretical and moral level and consequently did not appeal to the idealistic elements in the Party. Here, at last, was an attempt by the Right to meet the moral arguments on their own plane and in their own context. Socialist Union not only attacked rigid dogma as such, but also attempted to replace certain doctrines by others. It argued a moral case from the social-democratic Right, a rare and refreshing phenomenon.

Socialist Union's success in rationalising the Leadership's position in its first publication is borne out by the semi-official backing it received. James Griffiths[1] wrote a foreword to the book and together with Morgan Phillips, then General Secretary of the Party and supposedly responsible only for official documents, launched it at a press conference. Attlee, too, strode enthusiastically into the act. He was the main speaker at a meeting officially called to introduce the booklet and its collective authors. He broke with his traditional neutralism between factions and was enthusiastic in his remarks about the new publication. Before publication date he read the proofs and wrote the following letter to *Socialist Commentary*: 'I have read this with great enjoyment and admiration. It certainly expresses in far better language than I command the views which I hold and the faith I believe.'[2] In his speech launching publication Attlee noted two aspects of the work with which he agreed: the rejection of the myth of the inevitability of socialism and the emphasis on the spirit of fraternity. He also attacked those who considered nationalisation as synonymous with socialism and underlined another fundamental point in the book: the confusion that existed in many sections of the Movement over purpose and method. Nevertheless, the Leader of the Party, although appearing to side strongly with Socialist Union, attempted to maintain his neutrality by accepting the views expressed in the booklet only in so far as they coincided with his ethical beliefs, the coincidence being substantial, and by making no specific attack upon the Left in his remarks.

The non-Labour press interpreted the reception that

1. Griffiths was at that time 'Shadow' Colonial Secretary.
2. *Socialist Commentary* documents.

Socialist Union received rather differently. The *Manchester Guardian* stated that 'yet, since no one in the Labour Party can dissociate himself from the brawls of party life let alone the present debate with the Bevanites, it is easy to see that Mr Attlee will be gladder than Mr Bevan will be at the restraint of Socialist Union and its works'.[1] The *News Chronicle*[2] and *The Times*[3] echoed this sentiment, but it was the bitter attack on the document by *Tribune* that indicated Socialist Union's antipathy to 'Bevanite' thinking. Under the title of 'Sunday School Socialism', *Tribune* said that *Socialism: A New Statement of Principles* was 'a typical example of that "fresh thinking" which consists, not in producing new ideas or fresh approaches, but in watering down distinctive socialist ideas with the muddy stream of liberal traditionalism'.[4]

Although this particular work of socialist 'liberal traditionalism' received great acclamation and caused substantial controversy, Socialist Union's later publications presented just as important a case for revisionist thinking. In May 1953 the second Socialist Union booklet was published, this time on foreign policy.[5] It was an attempt to apply the principles outlined in the first publication to world politics. Although it weaved certain issues – the rule of law, the equality of nations and the problems of underdeveloped communities – into a coherent foreign policy, it tended to reject the concept that there could be a specific *socialist* foreign policy. For instance, it said: 'Socialist principles cannot provide in advance the cut and dried solutions to detailed problems, which some people may be looking for. But, as we have shown, they can provide what is of inestimable value – a set of values.'[6] In short, the world is too complex for old-fashioned socialism.

Socialist Union's final contribution, *Twentieth Century Socialism*, was published in 1956 and was a practical elaboration in all

1. *Manchester Guardian* (27 Jun 1952).
2. 'The group makes the first thorough attempt to state the position of the non-Bevanite wing of the Party.' *News Chronicle* (27 Jun 1952).
3. *The Times* compared the new booklet to *New Fabian Essays*, and stated that both contributed to 'an open rejection of both the collectivism of the early Fabians and the common definition of Socialism as the nationalisation of the means of production, distribution and exchange' (27 Jun 1952).
4. *Tribune* (11 Jul 1952) p. 3.
5. *Socialism and Foreign Policy* (1953).   6. Ibid. p. 77.

fields of policy of the principles laid down in 1952. However, at this particular period the ideological and intellectual debate in the Party centred around Crosland's book, *The Future of Socialism*, as this was a more poignant attack on fundamentalism than anything produced by Socialist Union. This should not underrate the vital contribution that both *Socialist Commentary* and Socialist Union made to the growth of revisionism in the early fifties.

During the high-tide of Bevanism, *Socialist Commentary* willingly served as a focus for the political and strategic thinking of the Right. Its role as a participant in the inter-Party rhetoric and factionalism of the period was vital in ensuring that the Left did not have a monopoly in the field of day-to-day political warfare. Socialist Union's contribution was possibly more important in the long run, as it provided a major contribution to the growing philosophical justification for decent, moderate, parliamentary socialism. In adding a moral dimension to a position which had been too often based upon practical political justification, Socialist Union took much of the potency out of the Left's arguments. After Socialist Union the Left could never legitimately claim a monopoly of morality.

Dr Hinden's group put a heart into the philosophies of the Labour Right.

Socialist Commentary, Socialist Union and the *New Fabian Essays* provided a watershed in British democratic-socialist thinking. The policy documents of the Party, *Let Us Face the Future*, 1945; *Labour Believes in Britain*, 1949; and *Labour and the New Society*, 1950, were certainly not fundamentalist programmes yet they represented only a modernisation, mainly at the hands of Morrison, of the 'Webbism' of the 1930s. Many of the basic assumptions of earlier socialism remained, particularly with regard to social and economic analysis. The 'new thinkers' of the early fifties represented a partial break with this past; a break that was to be finalised in 1956 by Crosland's *The Future of Socialism* and Strachey's *Contemporary Capitalism*.

CROSLAND AND STRACHEY: THE FINAL BREAK WITH THE LEFT

Nothing said in the fifties and sixties, whether before or after the 1959 election, was basically new to revisionist thinking. The reaction against Marxist thought and analysis within the social-democratic Left found its first philosophical and intellectual basis in Eduard Bernstein.[1] In the 1940s with the growth and predominance of Marxist intellectual thought, only Evan Durbin produced a revisionist answer[2] although a number of young intellectuals produced works on social reform.[3] Also, Tawney was prominent with his non-Marxist attitude to public ownership and control. Nevertheless, it was not until the mid-1950s that any systemised revisionist writings appeared. In the early fifties attempts were made to place public ownership in a revisionist context, and Patrick Gordon Walker and Roy Jenkins produced books which differed fundamentally from the Marxist Left in their interpretation of socialist principles. *Socialist Commentary* was the main organ of the so-called 'new thinking' during this period. However, it was not until the publication in 1956 of Crosland's book[4] that any comprehensive and integrated post-war revisionist case was argued. At about the same time Strachey produced the first of his trilogy of works on democratic-socialism that was to finalise his break with Marxism.[5] Together with these important works, a large number of revisionist pamphlets and articles were published during the fifties, most of which appeared either in *Socialist Commentary* or *Encounter*. The Fabian Society, although more broadly based, also published many of these revisionist tracts,

1. Particularly important were: E. Bernstein, *The Suppositions of Socialism and Problems of Social Democracy* (Stuttgart, 1899), and E. Bernstein, *Evolutionary Socialism: a criticism and affirmation* (Independent Labour Party Library, London, 1909).
2. E. F. M. Durbin, *The Politics of Democratic Socialism*.
3. E.g. D. Jay, *The Socialist Case* (1937), and H. Dalton, *Practical Socialism for Britain* (1935).
4. C. A. R. Crosland, *The Future of Socialism* (1956).
5. J. Strachey, *Contemporary Capitalism* (1956). In the 1930s Strachey had produced two works – *The Nature of Capitalist Crisis* (1935) and *The Coming Struggle for Power* (1933) – which established him as a rigorous Marxist thinker.

D

one of the most important being by the then future Leader of the Party, Hugh Gaitskell.[1]

From among this flood of literature in the mid-fifties Crosland's and Strachey's contributions were by far the most significant. The two men stand out as intellectual giants, for their work was more than simply a logical development of the writings following the post-1951 defeat. In fact they represented the final break, in intellectual terms, with the Marxist legacy within socialist thinking. Crosland had two aims. First, to prove the irrelevance of the Marxist analysis to contemporary Britain, and second, to set out the revisionist case in a comprehensive manner. The upheaval that he caused in socialist intellectual circles and the theoretical debate within the Party that he instigated, is the mark of his success. Few would disagree with the contention that *The Future of Socialism* was the greatest single contribution to democratic-socialist thought produced since the war. Strachey's work, on the other hand, was more restricted in scope but dealt effectively and cogently with an analysis of the then present capitalist economic system, and the conclusions that should be drawn from such an analysis.

Crosland and Strachey attacked Marxism at its heart. They said that the world had changed. Crosland seemed to react against the Left more violently than did Strachey, and his works, although logical and well-reasoned, contained at times elements of a personal vendetta. His incisiveness and poignancy were salutary and predictably wounding to those who did not share his views. He became the Left's principal 'bogy-man' after Gaitskell.

Strachey, on the other hand, possibly because of his communist past and his more literary and detached style, did not evoke such extreme reactions in his opponents. He was a disillusioned Marxist with a resigned air about him, and his attack on his old beliefs was less frontal and consequently received less publicity. Nevertheless his role was as vital as Crosland's. They both managed to isolate the key issue – the change in economic power-relationships in post-war Britain – and in so doing prodded the central nerve in contemporary democratic socialism.

1. Gaitskell, *Socialism and Nationalisation*.

The Transfer of Power

Vital to the revisionist position during this period was its insistence that the nature of capitalist economic organisation had changed since the twenties and thirties. It argued that a fundamental transfer of power had occurred which the Marxist wing of the Party did not appreciate. This transfer had been threefold. First, the old-style capitalists no longer fulfilled an entrepreneurial function and this removed the owners of industry (the old-style capitalists) from economic decision-making. The influence of Burnham's *The Managerial Revolution* was considerable in this respect, although Crosland was careful not to over-emphasise the changes:

> As a result, although the ultimate power of course remains in the hands of the top 'lay' management, more and more influence passes to the technical experts and specialists. . . . This partial change in the character of the decision-making function naturally calls for men with a different outlook . . . from the traditional capitalist.[1]

The loss of economic power by the old-style capitalist class, it was argued, was a function of the growing scale of modern industrial and service enterprises. Strachey argued it historically:

> The hand-loom weaver owned the tools of his trade and ran his own business. So for that matter did the Lancashire mill owner – the representative figure of the capitalism of, say, a hundred years ago. He differed from the hand-loom weaver only in that he did not himself work directly at the productive process. . . . But in the year 1862, in Britain, a further change began. The Joint Stock Company with limited liability came into existence. The modern class or category of shareholders was born. . . . And this new race of beings had, and have, the distinguishing characteristic that they own, but do not conduct, the main body of the economic activity of the country. Another new race of men, the managers or directors, who conduct but do not own, had consequently to be born.[2]

The growth of monopolies and restrictive practices added strength to this argument, not only because it consolidated

---

1. Crosland, *Future of Socialism*, p. 15.
2. Strachey, *Contemporary Capitalism*, p. 35.

managerial, as opposed to capitalist, decision-making in industry, but because it changed price-determination. No longer, it was argued, were prices determined by competition, but rather they were fixed by conscious decisions of groups. This change led Strachey to write that 'such a change nullifies some of the basic principles of capitalism'.[1]

This basic change in the capitalist system was important not only in itself but also because it led, at the hands of Crosland and Strachey, to a new theory of profit. The decline of capitalist control and the growing separation of shareholders and managers in the large companies, led to a new motivation for profit. The salaries of the managerial class were not dependent upon the level of profit and therefore high personal consumption ceased to be a motive. Rewards to shareholders were also insignificant as a motive. Instead, revisionists placed an emphasis upon social prestige as a motivating factor, but accepted that one of the criteria for success and prestige in modern industrial enterprise continued to be the level of profit. Once it was accepted that social prestige was, among other aims, a central desire of the modern entrepreneurial class, then it was argued that other types of action, aside from profit, could gain this prestige for the manager. Factors involved in attaining industrial status were changing. They now involved: a reputation as a progressive employer, an initiator of profit-sharing schemes, a patriotic stance on exports or a devotee of higher production.[2] This did not suggest that profits had ceased to be the predominant motive, but it indicated that a new climate had been created in which the modern manager and economic decision-maker had adopted a 'less aggressive pursuit of maximum profit at all costs'.[3]

This so-called 'managerial revolution', which played such an important part in Crosland's and Strachey's political thinking, was first mooted from a socialist viewpoint as early as 1950 by R. H. S. Crossman.[4] Crossman is not usually considered a revisionist, mainly because within the context of the Party he

1. *Contemporary Capitalism*, p. 27.
2. Crosland, *Future of Socialism*, pp. 35–6.
3. Ibid. p. 36.
4. R. H. S. Crossman, *Whither Socialism?*, Fabian Tract No. 286 (1951), particularly pp. 11–14.

allied himself on many occasions with the Centre and Left against the Right. Nevertheless, many of his views, especially in the early 1950s, questioned and refuted many of the Left's Marxist tenets. In a Fabian Tract Crossman developed the thesis that property-ownership had become irrelevant as a social or economic power factor. By 1952, having recognised this new phenomenon, Crossman was warning against dangers inherent in it:

> But overshadowing these two questions [inflation and collective bargaining] is the threat of the managerial society. . . . The main task of Socialism today is to prevent the concentration of power in the hands of either industrial management or the state bureaucracy.[1]

Surprisingly, no similar warning appeared in the writings of any other major revisionist thinkers.

Crossman's importance lies not only in the fact that he recognised the new managerial power structure, but also that he engaged in a consistent campaign against what he considered to be an inevitable product of the new situation – an increase in arbitrary industrial power and totalitarian economic control inherent in the growing gulf between managers and workers.

Another aspect of this transfer of economic power was external to the business class. The seller's market for labour that had existed in the nation ever since the war had helped to bring about a transfer of power from management to organised labour. The most conspicuous aspect of this change, to Crosland, was the new relationship between the trade unions and the Conservative Governments of the post-war period:

> Here one can speak, without exaggeration, of a peaceful revolution. One cannot imagine today a deliberate offensive alliance between Government and employers against the Unions on the 1921, 1925–6 or 1927 models. . . . Instead the atmosphere in Whitehall is almost deferential, the desire not to give offence positively ostentatious.[2]

1. Crossman, 'Towards a Philosophy of Socialism', in *New Fabian Essays,* ed. Crossman, p. 27.
2. Crosland, *Future of Socialism,* pp. 13–14.

The third, and possibly the most important, aspect of the transfer of power that was observed in revisionist writings was the transfer from the capitalists to the state. Strachey tended to attribute this change to the growth of monopoly power: 'Whenever and wherever the process of concentration into large and few units reaches a certain point, the State itself becomes closely associated with the productive process.'[1] Crosland, on the other hand, saw the increased power of the state, that had been gained at the expense of the business class, as a consequence of the acceptance by Governments, both Conservative and Labour, of responsibility for areas that they had previously left to the free-market process; full employment, the rate of growth, the balance of payments and the distribution of incomes. If Crosland had been making this point in the 1960s he would probably have included prices and money incomes in the list.

Labour's post-war nationalisation measures had also played an important part in transferring power from the business class to the state. Crosland was dubious, however, as to whether the state had really gained commensurately with the loss of the business class. He felt that economic decisions in the public sector had passed out of the hands of the capitalist class into the hands of a new, largely *autonomous* class of public industrial managers.[2]

This gradual but definite erosion of the power of the business-ownership class, had consequences for political and economic analysis. It heralded the separation of *ownership* and *control*. Gaitskell illustrated this in an excellent work in 1955:

> The nationalisation of an industry means that it is both publicly owned and publicly controlled. But Socialist thinkers and writers have from time to time put forward the notion of public control without ownership, and also – though less frequently – the idea of public ownership without control. The latter . . . was hinted at by Dr Dalton in his *Inequality of Incomes*; the former has had, of course, much wider support. . . .[3]

This idea of the separation of ownership from control is funda-

1. Strachey, *Contemporary Capitalism*, pp. 32–3.
2. Crosland, *Future of Socialism*, p. 11.
3. H. Gaitskell, *Recent Developments in British Socialist Thinking*, Lecture, 26 Nov 1955 (1956) p. 29.

mental to an understanding of the revisionists' approach to the question of nationalisation. If ownership and control were not synonymous, then in order to fulfil its responsibilities the state would have no need to expropriate existing private property. Socialist ideals could be achieved simply by controlling and manipulating the economy and the tax-system.

Ownership therefore had become largely irrelevant as a means. It was surely never an end!

The New Position Regarding 'Ends'

The aforementioned analysis of the capitalist economic system was central to the rejection of public ownership as the main tool for the realisation of socialist ideals. Indeed, the central criticism put forward by revisionists of those in the Party who advocated massive public ownership as an ultimate goal was that they were confusing means and ends.[1] To the revisionists public ownership had no *intrinsic* value and therefore could not be considered an ideal. It could, however, play an important part in *achieving* long-term aims; one of the important by-products of the public-ownership controversy was the re-evaluation of means and ends, within a social-democratic framework.

The question was often asked: what do revisionists stand for? Do they have ultimate aims and a vision of a new society? The answer was simply that they had different ultimate aims from those of the Left. They certainly rejected public ownership as a first principle, but erected other ideals in its place. Six basic first principles of British democratic socialism emerge from a study of the works of Gaitskell, Crosland, Crossman, Jay, Jenkins and Strachey. Most of these, however, are simply a reiteration, in the contemporary context and language, of those propounded earlier by Bernstein and Durbin.

A major first principle, or rather value (it has less strident connotations), was a loose amalgam of equality, social justice and the idea of the 'classless society'. Much of this is summed up by G. D. H. Cole in a passage, often quoted by Gaitskell

1. For a detailed analysis of the confusion of 'means and ends' read D. Jay, *Socialism in the New Society* (1962) ch. 1.

and Crosland, in which he thinks of socialism as being 'a broad, human movement on behalf of the bottom dog'.[1] This whole concept, and its sub-concepts, were, of necessity, extremely vague. Nevertheless, two major strands can be seen. The first of these was a revulsion at material poverty and inequality and the accompanying need to alleviate it by social welfare. Crosland put it thus: 'The relief of distress and the elimination of this squalor is the main object of social expenditure; and a socialist is identified as one who wishes to give this an exceptional priority over other claims on resources.'[2] This was obviously an aim of the twenties and thirties that had not yet been realised and therefore was still worth fighting for. Douglas Jay, in 1937, had devoted practically the whole of his first major work to the alleviation of poverty and hardship through a redistribution of wealth made possible by a 'socialist' taxation system.[3] The promotion of welfare had been a long-standing revisionist aim. In fact, it found its way into the new amplification of aims passed by the National Executive Committee of the Party in 1960.[4] All this, however, was mainly a negative response to a given situation. More positive than this was the second strand, more abstract but nevertheless just as real; the ideals of equality, social justice and the concept of the 'classless society'. These concepts, although separate, were inter-involved. Obviously social justice involved the concept of equality and the concept of the classless society involved both equality and social justice. Unfortunately very little attempt was made to identify these concepts individually and much of the writings of the period involved an appeal to a vague combination of all of them. Equality, for instance, was rarely analytically subdivided into its economic, social and political aspects. Nevertheless, the continual emphasis on equality as an end, as opposed to public ownership or class conflict, does help to illuminate revisionist thinking. Roy Jenkins, for instance, saw equality as the concept that differentiates socialism from both liberalism and communism, and

1. G. D. H. Cole, *A Short History of the British Working-Class Movement*, vol. III (1948) p. 22.
2. Crosland, *Future of Socialism*, p. 77.
3. Jay, *The Socialist Case*.
4. *NEC Statement* (Mar 1960) para. (e).

pronounced that 'where there is no egalitarianism there is no socialism'.[1] Crossman, in the same set of essays, elevated the concept to what he considered the prime aim of socialism:

> The Socialist measures this progress of social morality by the degree of *equality* and respect for individual personality expressed in the distribution of power and in the Institutions of law and property within a State. *This standard* indeed, is what we mean by the Socialist ideal.[2]

All revisionists agreed that a greater degree of material equality was needed, based upon a more equitable distribution of wealth, but most of them laid greater stress upon social equality. This idea was a distinguishing characteristic of leading revisionists. It propounded that not all personal or group antagonisms and resentments were based upon an economic root. It was best summed up by Crosland:

> Nevertheless the case for greater equality can still rest firmly, as I believe, on certain values or ethical judgements of a non-economic character; on a belief that more equality, even though carrying few implications for the sum of economic satisfaction, would yet conduce to a 'better' society.[3]

The sort of equality Crosland is aiming for here is concerned with status not wealth. It involves an attack on privilege in a social rather than in an economic sense. It is an attempt to break down the restrictive social barriers that lead to frustration and resentment by certain groups, even though those groups may have either achieved, or are near achieving, a greater degree of economic and financial equality. The Socialist Union publication of 1956 put the same point slightly differently:

> Every person, no matter what his origins or endorsements, wants to make the most of his life in his own way. His claim to do so . . . deserves the same respect as the next man's. . . . It is an equality that rests simply and surely on their common humanity. Social privilege is the failure of society to accord this equal respect to the claims of all its members.

---

1. Jenkins, 'Equality', in *New Fabian Essays*, p. 69.
2. Crossman, 'Towards a Philosophy of Socialism', in *New Fabian Essays*, p. 10. (Italics mine.)
3. Crosland, *Future of Socialism*, p. 125.
  *

Here again, the argument is purely social and can be divorced from economic associations. This divorce illustrates one of the major differences between the revisionist and the Marxist analysis.

Before leaving the question of equality it is important to understand that revisionists did not accept, without at any rate major qualifications, the idea of 'equality of opportunity'. They rejected the concept of 'all equal at the starting gate' because this involved the acceptance of rabid competition during the race. Equality meant the continual bolstering, all along the course, of those who may fall behind.[1]

Another important socialist aim stressed by the revisionists was the ideal of the co-operative society, used both in the social and in the economic sense. Bound up with this idea was an appeal to fellowship and a rejection of both the social and economic individualism of the capitalist system. Perhaps William Morris was the originator of the idea when he said, 'Fellowship is life, lack of fellowship is death'.[2] Socialist Union, with its ethical foundations, placed great import upon this aspect of socialist thinking – the 'brotherhood of men' being an integral part of it.[3] Crosland, however, disagreed with the importance of the 'co-operative' aspiration. He accepted that society would be 'better' if there was a greater awareness of a co-operative social purpose, but he did not feel able to include this ideal in what he considered a definitive statement of socialist aims or as part of his goal. Crosland doubted whether the wholesale pursuit of the co-operative ideal would not lead to losses in other directions – personal independence, privacy and an increased standard of living.[4] Implicit in this was his view that economic growth was still based to some extent upon incentives. Incentives were founded upon competition not co-operation. If co-operation led to economic growth well and good; if not then co-operation must be jettisoned. The 'cake' must grow larger before it can be shared!

Despite Crosland's doubts, other thinkers continued to stress

1. See: (a) Socialist Union, *Twentieth-Century Socialism* (1956) p. 25; (b) Crosland, *Future of Socialism*, pp. 150–69; (c) R. H. Tawney, *Equality* (1931).
2. Quoted in *Twentieth-Century Socialism*, p. 53.
3. See *Socialism: A New Statement of Principles*, p. 35.
4. Crosland, *Future of Socialism*, p. 76.

co-operation as central to socialist aspirations.[1] It would be misleading to think of this ideal as peculiar to right-wing thought in the Party. Co-operation was an important aspiration of the old Independent Labour Party and of the Christian Socialists. For instance Walter Padley, President of USDAW and the most colourful living exponent of Christian socialism, saw 'the co-operative ideal' as crucial to his particular socialist faith.[2]

A further element in the 'co-operative syndrome' was the non-Marxist socialists' emphasis on social harmony, as opposed to social divisiveness. This view dismissed the need for class conflict as a prerequisite for socialist advance.

Growing out of the 'co-operative spirit', the idea of participation also came to be elevated into an ultimate end but mainly with an industrial connotation. The need for greater responsibility and participation by workers in economic decision-making was seen as intrinsically good as well as conducive to higher productivity.[3] Not surprisingly, though, the precise form of this greater worker participation was not elaborated upon.

Labour Party revisionism was therefore exceedingly egalitarian and democratic. It loathed élitism and its social, political and economic consequences, but remained an essentially negative response to what was considered a divided and class-ridden society. An exception was Crosland, who, although deeply concerned about the education system perpetuating this élitist structure, also made a positive contribution to Labour Party thinking by his detailed analysis of the virtues of comprehensive education.[4] Before 1956 no one in the Party had thought deeply about the role or structure of education and its vital position, as a conditioner of attitudes and perpetuator of class barriers.

As important as equality to revisionist socialists was the concept of freedom, both personal and political. This wooly and vague term was used unsparingly in conjunction with equality, as a means of defining what socialism meant. For example,

---

1. See Gaitskell's speech, *LPACR 1959*, p. 111.
2. *USDAW ADM Report*, 1960, p. 63.
3. See Crosland, *Future of Socialism*, pp. 274ff.; also, *Twentieth-Century Socialism*, ch. 10.
4. See Crosland, ibid. ch. 10.

Douglas Jay wrote, 'Socialists believe in Liberty, political and personal as firmly as they believe in Equality'.[1] Also, Socialist Union stated, 'Socialism is not only about Equality; it is also, and even more fundamentally, about Freedom'.[2] The revisionist attitude to freedom can be divided, albeit unsatisfactorily, into two types. First, freedom was seen in a narrow political sense as an absence of totalitarian and arbitrary rule. Secondly, it was seen as the enlargement of the area of choice open to an individual with particular reference to the individual as consumer.

It is unfair to treat political freedom as the special preserve of revisionists. Every non-Marxist, and even many Marxist socialist thinkers, accepted the idea of the democratic process. Nevertheless, only the revisionists elevated this democratic process (in the Western sense) to an absolute. Evan Durbin, in his book *The Politics of Democratic Socialism*, attempted to show that it was impossible to achieve socialism through non-democratic means. Indeed, revisionists seemed to cling rather narrowly to the need for a two-party system as a prerequisite for political freedom, although many of these simplistic arguments were often obscured by the use of sophisticated language.[3]

This rigid belief in the Western democratic process with the party system and preferably parliamentary government, often led right-wing thinkers to be much more 'electorate conscious' than their opponents. It led them also to think of political compromise as good in itself and as a manifestion of concern for the views of those who were not in agreement with them. A thoroughly doctrinaire approach, it was considered, had within it the seeds of intolerance and totalitarianism. But it is incorrect to think of the revisionists as being without doctrine (indeed this chapter has been analysing their contribution to it). Instead, what doctrine they had was never held rigidly; it could always be diluted by their other beliefs, particularly tolerance and compromise. The basic humanism of their approach precluded too rigid an application of their beliefs. People took precedence over political abstractions. Nevertheless it is hard for politics to be given any direction without ultimates, and revisionists possessed their fair share of them. If there was an ultimate commitment then it was to political freedom and all it entailed. Gaitskell suggested that revisionists 'were equally devoted to democracy and personal freedom. . . . They believed in tolerance and they understood the need for compromise. . . .' Thus political freedom, in the context of Western democratic institutions, became, under the influence of Durbin, Tawney, Cole, Dalton and Gaitskell, a central revisionist-socialist value.

Personal freedom was the other element involved and this centred upon the need to maintain checks against arbitrary power. In the economic field it manifested itself in the need for greater consumer choice.[1] Freedom in this sense was not seen simply in a negative context, as the absence of restraint,[2] but as something that needed to be enlarged. Not only should socially and economically imposed restraints upon the individual's freedom be eliminated, but all individuals should have their area of choice positively extended.

It is hard to understand how all this can be squared with the large amount of state and social interference that would be necessary in order to achieve the greater equality that so many of the revisionists yearned for. To be fair, they realised this dilemma but seemed unable to resolve it. The most they could do was to accept a loose mix of freedom on the one hand and equality on the other. As with all those who end up in this position, they reclined into moderation and common sense. They adopted values or ideals, as opposed to principles – for the latter were too absolute for them and would lead them into conflicts.

If, however, a choice had to be made between freedom and equality, then most of the revisionists would plump for freedom. They emphasised equality so much because within the framework of mid-twentieth-century England, freedom, and particularly its political branch, was a constant.

1. See particularly *Twentieth-Century Socialism*, ch. 4.
2. Crosland placed great emphasis upon removing socially imposed restrictions on the 'individual's private life and liberty' (p. 355). He advocated a more liberal attitude towards such moral issues as divorce-law proceedings, homosexuality and capital punishment.

To all these ideals should be added their racial and international implications. The Labour Right, together with most other socialist thinkers, stressed a rejection of discrimination based upon grounds of race, colour or creed. Also, it affirmed its belief in international order as a prerequisite to a stable and peaceful world.[1]

These then are the basic socialist ideals as put forward by revisionist thinkers. Two basic common strands can be detected. First, there is notable lack of emphasis on economic analysis or prescription. Ethical and moral judgements abound and much of the social prescription has no economic root. Naturally, public ownership is not considered as an ideal. Secondly, the idea of tolerance and compromise involved in the concept of political freedom lessens the rigid adherence to any doctrine. Of course revisionism has its doctrines, but it is 'non-doctrinaire', not in the sense of being less absolute, but in the sense of being less rigidly and ruthlessly applied.

It could be argued that the fundamentalist wing of socialist thought would agree with all these aspirations of revisionist thinking. Indeed they would, but they would consider the lack of an economic and class interpretation as a fundamental mistake. It is this difference between revisionists and fundamentalists that formed the basis of the public-ownership controversy. To fundamentalists public ownership, and the eradication of capitalism, was central to changing the economic structure – upon which, in their language, all other infrastructures were erected. The revisionists did not see this major structural economic change as necessary to fulfil their ideals.

The New Position Regarding 'Means'

Revisionists never dismissed public ownership as an important means by which their ideals could be realised. But, as Jay argued, 'Public ownership is a *means* to social justice, and only one means at that; and "nationalisation" is *only one form of public ownership.*'[2] This contention that public ownership was only one of the means towards reaching a socialist goal inevi-

1. See Appendix II, (a) and (c).
2. See D. Jay, *Beyond State Monopoly*, Fabian Tract No. 320 (1959). (Italics mine.)

tably lead them to expound the most controversial point of all – the acceptance, for all time, of the mixed economy. As early as 1953 Roy Jenkins, when he was still only feeling his way towards a revisionist position, put it rather bluntly: 'A mixed economy there will undoubtedly be, certainly for many decades and perhaps permanently, but it will need to be mixed in very different proportions. . . .'[1] By 1960 this view had become incorporated in official Party doctrine.[2]

Together with the mixed-economy idea, the view that public ownership involved not only the public corporation but a whole host of other forms of ownership, including the government shareholding concept, was accepted. Nevertheless, the main battle was soon to be won with the NEC publication of *Industry and Society* in 1957. The direct attack on Clause IV,[3] implied by the mixed-economy argument, however, was not to be so successful.

Public *ownership* was relegated in importance as a socialist 'means', because public *control* had within it most of the tools needed to achieve the revisionist view of socialist society. Ownership and power were no longer synonymous, and therefore the State had no need to take over the vast majority of privately-owned concerns, for it could control the economy by weapons already in existence.[4]

One of the major weapons was fiscal policy. Jay particularly saw the taxation weapon as fundamental to the redistribution of wealth within society.[5] Another allied concept, but one that tackled the problem from the other side, was social-welfare policy. All the major revisionist writers paid great attention to this method of increasing equality, but the writings of Professor Titmuss in this field remain to this day the major contribution.[6] Social welfare, and indeed full employment could only be

---

1. R. Jenkins, *Pursuit of Progress* (1953) p. 105.
2. See p. 169 below.   3 See p. 160 below.
4. For an analysis of these weapons see *Twentieth-Century Socialism*, ch. 13.
5. See Jay, *The Socialist Case* and *Socialism in the New Society*. Also, Crosland, p. 224, and Gaitskell, *Recent Developments in British Socialist Thinking*, p. 25.
6. See R. H. Titmuss, *Essays on the Welfare State* (1958), and 'The Irresponsible Society', an additional chapter of *Essays on the Welfare State* (1963). We have seen earlier that social welfare was considered by some revisionist thinkers as an 'end' in itself. Others considered it as a 'means' to greater equality. Revisionists themselves were often confused as to the precise separation of 'ends' and 'means'.

pursued, however, within the framework of a planned economy. Central and regional planning therefore became more important as a means whereby left-wing governments could achieve a greater measure of social justice and equality. The theoretical background for the planned economy was produced by Keynes,[1] but revisionist thinkers elaborated on the theory, in a political context, and added a whole new range of economic controls both direct and indirect. The outcome of all this was the 'managed' or 'controlled' economy. Democratic planning became the alternative to complete state ownership. The wartime and post-war experiments in detailed planning, however, provided serious arguments in favour of less bureaucracy and greater mobility in the allocation of resources within the economy. Crosland rejected certain aspects of the post-war experiment: 'This necessarily involves an intricate complex of licensing, rationing and allocation controls. . . . They deny the consumer a free choice of goods and suppliers . . . they involve an excessive growth of bureaucracy.'[2] He went on to make a major break with fundamentalist thinking in advocating the price mechanism as the most satisfactory system of distributing the 'great bulk of consumer goods and industrial-capital goods'.

The case for further intervention in the private sector was based upon the need for the Government to stimulate expansion in the economy and to help the balance-of-payments position – when what he calls 'social' and 'private' costs appear to diverge. A basic agreement between Crosland and free-market economists can be seen here in the method of analysis.[3] They differed only over the amount of emphasis to be given to social as opposed to private costs. Indeed, as Crosland himself put it,

> the issue of planning is not now one of the fundamental differences between Right and Left. Naturally important differences of emphasis remain, productive of much political heat. But generally the issue now is not whether, but how much, and to what purpose, to plan.[4]

---

1. See J. M. Keynes, *The General Theory of Employment, Interest and Money* (1936).
2. Crosland, *Future of Socialism*, p. 343.
3. See E. Powell, *A Nation Not Afraid* (1965).
4. Crosland, *Future of Socialism*, p. 344. Times have changed. Large sections of Conservative thought now almost totally reject all economic planning.

The tool of planning, in order to achieve economic growth and efficiency, was certainly a legitimate weapon for the revisionists, whereas the Right[1] would tend to feel that growth would be more readily achieved under a totally free system. Economic growth itself became very important. Revisionists were not content simply to redistribute an existing 'cake', but wanted to concentrate on making the 'cake' larger. The unsolved question, however, remained: would the short-run disadvantages (in terms of equality) associated with enlarging the cake, outweigh the long-term advantages of a higher gross national product?

Two major points emerge from this analysis of the revisionist approach to contemporary capitalism and the methods that they argued were necessary in order to achieve their ideals. First, although the revisionists were subjected to continual attack in a propagandist sense from *Tribune*, no comprehensive and detailed alternative analysis or prescription was put forward. The *New Left Review*, on the one hand, and Emile Burns, in a cogently argued polemic, on the other,[2] made sporadic raids upon the revisionist approach. They failed. First because of the sheer quantity of revisionist writings of the fifties; and secondly because in answering them they too often lapsed into abuse and polemics.

But a major criticism of the revisionists remains. In their attempt to define their ultimate ends they remained conspicuously vague. Concepts such as equality and social justice are indeed hard to define in any precise way. Perhaps a more realistic explanation of this inability to be precise lies in the revisionists' distrust of what Max Weber has called the 'ethics of ultimate ends'. Patrick Gordon Walker illustrated this view when he said that progress cannot be judged in an absolute sense because 'we would be guilty of making our own subjective and unstated standards masquerade as absolutes'.[3] It was put perhaps even better by Bernard Crick, although in a negative and more polemical form:

The idealists of the rank and file of the *New Left Review* will

---

1. Used in this sense to denote free-enterprise economists.
2. E. Burns, *Right-Wing Labour* (1961).
3. P. Gordon Walker, *Restatement of Liberty*, p. 180.

remain inevitable dupes of the old Marxists so long as they believe in being absolutely right about somebody else's business.... The ethic of ultimate ends in politics is, at its best, the phariseeism latent in pacifism; at its worst, it is the ruthlessness of Stalinism. Vision is needed, but it needs to be a persuasive vision, not a strident, intolerant, denunciatory vision.[1]

Here, however, we can see a new ideal emerging – that of tolerance, conciliation and compromise. Indeed, this was the ideal behind the obsession with democratic forms that many revisionists portrayed. Strachey, for instance, was particularly rigid in his defence of the 'democratic process', although in his case it may have been because of a revulsion against his Marxist past.

1. B. Crick, 'Socialist Literature in the Fifties', in *Political Quarterly* (Jul–Sep 1960) p. 367.

CHAPTER FIVE

The Success of the 'New Thinkers'

The sluggish giant is not always slow to incorporate new ideas into its bloodstream. The 'new thinking' of the early 1950s, and the ideas circulated by Crosland, Gaitskell, Strachey and others in the mid-1950s, culminated in 1957 in the adoption by the whole Labour Movement of the policy document on public ownership, *Industry and Society*.[1] This was a thoroughly revisionist document, and its publication would have been inconceivable had it not been for the groundwork carried out by revisionists following the defeat of the Party in 1951.

The adoption of *Industry and Society* also marked the end of the 'consolidationist' approach to public ownership.[2] A feature of the earlier 'consolidationist-fundamentalist' debate was an awareness by many on the revisionist wing of the Party of the inadequacy of Labour's public-ownership proposals in general and of the 'state-board' system in particular. Also, *New Fabian Essays* and Socialist Union publications created an atmosphere in which a reappraisal of party thinking on public ownership was possible. The loss of the election in 1955 made this reappraisal both urgent and necessary.

The debate following the 1955 election was different in kind from that following the 1959 election. 1959–60 saw a fundamental confrontation over principles following an assault by the Gaitskellites upon what many considered to be the Party's soul. Established and enshrined traditions were at stake in 1959,

1. *Industry and Society: Labour's policy on future public ownership* (1957).

2. It is not surprising therefore that Morrison, the architect of 'consolidationism', opposed, at the 1957 Party Conference, the adoption of *Industry and Society*. See his speech, *LPACR 1957*, pp. 135–6.

whereas in the post-1955 situation no such direct attack was made.[1] Instead of a frontal assault the Party witnessed the growth of new concepts and ideas, some of which actually envisaged the enlargement of the public sphere. This helps to explain the 'quiet revolution' inherent in the adoption of *Industry and Society*, for instead of denying the importance of the future role of public ownership, it presented alternative types of common ownership to the Movement.

The quietness of the revolution, however, should not overshadow its significance. The adoption of *Industry and Society* together with its sister publication, *Public Enterprise*, consolidated three important trends in Labour thinking. All three of them contained elements of revisionist thought.

The first important trend was concerned with what I have already described as the growing 'critical faculty' in the Movement towards aspects of the nationalised industries. We have already seen how Davies, Gaitskell and *Socialist Commentary* began this process and how Crosland added to it in his major work of 1956.[2] Many of the criticisms levelled at the existing nationalised industries by the above writers were echoed by *Public Enterprise* in May 1957. Some of the ideas in that document regarding the organisation, structure and financing of the nationalised industries showed their influence. Also their particular pleas regarding devolution in management, greater joint consultation between management and worker and more consumer-orientation found expression in the document. For instance, Davies suggested that one of the reasons for the inadequate public relations of the publicly owned industries was lack of public awareness regarding the Consumer Councils. He suggested that 'the present need is to publicise to greater effect the existence of these Consumer Councils, their purpose and activities'.[3] Five years later the official document stated: 'We have no doubt that the chief weakness in consumer consultation is that too few consumers know that it exists. There is urgent

---

1. A distinction should be made between a political and a theoretical debate. As we have seen from the last chapter the mid-1950s witnessed the climax of the intellectual debate over public ownership. This did not manifest itself in a political form until the crisis over Clause IV, described in Chapter Eight.

2. Crosland, *Future of Socialism*. See particularly ch. xvii.

3. Davies, *Problems of Public Ownership*, p. 27.

need for better publicity about the work done by the Councils and the service provided for consumers.'[1]

The ideas in *Public Enterprise*, however, were not the sole preserve of the revisionists. *Keeping Left*, for instance, considered that, 'We cannot disguise the fact that the public corporations have not, so far, provided everything which socialists expected from nationalised industries'.[2] Left-wing criticism of the system, however, laid stress upon the lack of worker participation in the industries whereas most of the revisionist tracts, while admitting that greater consultation should be attempted, placed emphasis upon the need for increased efficiency and better public relations. *Public Enterprise* paid only scant regard to the question of labour relations and concerned itself primarily with questions of management and finance.[3]

The second important trend of 1957 was the further progress made towards conditioning the Movement to accept forms of public ownership other than nationalisation. *Industry and Society* made a totally new breakthrough in this field by advocating the community shareholding principle. This was a radical departure as no official document had spelt out in detail this idea before, although some (particularly *Labour and the New Society*) had produced a large number of alternative systems of public ownership.

Two methods of community shareholding were proposed. *Industry and Society* advocated a system whereby death duties should be paid in shares and land rather than in cash.[4] Dalton had originally conceived the idea with respect to land[5] and both Gaitskell and Crosland extended this to equity shares.[6] Gaitskell was probably the first political writer to advance

1. *Public Enterprise*, p. 36.
2. *Keeping Left*, p. 29. Crossman, a signatory of *Keeping Left*, also made an individual contribution to the re-evaluation of the nationalised industries. He was particularly interested in the workers'-participation system of West German publicly-owned industry. See Crossman, *Socialism and the New Despotism*, p. 14.
3. Only one of the 30 'conclusions' arrived at in the document referred to labour relations.
4. *Industry and Society*, p. 40. This idea was originally proposed in *Towards Equality: Labour's policy for social justice* (1956), but it received little attention.
5. See H. Dalton, *Inequality of Incomes in Modern Communities* (1920).
6. Crosland, *Future of Socialism*, p. 236, and Gaitskell, *Socialism and Nationalisation*, p. 35.

this view, as most of the work on his 1956 Fabian pamphlet *Socialism and Nationalisation* was completed by 1953. In it he suggested that the state could become the owner of industrial, commercial or agricultural property 'either by taking in death duties – not cash or bonds but equity shares or real estate – or, by using the proceeds of a budget surplus to purchase equity shares. . .'.[1]

The other method of community shareholding mentioned in *Industry and Society* also had its political origins with Gaitskell and Crosland. Gaitskell suggested that:

> a gradual extension of the public ownership of property . . . could undoubtedly be carried through without a great extension of the list of nationalised industries. It would no doubt be necessary to set up one or two new public Corporations which would in effect be large investment trusts – not so different in their operation from the insurance companies or some other financial institution.[2]

The precise nature of the public corporation envisaged by Gaitskell was worked out in *Industry and Society*. It involved a National Superannuation Fund under the control of independent trustees, who would invest the surplus of contributions over pension payments.[3]

These two new methods of increasing community ownership of industrial shares met with considerable opposition from within the Party. Many people on the Left did not see this new system as increasing public ownership, but rather as creating a situation whereby 'a future Labour Government is going to be a hostage bound hand and foot to the capitalist system'.[4] This view was not confined only to the Left. There were a considerable number of trade union MPs, some with governmental experience in the period of 1945–51, who considered this new method a betrayal of 'Morrisonian' public ownership and as a compromise with capitalism.[5]

1. Gaitskell, op. cit.   2. Ibid. p. 42.   3. *Industry and Society*, p. 40.
4. M. Edelman, *LPACR 1957*, p. 132.
5. E.g. Shinwell said at the 1952 Conference: 'We either take this way, the capitalist way – for, after all, it is the capitalist way, not likely to be seriously objected to by the Tories – after all, to invest in private undertakings, bolstering up shares, becoming shareholders and investors, all the capitalist bag of tricks will not alarm them unduly. I say it is either this way or to stand firmly by our fundamental principles.' *LPACR 1952*, p. 140.

Two further points emerged from the discussions surrounding the new state shareholding system. First, the Left were worried about the implications of the new system upon the collective bargaining situation. The fact that a future Labour Government should become an interested party in an industrial dispute (because of its shareholdings it would be acting the role of employer) was seen as 'unsocialist'. This was an unsound criticism because the official document had made it clear that the proposed trustees would be independent of government control and would 'be able to invest in whatever manner they consider will best safeguard the interests of contributors'.[1] A further point of controversy arose out of an idea put forward by Douglas Jay that the profit from these state shareholdings should be used to reduce taxation.[2] Although this view did not find its way into the official document it caused some controversy at the Party Conference. It was argued that profit-making was a 'capitalist' phenomenon and that it was inconceivable for socialists to advocate profits accumulated 'at the expense of the worker'.[3] Roy Jenkins answered this criticism by refuting the idea that profit was purely a feature of privately-owned industries and that some form of surplus was needed in order to finance development without recourse to borrowing from outside the industry.[4] However, this apparently sensible argument failed to convince those with an emotional distrust of private property.

It is apparent that the community-shareholding principle, although increasing the area of public ownership, was an infringement of the belief held by many in the Movement that socialist action should be divorced from any participation in the 'capitalist' economic and financial structure. Furthermore, the proposals in *Industry and Society* that this participation should not involve the state control of companies in which it had

1. *Industry and Society*, p. 40.
2. Letter to *The Times* (26 Jul 1957) p. 11e.
3. *LPACR 1957*, p. 132.
4. Jenkins said: 'I do not know how you can run industry without making some form of profit, even although they call it a surplus. The nationalised industries also make a profit, even though they call it a surplus. I wish the National Coal Board were allowed to make a bigger profit, so that they could finance more development out of their own resources. . . .' Ibid. p. 152.

invested caused further resentment.[1] Gaitskell had earlier refused to commit himself on the degree of control envisaged. When referring to his proposed public corporations he had said, 'How far they would exercise control over the companies in which they held shares is not a matter on which it would be wise to be dogmatic now'.[2] Jenkins, however, was more decided on the matter:

> I do not think it would be possible to exercise an effective control over the policy of those firms even if you owned them. How are you going to do it? They would presumably be responsible to the President of the Board of Trade. The Minister of Fuel and Power already has enough difficulty in controlling three nationalised industries. How the President of the Board of Trade in a future Labour government is going effectively to control a majority of the 512 I do not know.[3]

Another aspect of this new approach to public ownership was the question of 'competitive public enterprise'. This was the system whereby the state would acquire direct control of individual firms within given industries rather than national-ising the whole industry, as had been the pattern after the war. As we have seen from an earlier chapter this idea was not new to official Party thinking, but *Industry and Society* continued the campaign to make this approach acceptable.[4] Many revisionists helped to publicise this idea, but perhaps the most detailed and well-argued case appeared in *The Future of Socialism* (pp. 332–9). Crosland was optimistic regarding the successful operation of such companies, but remained sceptical about the criteria used for selecting which companies within an industry should be taken over.

1. J. Campbell (NUR), who moved the reference back of the official document, stated: 'When he [Harold Wilson] talked, as he did, over this new approach to the problems of the day, for example, about obtaining control through purchase of shares without participating in the management. . . . This is power without responsibility, the prerogative of the harlot down through the years.' Ibid. p. 131.
2. Gaitskell, *Socialism and Nationalisation*, p. 35.
3. *LPACR 1957*, p. 153. The figure 512 referred to the number of firms con-sidered for control in the motion being debated at the Conference.
4. 'Thus it may be that public ownership of a single firm will suffice to break a production bottleneck or restore competition in a monopolised industry. It may be that new industries, like atomic energy, can be pioneered from the start under public ownership. It may be that public participation in a private firm can be secured through State investment in it.' *Industry and Society*, p. 47.

The growth of these other methods of public ownership[1] – a means of achieving greater equality and a more equitable distribution of wealth – was only one aspect of the revolution inherent in the adoption of *Industry and Society*. Possibly more far-reaching was the contention that there existed methods of governmental control which provided an alternative to public ownership as a means of furthering socialist aims.

One such method of government control was fiscal policy. As we have seen, Jay[2] had pioneered the cause of taxation as a major socialist instrument in the search for equality and by 1957 this had become central to official Party policy. *Industry and Society* argued that increased 'democratisation' of private ownership (i.e. profit-sharing and dividend-limitation) was inadequate for the purpose of achieving greater equality of wealth. Instead a capital gains tax was proposed. It was further argued that as capital gains resulted in augmenting wealth and spending-power they should therefore be treated in exactly the same way as other forms of personal income. It took eight years for this suggestion to be implemented as national policy!

Here again the influence of the revisionists is easy to discern. In a lecture in 1955, Gaitskell considered that 'he [the modern socialist] is also impressed with the extent to which capital gains free of tax have preserved inequality, and he feels that the British system is out of date and anomalous, and should if possible be brought into line with other countries, such as the U.S.A. and Sweden'.[3] Crosland likewise considered this tax necessary:

> Moreover, apart from considerations of logic and equity between taxpayers, there is a clear redistributive case for taxing capital gains. They accrue only to those who already own property; and the present distribution of property ... is not only highly un-equal, but also, since so high a proportion is inherited, the least defensible aspect of inequality. Thus all the evils inherent in the

---

1. A surprising omission from *Industry and Society* was the idea of municipal enterprise. Indeed the Party was committed to a massive increase in municipalised housing by the adoption of *Homes for the Future* (1956) at the Conference of 1956.
2. See Jay, *The Socialist Case*.
3. Gaitskell, *Recent Developments in British Socialist Thinking*, p. 20.

maldistribution of private capital are magnified by the exemption from tax of the gains to which that capital gives rise, and which still further increase the inequality of purchasing power; and a tax on these gains is therefore wholly to be desired on socialist grounds.[1]

The introduction of the capital gains tax into the official Labour vocabulary was a singular success for revisionist-socialist thinking. A further success was the acceptance by an erstwhile suspicious Party of the need to work within the capitalist system and thereby accept the permanence of the mixed economy. Share-buying and profit-making by the state had previously been alien to many socialists and its acceptance in 1957 was a measure of the influence of revisionist thinkers on official policy.

Another important breakthrough for revisionism was that *Industry and Society* at no point referred to public ownership as an ideal in itself. Indeed, in the introduction the document stated that 'public ownership has always been regarded by British Socialists as a *means* towards achieving the ultimate ideals of socialism'.[2] An interesting feature of the debate over *Industry and Society* was that some members of the NEC, in order to persuade Conference to accept the document, deliberately downgraded this aspect of it. When referring to public ownership Harold Wilson said of his NEC colleagues, 'We found that though the faith was a common one, we varied in the emphasis we put on particular reasons for it.'[3] It was quite obvious, however, that 'the faith' was not a common one, for a vital message of *Industry and Society* was that public ownership was not a question of 'faith' but rather of method.[4]

Two consequences flowed from this rejection of public ownership as an end in itself. First, the separation of means and ends became an important discussion point in a Party that had for so long refused to isolate them from each other. Secondly, once this separation had been accomplished, it was

1. Crosland, *Future of Socialism*, p. 241.
2. *Industry and Society*, p. 7. (Italics mine.)
3. *LPACR 1957*, p. 129.
4. Quite apart from this, the Leader of the Party had on many occasions (i.e. at the Party Conference of 1955, *LPACR 1955*, p. 175) made clear that his own first principles did not include public ownership.

'equality' rather than 'public ownership' that emerged as the major socialist ideal, a process that the Gaitskellites could feel well pleased with. They had re-established Labour as an egalitarian party.

This, therefore, was the measure of success that revisionist thinking had achieved in the Party. Also, surprisingly little sacrifice in terms of Party unity or dissent was entailed in the process of persuading the Movement to adopt these views.

THE ADOPTION OF 'INDUSTRY AND SOCIETY'

Following the defeat of 1955 Labour set up a whole series of study-groups with a view to setting in motion a round of policy documents that would be presented over a period of three years to the Annual Conferences of the Party.[1] Although one resolution at the 1955 Conference wanted a special committee set up to deal with this re-examination,[2] the NEC managed to restrict the policy-making to its own Home Policy sub-committee, thereby keeping it in its own hands. In turn this sub-committee left the drafting process to study-groups which consisted entirely of members of the NEC.[3]

An analysis of the composition of the two study-groups which dealt with public ownership shows that on each of them the Right had a majority. For instance, out of the 10 full members on the study-group dealing with *Public Enterprise – Labour's review of nationalised industries*, only 3 (possibly 4) were associated with the 'expansionist' school of the early 1950s.[4] Similarly the study-group on *Industry and Society* produced a pro-Leadership majority although in this case the Left were better

1. Documents concerning Equality, Housing and The Individual's Relation with Society were presented in 1956. In 1957 Security and Old Age, The Nationalised Industries and the Future of Public Ownership were considered. In 1958, policy documents relating to The Atomic and Automatic Age, Agriculture and Education were discussed.

2. Harrow Borough Labour Party proposed this in Composite Resolution No. 88, *LPACR 1955*, p. 119.

3. Some outside experts were brought into the preliminary discussion – but only in the form of 'co-opted membership'.

4. They were Aneurin Bevan, Tom Driberg and Ian Mikardo. Harry Nicholas (NEC representative of the TGWU) was not involved in the debates surrounding the 'shopping-list' controversy, although his views on public ownership were considerably to the left of Gaitskell's.

represented.[1] Nevertheless, both study-groups reported back to the full NEC where the final decision regarding publication was taken and in this arena the Right, bolstered by the trade union section, could manage an almost two-to-one majority.

This helps to explain the lack of specific candidates scheduled for nationalisation. *Challenge to Britain* (the policy document of 1953) had listed Mining-machinery, Aircraft and Land as ripe for certain forms of public ownership. *Industry and Society* made no reference to these industries at all and apart from Steel and Road Haulage advocated nothing specific. Indeed the reason given for lack of further specific candidates seemed fairly hastily prepared:

> In recent years inquiries into the problems and organisation of several other industries have been undertaken by the Labour party, by the TUC and by other groups in the Labour movement. Although much useful spade-work has been done, many of the facts upon which judgement must be based are simply not available to an Opposition Party; and – an additional complication in a period of great industrial development – the facts themselves can rapidly change.[2]

In fact it was a stalling operation and was seen as such. Being in opposition did not hinder the NEC from making definite commitments on Steel and Road Haulage, both of which were in exactly the same position as many other industries regarding ascertainment of data. In fact the NEC would have preferred to include no specific public-ownership recommendations at all, but for reasons of Party harmony felt obliged to list Steel and Road Haulage. This view is supported by Morrison who found the document 'confusing', 'too clever by half' and suggested that 'it is trying to please so many wings of the Movement that it will have no wings to fly with itself'.[3] This view may have been unfair, and based upon Morrison's resentment at his old philosophy being ditched, but the document was indeed vague and left itself open to numerous interpreta-

---

1. NEC members of the study-group included: Griffiths (Chairman), Bevan, Brinhan, Castle, Cooper, Driberg, Gaitskell, Gooch, Greenwood, Mikardo, Nicholas, Padley, Skeffington, Tallon, Wilson. There were no co-opted members.
2. *Industry and Society*, p. 46.
3. *LPACR 1957*, p. 136.

tions.[1] The pledge from the NEC that the new proposals for share-buying were not an alternative to nationalisation further complicated the issue.

This confusion over the exact meaning of certain aspects of the document produced a varied response from the Left after its publication in July of 1957. Immediately following the publication and the accompanying press conference, *Tribune* gave what amounted to a cautious endorsement of the statement but remained suspicious on the question of interpretation: 'We do not say dogmatically that the words mean nothing. What we do say with absolute assurance is that no one can state for certain what they mean.'[2] Frank Cousins, on the other hand, was more certain as to the meaning of many of the passages in *Industry and Society*. He said of his union:

> We are not prepared to accept a statement which is a substitute for present methods of public ownership. . . . But the Labour Party has made it clear that it intends to use the form of public ownership most suited to the particular industry. If that is so then we will endorse the statement.[3]

At that time Cousins did not seem to realise that the document before him, as well as down-grading the principle of public enterprise in general, referred to 'firms' as opposed to 'industries' in connection with future proposals. Nevertheless, the fact that Cousins could support the document shows that its vagueness contributed greatly to Party unity. Facing both ways is not always a political liability.

Enthusiasm for the document came from another strange quarter – Ian Mikardo. His membership both of the NEC and of the sub-committee's study-group that drafted *Industry and Society* may have limited his ability to criticise it. Nevertheless, in the early stages following publication he believed that the 'total public ownership of the large firm sector'[4] could be

1. E.g. the phrase (*Industry and Society*, p. 57): 'We reserve the right to extend public ownership in any industry or part of industry which, after thorough enquiry, is found to be seriously failing the nation', can be open to many interpretations. An interesting emphasis is placed upon 'seriously' in the quoted phrase. All previous documents had simply referred to 'failing the nation'.

2. Editorial in *Tribune* (19 Jul 1957).

3. *TGWU Biennial Conference Report 1957*. This forms part of the *TGWU Record* (Aug 1957).

4. *Tribune* (19 Jul 1957) p. 5.

achieved within the framework of the policies outlined in *Industry and Society*. Even a cursory study of the relevant sections of the document would illustrate that Mikardo's thesis was extremely optimistic:

> The Labour Party recognizes that, under increasingly profes-
> sional managements, large firms are as a whole serving the nation
> well. Moreover we recognize that no organisation, public or
> private, can operate effectively if it is subjected to persistent and
> detailed interventions from above. We have, therefore, no inten-
> tion of intervening in the management of any firm which is doing
> a good job.[1]

Mikardo continued to support the document, he could do little else as an NEC member, but blamed Gaitskell, Wilson and Crossman for 'playing the programme down'.[2] He obviously assumed that *Industry and Society* contained fundamentalist pro-posals and, for a short time, it seemed as if this exercise in political *double entendre* was going to work.

By the time of the Party Conference, however, many of the left-wing elements that had originally given the document support had a change of mind. For instance, *Tribune* published a leading article stating that in its view the document should have been 'referred back'.[3]

Conference passed *Industry and Society* by 5,383,000 to 1,442,000 votes. The size of this majority was a result of the overwhelming support given to the document by the larger trade unions. Only one member of the 'big 6', the NUR, voted against the NEC's proposal for adoption of the report.[4]

Four out of the other five major unions were well content with the new policy document and both Birch (USDAW) and Carron (AEU) reported their views to the Conference. The TGWU, however, found itself in an extremely ambiguous position. Its delegation cast one million votes for the document, but its General Secretary remained highly critical of many aspects of it. He suggested that 'you do not necessarily get

---

1. *Industry and Society*, p. 49.   2. *Tribune* (26 Jul 1957) p. 5.
3. Ibid. (4 Oct 1957) p. 1.
4. The NUR also moved the following resolution: 'This Conference affirms its belief in the common ownership of all the basic industries and means of production and deplores the present tendency to deviate from these accepted Socialist prin-ciples. . . .' *LPACR 1957*, p. 131.

socialism with nationalisation but you do not get socialism without nationalisation'.[1] On this criterion, therefore, *Industry and Society* was very far from being a socialist document!

Some of the ideas propounded in *Industry and Society* found their way into the Party's election manifesto of 1959.[2] Nevertheless this manifesto was very similar to previous ones, for it advocated the re-nationalisation of Iron and Steel and long-distance Road Haulage and stated that 'where an industry is shown, after thorough enquiry, to be failing the nation we reserve the right to take all or any part of it into public ownership if this is necessary'.[3]

Therefore, in practical electoral terms the Party's public-ownership proposals had changed little in ten years. In its more detailed and analytical works on public ownership, however, there had been a significant change in emphasis. *Industry and Society* was a far less fundamentalist document than *Challenge to Britain* (1953), its immediate predecessor. The Party's more flexible descriptive and prescriptive attitude to common ownership was not easily translated into electoral terms, and therefore the Party's 'image' remained much the same as it had always been: that of a doctrinaire, nationalising Party. But a case existed for the contention that in real terms the Party had changed its attitudes but had received insufficient public credit for it.

In fact, the public hardly realised that any such controversy had taken place, and it was not until Gaitskell raised the issue of Clause IV in 1959 that the question of common-ownership ever reached the headlines.

Labour's quiet economic policy revolution was submerged beneath the more colourful and dramatic convulsions over foreign policy and defence.

1. Ibid. p. 143.
2. E.g. 'We shall also ensure that the community enjoys some of the profits and capital gains now going to private industry by arranging for the purchase of shares by public investment agencies such as the Superannuation Fund Trustees.' *Britain Belongs to You!* (1959).
3. Ibid.

CHAPTER SIX

The Spectre of
Ernest Bevin

THE REJECTION OF 'A SOCIALIST FOREIGN POLICY'

The Labour Movement lived with Ernest Bevin in a state of confusion. As Foreign Secretary his policies cut deeply across many traditional socialist attitudes to foreign affairs. His ardent support of the American Alliance and his tough and entrenched opposition to any further Soviet expansion naturally led to a reappraisal of what a socialist foreign policy should be. This process produced a school of thought which clashed violently with traditional beliefs and upset many hallowed assumptions. In the forefront of this new approach was a group of young, right-wing intellectuals whose sympathies on foreign-policy questions were with the Leadership and whose writings and speeches were ruthlessly analytical. What Douglas Jay, Anthony Crosland and Roy Jenkins were attempting to do to British democratic socialism on the home front, Denis Healey, Christopher Mayhew, Reginald Prentice, John Strachey and Kenneth Younger and others were attempting in the field of foreign policy.

These 'new thinkers' used their arguments very often as a justification for the Leadership's foreign policy proposals and as a reaction to the assaults on them from the Left of the Party. Their fundamental thesis centred around a rejection of the notion that foreign policy decisions could and should always be firmly based upon socialist principles. They dismissed the notion that 'a socialist foreign policy'[1] could be a viable con-

1. There are many examples in the early 1950s of attempts by the Left of the Party to construct a 'Socialist foreign policy'. Many of them placed an emphasis on different aspects of British relations with the world but all were agreed that a foreign policy should be based upon certain, defined, socialist principles.

cept in international affairs. This reference to certain well-defined principles as the basis for international action was often the ground upon which the Left and the 'Bevanites' chose to debate with the Leadership. The defence of the Party's official position with regard to the United States, NATO, British and German rearmament and SEATO was not easy, and often hypocritical, when justified by socialist language and rhetoric. After all, could a socialist really support German rearmament? The major effect of the young revisionists was that, being free from the restraints of leadership, they boldly shifted the assumptions upon which the controversy existed.

Many revisionist political thinkers believed that traditional ideology should play no part in foreign-policy decision-making, and in its place they erected the 'power-political' approach. Mayhew declared in June 1950: 'It is not ideology, but logic and common sense which point the way to a broad rather than a narrow approach to the unity of the West.'[1] Healey was much more direct than this; he continually attempted to show that the failure of the Left to produce a coherent foreign policy was based upon both their rejection of the 'power-political' approach and their utopianism:

> It [the party] has too often fallen victim to Utopianism. In particular, it tends to discount the power elements in politics, seeing it as a specific evil of the existing system rather than a generic characteristic of politics as such. The liberal utopian believes that if left to themselves men will automatically act for common interest. The Marxian utopian exaggerates the influence of economic factors on human behaviour and believes that all social evils stem from a bad system of property relations. *In both cases deprecation of the power factor entails an inadequate understanding of the techniques of power.*[2]

Inherent in this propagation of a non-ideological approach to world affairs was a realisation of the inability of the British Government *alone* to take firm stands. World politics, as opposed to internal affairs, entailed the restraining elements of foreign powers. In foreign policy, affirmation was not enough.

1. Mayhew, 'British Foreign Policy Since 1945', in *International Affairs* (Oct 1950). This was a transcript of a speech he delivered at Chatham House on 27 Jun 1950.
2. Healey, in *New Fabian Essays*, p. 162. (Italics mine.)

E

All serious students of international affairs saw this clearly and it was also the unhappy conclusion of those thinkers in the Party who, while adopting fairly radical and Left policies at home, were considered right-wing on foreign policy.[1]

This view ran directly counter to the views of those who believed that a distinctive 'socialist foreign policy' was not only desirable but also possible. A good example of this thought-process was a motion, moved at the 1952 Party Conference by John Mendelson, which stated: 'We can best serve the cause of peace by sticking to our distinctive socialist principles and refusing to subordinate them to American, Russian or any other pressures.'[2] The neutralism inherent in this motion, together with the view that 'socialism' was somehow ideologically midway between 'capitalism' and 'communism', was strongly rejected by revisionist foreign-policy thinkers who contended not only that British neutralism would alter the balance of power in the world, but also that Britain had a greater identity of interest with the United States than with the Soviet Union.[3]

As well as condemning 'equidistant' theory, revisionists were also suspicious of the Left's blanket moral condemnation of nuclear weapons and nuclear war. They considered that the term 'evil' when applied to nuclear weapons, or the contemplation of using nuclear weapons, was a truism accepted by all shades of opinion and therefore irrelevant as an issue. It was also suggested that the force of the moral argument against nuclear war often hindered politicians from thinking about and analysing in depth the nuclear situation.[4] The moral and emotional climate of the time did not, however, have much effect upon revisionist defence thinkers who continued to study in depth the issues involved. More often than not this analysis resulted in a defence of the balance of power and deterrent

1. E.g. Michael Stewart's views on public ownership in the early fifties were 'expansionist' in nature, but on foreign policy and defence he was an ardent supporter of the Leadership. He even advocated that in certain circumstances the West should be the first to use nuclear weapons. *Policy and Weapons in the Nuclear Age*, Fabian Tract No. 296 (1955).

2. Composite Motion 20, *LPACR 1952*, p. 116.

3. For revisionist attitudes to neutralism see Healey, *Neutralism*, and Chapter Nine of this work.

4. See F. W. Mulley, *The Politics of Western Defence* (1962) ch. 2, and J. Strachey, *On the Prevention of War* (1962) ch. 4.

theory. Revisionist defence thinking culminated with two important works by Mulley and Strachey in 1962.[1] They both had reservations about certain aspects of deterrent theory (for instance, the concept of massive retaliation as advocated after 1957) but basically supported it as a guarantee of peace.

Therefore the rejection by revisionists of the viability of the concept of a 'socialist foreign policy' was largely based upon an awareness of the power element in international affairs, and the vital distinction between the freedom of action of a government at home and the restrictions imposed on it in its dealings with foreign powers. A suspicion of any generalised condemnation of nuclear weapons and an abhorrence of ideological motivation in foreign policy were also important influences.

Nevertheless, much as they distrusted it, the ideological element was not totally absent as an ingredient in the foreign and defence thinking of the revisionist socialists. Although they preferred to think of themselves as primarily strategic practitioners, subtle doctrinaire attitudes were inherent in their views of both the United States of America and the Soviet Union. Labour's divided attitude to the two post-war super powers is vital to an understanding of its split personality on foreign affairs.

The Left's antipathy towards the foreign policy of the United States was as much a result of reaction to America's own internal social, political and economic system as to the specific foreign-policy decisions of her administrations. Also, the Left was often naïve about the United States, as the following speech by the mover of the Lambeth Norwood resolution[2] at the 1952 Party Conference illustrates:

There are two Americas: the America of Socialism and the America of reaction. Unfortunately the America of reaction, led and dominated by 60 monopolistic families, control [sic] the American economy.[3]

This may have been a simple view but many articulate members

1. Ibid.
2. This motion, in the form of an amendment to the NEC policy document, asked the Conference to withdraw from the NATO Alliance.
3. *LPACR 1952*, p. 119.

of the Labour Left were also deeply worried about what they considered 'reactionary elements' at large in the United States.[1]

Those on the Right of the Party, however, far from being disturbed by the internal situation in the United States, shared Mayhew's contention that 'the close alliance with the United States was a pleasure, but also a necessity'.[2] Healey attempted to show that the United States had changed since the 1930s:

> A lot of it [anti-Americanism] is based upon a failure to realize how much America has changed in the last 20 years. America is not run by Wall Street. Wall Street has lost every election in the last 20 years.[3]

Some revisionists attempted to appease anti-American feeling by emphasising the importance of the American Labour Movement, and the connections between the trade unions and the Democratic Party, as a bulwark against 'reactionary' elements in the American political system. Also, they argued that the United States had been much more successful than many European nations in restraining monopoly capitalism.[4] Crosland, however, was far less sympathetic to left-wing anti-Americanism than many of his friends, and was determined not to appease it. He considered that 'too many emotional prejudices are involved, and judgments are based upon immense subconscious efforts at projection and displacement'.[5] He was an ardent admirer of the American economic and social system and came to the tentative conclusion that it would develop in the direction of 'statism' (a euphemism of his for a mixed economy and a pluralistic society), a phenomenon he found fairly acceptable. There was also general praise on the Right of the Party for the comparatively egalitarian educational system of the United States and the high degree of equality of opportunity in industry. Also the institution of the American capital gains tax, as a method of redistributing wealth, was seen as a desirable practice well in keeping with democratic-socialist principles.

1. See particularly the speech of J. Mendelson, ibid., p. 116.
2. Mayhew, 'British Foreign Policy Since 1945', p. 477.
3. Healey, *LPACR 1952*, p. 123.
4. Strachey, 'Tasks and Achievements of British Labour', in *New Fabian Essays*.
5. Crosland, *Future of Socialism*.

This positive enthusiasm for certain aspects of the internal situation in the United States found little declared support among the Leadership of the PLP or the NEC. The Leadership, understandably, were more concerned with defending the foreign policy of the United States and Britain's membership of NATO than with praising American economic and social phenomena. Gaitskell particularly was deeply committed to the support of American foreign policy even in relation to the Far East and the Korean War, and this led him to threaten resignation in February 1951 unless the Government supported an American resolution at the United Nations branding China as an aggressor.[1] Indeed, overt support for virtually every vicissitude of American foreign policy was another aspect of the revisionist-socialist position. It was not because of a pragmatic calculation of each issue as it arose, but because the Leadership were often forced into this position by their repeated acquiescence in the general lines of post-war American international policy.

Many sections of the Labour Left were at their most extreme when denouncing American foreign policy, particularly at the time of the Korean War. They often referred to what they considered the hysteria of the American leaders and tended to blame them for aggressive policies.[2] The revisionists read American actions in a different way:

Are we tying ourselves to a dangerous and incalculable ally? There have certainly been times when this seemed possible. American policies in the Far East, for example, have awakened deep misgivings and when some Americans talk of a war of liberation we darken with forebodings. But a nation must be judged on general lines of policy and not on aberrations from it. In spite of all the commitments she has taken overseas, America is not by and large threatening the rights of other nations or oppressing their peoples. Those who talk of interventionist wars are a minority, repudiated by Americans themselves. The U.S.

---

1. Unpublished private papers of Hugh Dalton.
2. A typical example was this statement by S. O. Davies MP. He referred to 'the hysteria which exists among American leaders, the deliberate, grotesque persecution of outstanding Americans, their fantastic doings in the guise of uprooting un-American activities, and the terribly dangerous megalomania of such people in whose possession are the most horribly destructive weapons which have ever cursed this world of ours'. *Hansard* (5 Jul 1950).

has worked loyally within the United Nations; she has not been guilty of any aggression. There is no convincing case for opposing this alliance on the grounds of socialist principle.[1]

This is virtually a definitive statement of the right-wing and revisionist attitude to American foreign policy. But the view that the United States was basically peaceful was not the only reason for sympathy for and identification with her international policy. An equally important motive was the view that there was an identity of interest between Britain and the United States.

This identity of interest, according to many right-wing thinkers, lay in the defence of Western democracy. Revisionists saw the democratic systems of the United States and Britain as being a more important common factor than the socialist elements of the Soviet Union and the British Labour Movement! Some even went so far as to argue for organic unity between all non-communist forces against the Soviet Union and her associates.[2] Others, like Lucjan Blit, wondered, 'Why do some Labour people see only the grey colour of indifference in the clash between communist and democratic forces in the world?'[3]

Apart from this basic ideological cleavage, revisionists broke with the Left because they considered that the consequences (even in terms of the furtherance of the Left's own political ends, some of which revisionists shared) were not thought through with sufficient clarity. The alienation of the United States by Britain, it was argued, would either lead them into an isolationist posture or, alternatively, into alliances with Spain or Germany as a plank of American European policy. Healey used this argument, at a Fabian conference in the summer of 1951,[4] to illustrate what he considered to be the illogicality of the 'Bevanite' position; namely, that it would drive the

1. *Socialism and Foreign Policy*, p. 54.
2. See D. Healey, 'Britain and Europe'. Also, Healey advocated an expenditure of 10% of the gross national income by Britain on the defence of Europe against Russian expansionism. See Healey, 'The Defence of Western Europe'.
3. L. Blit, 'Foreign Policy – Myth or Reality?', in *Socialist Commentary* (Aug 1952) p. 179.
4. Two speeches (by Denis Healey and John Freeman) on British attitudes to the United States were delivered at a Fabian conference in 1951. They are reproduced in *Rearmament – How Far?*, Fabian Tract No. 288 (1951).

Americans into the hands of even less 'socialist' elements and, indeed, into the hands of nations the Left considered positively 'reactionary'! Not only was the alliance necessary in order to prevent this happening but there were other good reasons for continued close co-operation with the United States. First, the Russian problem could not be solved without American help. Secondly, the problem of German reunification and demilitarisation could not be solved without United States participation. Thirdly, without the active economic backing of the United States the Commonwealth could not be held together. Finally, neither Britain's own economic problems nor those of the underdeveloped nations of Africa and Asia would be soluble without active American help.

Fundamental to the whole argument for close Anglo-American co-operation was its indispensability for world peace. Strange though it may seem today, Gaitskell consistently argued that a split between the United States and Britain would significantly alter the balance-of-power situation in the world and thereby bring war nearer.[1] Although Gaitskell was also ideologically committed to the United States, this 'balance-of-power' argument was purely a technical appraisal of the effects on the two power blocs which would result from a major shift by one of their major allies.

On the whole these were fairly sophisticated arguments, and they also involved home truths unacceptable to large sections of the Party. Attlee and the Shadow Cabinet, quite naturally, arrived at the same conclusions by a more acceptable route: fear of the Soviet Union. They used as their *raison d'être* for the NATO alliance an awareness of the Soviet threat to Europe and the aggressive nature of international communism, rather than any sympathy for American institutions or social developments. Therefore, both the Leadership and the younger revisionist intellectuals, together with the majority of the trade union bosses, agreed on the nature of Russian foreign policy and the consequences of it in terms of Britain's position and the policy of the Labour Movement. A typical NEC view was one of disappointment at the development of the Soviet

---

1. See H. Gaitskell, 'The Search for Anglo-American Policy', in *International Affairs*, vol. 32, no. 4 (Jul 1954).

state and of a resigned and reluctant antipathy towards the revolution there. This attitude is well illustrated by James Griffiths in his summation of the 1952 debate on foreign policy at Party Conference:

> I am the generation of 1917; I well remember the revolution; I remember how the British Labour and Trade Union movement fought for the right of the Soviet Union to develop its own way, and a comrade whose memory we cherish and who afterwards was so often attacked – Ernest Bevin – played a vital role in that matter. Right through since, we have sought co-operation. It is not our fault that we failed.[1]

On the issue of communist aggression there was little dissension in the Party. A majority of the 'Bevanites' accepted the views of Bevan himself on the matter. He was a dedicated anti-communist, consistently opposed to Soviet expansionism, and critical of international communist methods in many of the Eastern European nations.[2]

It is a mark of the atmosphere of the age that both Left and Right of the Labour Party could agree so decidedly on a single issue. Revisionist opinion was exceptional only because of the extreme nature of its attacks on Soviet foreign policy. Healey, Stewart, Strachey and Younger remained firmly suspicious of Soviet intentions throughout the decade, particularly in the field of disarmament and arms control. In 1956 Healey argued that 'the main aims of Soviet foreign policy, as defined by Soviet leaders themselves, remain unchanged – to get Germany out of NATO, to get NATO out of Europe and to persuade the West to abolish all nuclear weapons while leaving conventional forces in being'.[3]

Everyone then was agreed on the Soviet Union – except for a few fellow-travellers. But in the changing post-war world the Labour Left, not only because of its socialism but also because

---

1. *LPACR 1952*, p. 138.

2. See Healey (ed.) *The Curtain Falls*. Certain Left-wing MPs did not accept this view of Bevan's. For example, see the speech of A. J. Irvine in the 1951 Defence Debate in the House of Commons, *Hansard* (15 Feb 1951) cols 482–8. Also, for an alternative view of socialist foreign policy with reference to Labour Party decision-making, see D. N. Pritt, *The Labour Government, 1945–51* (1963).

3. D. Healey, 'When Shrimps Learn to Whistle: Thoughts After Geneva' in *International Affairs* (Jan 1956). See also Strachey, *On Prevention of War*, pp. 215–44.

of a latent 'little Englandism' and disguised (often very disguised) nationalism, could not reconcile itself to American military and political domination of the West. Perhaps if the United States had not been the world's foremost capitalist power they would have thought differently. As it was, they continued to search for a neutralist posture, and made a forlorn effort to apply socialist principles to the international power-political system. In so doing they clashed bitterly with the Right on the two major foreign- and defence-policy questions of the early-fifties, British and German rearmament.

THE REARMAMENT PROGRAMME AND FAR EASTERN POLICY

The Korean War, and Britain's involvement in it, led to a huge increase in armaments expenditure. The worsening political situation in Europe aggravated the position further and the defence estimates for 1951 rose to the highest point, as a percentage of gross national product, yet reached in peace-time.[1] There is little doubt that the British Labour Government was responding to American pressure in imposing this increased burden, but there was also a genuine feeling that it was in the national interest that Britain's defences should be drastically increased.[2] Nevertheless the Labour movement received this sudden and drastic rearmament programme with incredulity and stunned surprise.

The Left and Centre of the Party attacked the rearmament programme on the grounds that the British economy could not afford it rather than because of any illusions about Soviet foreign policy.[3] The debate resolved itself into a calculation of how much sacrifice should be asked for in order to deter aggression. The main weakness of the Government's case was

1. It was announced in a Statement on the Defence Programme to the Commons by the Prime Minister that total defence expenditure for the year 1951–2 would be £1,300 million and that for the next 3-year period it would be £4,700 million. *Hansard* (29 Jan 1951) col. 584.

2. An alarming War Office circular was presented to the Cabinet on 4 Feb 1951, which bluntly stated that 'war possible in 1951, probable 1952'. Unpublished papers of Hugh Dalton.

3. See the *Tribune* pamphlet *One Way Only* (1951).

that it failed to make clear that a real sacrifice was called for in order to build up the nation's defences. It seemed content to propose that the economy could survive such severe pressure. This was later contradicted by events.

Nevertheless, the underlying case of Gaitskell, then Chancellor of the Exchequer, and the Right is defended by Joan Mitchell in the standard work on the period. Her defence of the then Government is based solely on political arguments. She tends to discount the social and economic views of those who argued against such escalated rearmament expenditure:[1]

> It is one thing to argue in general terms in the long run in favour of the value of social and economic defences against subversion; but quite another to expect standards of living (however high) or social services (however lavish) to resist the march of armies.[2]

This illustrates a fundamental difference between the Right and Left of the Labour Party. In the last resort the logic of the Leadership's case rested upon its belief that a nation is defended by its armed forces rather than by its social or economic health or its political system. This indeed is part of the classic basis of the power-political argument, an argument the Left found it impossible to accept.

The 'Bevanites', while accepting that Soviet foreign policy was aggressive, rejected the view that in the end resistance to it depended upon such a drastically increased level of armaments. This was a tenable position analysed from hindsight but open to grave risks in view of the world situation at the time.

With the advent of the Korean War in June of 1950 another issue appeared that threatened to divide the Party, particularly as it was confined to an area in which British policy had on occasions clashed with that of the United States. Surprisingly, however, little dissension resulted from the Labour Party's

---

1. Walter Padley (President of USDAW) put the economic case thus: 'efforts to achieve stability shall not be undermined in any country ... thereby weakening the will and ability of the peoples to prevent by democratic methods the growth of communist parties subservient to Russia'. *LPACR 1952*, p. 142. Padley was referring to economic and social stability. It was feared that economic growth and expenditure on the social services would suffer at the hands of vastly inflated armaments expenditure.

2. Joan Mitchell, *Crisis in Britain 1951* (1963) p. 205.

acceptance of the fact that the aggressor in this case was North Korea. The question of the Chinese intervention in the autumn was a different matter and the Cabinet itself was divided on the issue. Although suspicious of the intentions of General MacArthur the Labour Cabinet, after a prolonged debate, supported the United States at the insistence of Gaitskell and Morrison.

Although there was by no means unanimity in right-wing circles, those who supported the United States did so on the grounds of British national interest. They used the superficial *Realpolitik* argument that the worsening situation in Europe, which was of direct concern to Britain, obliged us to be loyal to the Americans in the Far East in return for their continuing fulfilment of their obligations in the European theatre. Inherent in this argument is a moral element that was usually foreign to right-wing international thinking. It had always been part of the 'power-political' approach that nations acted in their own self-interest (as they interpreted it) and did not respond to appeals to moral obligations. Apart from the fact that NATO was already in existence and therefore *treaty*, as distinct from *moral*, obligations existed for the American Government in Europe, it would seem that, irrespective of British policy in the Far East, the United States Government was bound, so far as her already declared national interest was concerned, to intervene in Europe in the event of Soviet aggression.

A more plausible revisionist argument for Labour's backing of American foreign policy in the Far East was the need to maintain Western solidarity in the face of Soviet and Chinese aggression. It was suggested that if the Korean War led to a break-up in Anglo-American relations this would be a victory for Soviet diplomacy. An editorial in *Socialist Commentary* suggested that:

> Russia's hope had evidently been that the entry of China into open conflict with the U.S.A. would undermine that unity, especially Anglo-American friendship, and induce the U.S. to abandon or weaken her share in the defence of Europe.[1]

Here again can be seen the view, possibly exaggerated, that

1. *Socialist Commentary* (Jan 1951) p. 1.

Britain was so vital to the whole Western alliance system that her 'opting out' of responsibilities in this direction would be catastrophic for the security of the West. This was a theme consistently used by Gaitskell during the defence debates following the 1959 election.

It would be a mistake, however, to assume that the Labour Right, obsessive as they were about Western unity, were totally subservient to the United States in all aspects of their Far Eastern policy. Attlee particularly was lukewarm in his support of United States policy towards Formosa. He argued that it would be dangerous for world peace if Formosa was used as a base for the assembly of arms against mainland China.[1] Also, British policy, under both Conservative and Labour Governments, differed from that of the United States on the question of Communist China's admission to the United Nations.

Nevertheless these differences were of a peripheral nature compared with the general support given by Labour, both in government and opposition, to American Far East policy.[2] The preservation at all costs of the Western Alliance, and the added fact that Britain could only exert influence on America if she were loyal to that alliance, was the motivation for this virtual *carte blanche* backing. The calculation that support in the Far East was necessary in order to keep the alliance alive in Europe was more contentious. The last two years of the Labour Government witnessed growing international tension and there is a certain amount of evidence to suggest that decisions taken by the Labour Cabinet were the result of the need for immediate action and took place in a highly charged international atmosphere not only in Korea, but also in Europe. Political action, particularly taken at such crisis periods, is not always a result of rational assessment (if indeed it ever is). It may be that because of the tensions of 1951 Labour over-reacted to the situation.

It seems, again with the advantage of hindsight, that this was one of the few occasions when the Left (or at least the more moderate elements among them) were proved right. The

1. *Hansard* (5 Feb 1952) col. 838.
2. For a detailed account of Labour Party attitudes to American Far Eastern policy see L. Epstein, *Britain – Uneasy Ally* (1953), particularly ch. 10.

Centre–Left position, the main proponent of which was Harold Wilson, was vindicated. The huge rearmament programme did strain the British economy almost beyond enduring, for even the newly-elected Conservatives under Churchill were forced to cut the programme somewhat. Here were early signs that Britain's world role was in conflict with her precarious economy.

The Labour Right's proper concern over Russian and Chinese expansion led them, in this instance, to overreach themselves and also, possibly, to lose the 1951 election. Their emotional and psychological antipathy to international communism temporarily obscured their better judgement about the internal economic and social balance to be made at home.

Three years later the Party, now in opposition, was faced with another emotive situation, the problem of West German rearmament.

LABOUR AND GERMAN REARMAMENT

The German rearmament controversy, as with the Common Market debate eight years later, was not an issue that lent itself to a convenient Left–Right interpretation. Both the Shadow Cabinet and the NEC were deeply divided and many prominent figures who normally would be associated with revisionist thinking were bitterly opposed to any form of German participation in Western defence.[1] An analysis of the arguments used in these debates is a further guide to the problems associated with foreign-policy formulation in a mass democratic-socialist party.

As early as 1951, following a series of declarations against the rearmament of West Germany,[2] the Labour Government accepted 'in principle' the need for a German military contribution to collective Western defence. The Prime Minister announced that 'We have accepted the need for a contribution from Germany, but the time, method and conditions will need

1. Both Dalton and Strachey were passionate opponents of a German contribution to Western defence. Also, Bevin, while he was Foreign Secretary, shared their views.

2. Defence Minister, E. Shinwell, had stated in July 1950: 'His Majesty's Government have repeatedly and in conjunction with her Allies, declared their opposition to the rearmament of Germany.' *Hansard* (26 Jul 1950) col. 470.

a good deal of working out.'[1] Even though this public acceptance was a departure from previous policy, the Cabinet's
view was that any application of 'the principle' should be
delayed at least until after the four-power Berlin Conference.[2]
Dalton, who was reluctant even to accept 'the principle' involved, was the main advocate of delaying implementation. Most
of his Cabinet colleagues were willing to follow this course.[3]

The conditions under which Labour would agree to a
German military contribution were laid down by Attlee in his
12 February speech. He argued that the rearmament of the
countries of the Atlantic Treaty should precede that of Germany, that arrangements for the integration of German units
into the defence forces of the West should be carried out in
such a way as to preclude the emergence of German 'militarism', and finally that there should be the agreement of the
German people to rearmament.[4] These conditions, particularly
during the period in which they could not be met, guaranteed
a minimal Party unity. There was no movement in favour of
immediate, unconditional implementation, and even Healey,
who was not unsympathetic to German rearmament, was
careful to stress the arguments against as well as those in favour
of a new German military contribution.[5]

By the summer of 1952, following the defeat at a PLP meeting
of the ratification of the European Defence Community
treaties, ideas were circulating on the revisionist wing of the
Party which were less hostile to German rearmament than
those expressed previously. Kenneth Younger had argued that
Britain should join the European Defence Community in order
to ease an eventual German participation[6] and by May of
1953 Socialist Union was more forthright still:

Western Europe must be made secure, and this demands a
contribution from the Germans. . . . West Germany must regain

---

1. *Hansard* (12 Feb 1951) col. 67.
2. Much of the background for this information is provided in the unpublished
papers of Hugh Dalton.
3. Morrison, however, complained of this delaying formula. Unpublished
Dalton Diaries.
4. *Hansard* (12 Feb 1951) col. 67.
5. See Healey, 'Defence of Western Europe', pp. 234–8.
6. K. Younger, 'Germany and Western Defence', in *Socialist Commentary* (May
1952).

political equality both for the sake of German democracy and also because the alternative – continued occupation – is simply not practicable. Political equality carries with it the right and the obligation of self-defence.[1]

This attempt to steer the Party towards some form of acceptance of German rearmament had its greatest supporter in Herbert Morrison. As early as 1951 Dalton complained that Morrison, then Foreign Secretary, had an obsession with German rearmament and that he offered no restraining influence on his even more enthusiastic Foreign Office advisers.[2] After Labour left office Morrison continued to press the Party to accept in practice what had already been agreed to in principle. The major opponent of this view in the Party hierarchy was, not unnaturally, Dalton. He tended to be bitter, extreme and emotional on the subject. He was convinced that 'German rearmament might prove to be an irrevocable step on the road to hell on earth.'[3] It is not surprising therefore that Dalton did not even accept 'the principle' of rearmament that was conceded very early on. Instead he argued that this was the result of United States pressure that should have been resisted.

During the first two years in opposition, Attlee, whose attitude to German rearmament was described by the *New Statesman* as 'discreetly ambiguous', was able to balance off against each other the opposing forces both in the PLP and in the Movement as a whole. The Leadership managed to defeat attempts to commit the Party to outright rejection of German rearmament[4] and yet, at the same time, remained opposed to its implementation. An NEC motion at the 1953 Party Conference urged that further efforts should be made to secure a peaceful unification of Germany before considering rearmament.[5]

This period of relative tranquillity ended after the failure of the Berlin negotiations between the Western powers and the

---

1. *Socialism and Foreign Policy.*   2. Unpublished Dalton Diaries.
   3. Dalton used this statement in a BBC party political broadcast on 15 Dec 1951. Unpublished Dalton Diaries. There is little evidence to suggest that his views had changed substantially by 1954.
   4. *LPACR 1953*, Resolution 21 was defeated.
   5. Ibid., see NEC motion, p. 151.

Soviet Union. Following the breakdown of negotiations in February 1954 the Shadow Cabinet decided to recommend to the full PLP meeting a motion in favour of an immediate German contribution to Western defence. It is interesting that only Chuter Ede, Callaghan and Bevan voted against this recommendation (Dalton was in hospital at the time), and, apart from the abstention of Shinwell, the rest of the Shadow Cabinet was unanimous in its support for the policy Morrison had been advocating since 1951.

The German rearmament question divided the PLP more equally than any other single issue since the war, even including the defence controversies of 1960 and 1961. At a full Party meeting on 23 February the Shadow Cabinet's motion, moved by Morrison, was passed with a majority of only 9 votes, and a further motion, moved by Wilson, to the effect that no German rearmament should take place without a further effort at East–West negotiations was only defeated by 2 votes.[1] It is not an idle exercise to speculate on the possible course of events that would have followed if Dalton had been present at the PLP meeting. Apart from the fact that his vote would have been important in itself, particularly on the Wilson motion, his position as a member of the Shadow Cabinet and his standing among many right-wing MPs might have been influential enough to tip the balance and to have defeated the Morrison motion. In order to have acted in this way, however, Dalton would have had to resign from the Shadow Cabinet. It appears that, but for his illness, he would have seriously contemplated such an act.[2]

The anti-rearmers therefore came very close to a PLP victory and this evenly-balanced polarisation became evident again in September 1954, at the Trades Union Congress when a pro-rearmament motion was carried by only 455,000 votes.[3] At the Labour Party Conference the following month the majority for German rearmament was even smaller – a mere 48,000

1. Unpublished Dalton Diaries.
2. Unpublished Dalton Diaries. Also, Dalton, Callaghan and Wilson carried their convictions through to the point of voting against the ratification of the Paris agreements within the Shadow Cabinet.
3. *TUC Report 1954*, p. 413. The voting was 4,077,000 for the General Council motion and 3,622,000 against.

John Strachey

Left:
Roy Jenkins

Right:
Anthony Crosland

The Labour Party of the early fifties: Morrison, Phillips, Greenwood and Attlee

The Labour Party of the late fifties: Bevan and Gaitskell reconciled at Brighton, 1957; seen here with Mrs Gaitskell

The 1959 General Election

Before the election – Gaitskell and his wife leave Transport House for an election tour of Essex. In the background, from left to right: Tom Driberg, Richard Crossman, Ray Gunter, and, next to Mrs Gaitskell, Morgan Phillips

And after the election – Gaitskell concedes defeat at the press conference

votes.[1] The fact that the German question divided the Party so evenly illustrates that many of the traditional right-wing elements deserted official policy. Nevertheless most of the major revisionist thinkers of the period remained convinced that a German contribution to Western defence was essential. A study of the arguments used in the debate helps to clarify their reasons for this stand.

The pro-rearmers were accused on four main counts by those who opposed their policy on the German question. The argument used by the centre politicians against official policy was that it did not insist that further negotiations with the Soviet Union on German reunification should precede rearmament. The prospect of a united Germany would be damaged if rearmament of the western section took place first.[2] All sections of the Party felt that German reunification was desirable,[3] but the Right argued that the Soviet Union had made further negotiations on the subject impossible because of their refusal to accept the allies' pre-condition of free elections.

The question of free elections provided an interesting example of the differences between Morrison on the one hand and the Left on the other. Both R. W. Casasola of the Foundry Workers' Union, the mover of the composite resolution at Conference against rearmament, and Ben Parkin MP suggested that the insistence upon free elections before negotiating was asking the Soviet Union to abdicate an issue of principle before coming to the conference table. This was considered unrealistic. Morrison contended however that the principle of free elections was not negotiable.

Irrespective of the question of free elections, the whole debate surrounding negotiations with the Soviet Union illustrates the optimism of certain sections of the Left of the Party

1. The Amalgamated Society of Woodworkers defied the mandate of its conference by voting for the 'official' position. Also, the Amalgamated Union of Building Trade Workers abstained, having voted against German rearmament at the TUC 1954.

2. This was argued by A. Birch (USDAW). *LPACR 1954*, p. 96.

3. Except Desmond Donnelly: 'I personally do not believe there is such a chance now. . . . Even if Russia and America completely changed their policies . . . the plain fact is that for a decade already Germany has been divided . . . two completely different social and economic systems have grown up.' Ibid. p. 104.

about Soviet intentions. Allied to this was a tendency to blame
the West for the failure of the four-power conferences. Morrison,
on the other hand, together with Healey and Younger, tended
to doubt that any advantages could be obtained from international dealings with the Soviet Union. This resulted in a
sceptical approach towards attempts at an East–West entente,
which were continually being pressed for within their own
Party. Healey and Morrison were naturally subjected to the
taunts of the Left for being 'intransigent cold-warriors'.

The possible rise of German 'militarism' became another
issue in the rearmament controversy. The Left, together with
the trade union section of the right-wing establishment, agreed
that there was a danger to be faced from this quarter. In 1950
Ernest Bevin displayed an alarming, but not uncharacteristic,
sentiment when he said, 'The Hitler revolution did not change
the German character very much, it expressed it . . . it [mili-
tarism] was latent there right from the days of Bismarck.'[1]
Morrison also accepted that there was a danger of such a
phenomenon inherent in the then situation, but that 'supposing we admit that, what is the best way to prevent it. . . .
Does not history tell us that if you crush a nation down, if you
treat them as untouchables, this is the best way to create a
national spirit and possible fascism'.[2] Therefore on both the
Right and the Left of the Party a measure of agreement was
reached that a revival of 'militarism' was always a possibility
to be reckoned with. The debate centred on how best to prevent
it from expressing itself.

This view that 'militarism' was a characteristic of the
German people, and a factor to be considered before a policy
was evolved, was rejected as an assumption in only one corner
of the Party, the younger right-wing 'intellectuals'. Reginald
Prentice exemplified their views well when he argued that:
'For years after the defeat of Napoleon they said, "The French
are a militaristic race and they will not be cured". It is not
true of them and it is not true of any people.'[3]

This 'militaristic' aspect involved in the German rearma-

1. *Hansard* (28 Mar 1950) col. 323. It is interesting to note that Churchill objected to this view. Ibid.
2. *LPACR 1954*, p. 106.   3. Ibid. p. 99.

ment problem was part of a more general distrust, particularly on the Left of the Party, of the aggressive nature of leading segments of West German society. Continual reference was made to 'Nazi' elements in high places in the Bonn Government and the 'revanchist' characteristics of many leading West German politicians. This was part of the argument used later on in the 1950s to persuade the Party to change its policy towards recognition of the German Democratic Republic (East Germany). Revisionists contended however that revanchist elements existed on both sides of the divided Germany and that in the West, at least, some attempt was being made to erect a stable democratic state based upon the multi-party system with the all-important element, to revisionists, of free elections.

Apart from the 'militarist' argument, traditional appeals to international socialist 'solidarity' were made in order to forestall rearmament. This entailed a reference to the views of the West German Social Democratic Party (SPD), which even as late as 1954 was considered by all factions in the British Labour Party to be akin, in terms of political aims, to the British movement.[1] Indeed the NEC motion on German Rearmament at the 1954 Labour Party Conference conceded the importance of this 'international socialist' approach by instructing the NEC to consult with other European socialist parties in an endeavour to draw up a common policy.[2]

On the specific question of the SPD both sides in the argument attempted to claim its allegiance. There was considerable truth in Parkin's contention that Herr Ollenhauer, the Leader of the SPD, would have voted, if he had been present, for the anti-rearmament composite resolutions as the SPD was on record as being opposed to German rearmament. Nevertheless, the SPD, at a meeting of the Council of the Socialist International at Amsterdam on 20-1 December 1954, together with the socialist parties of Belgium, Holland, Italy, Luxembourg, Norway, Denmark and France approved the London and

---

1. For an interesting account of the 'revisionist' trends in the German Social Democratic Party see Childs, 'The Development of Socialist Thought in the SPD 1945-58' (Ph.D. thesis, London Univ., 1961).
2. *LPACR 1954*, p. 92.

Paris agreements that made possible a West German contribution to allied defence.[1] By July 1955 all the members of the
Socialist International, save the neutral Swiss party, agreed to
a German military contribution.[2] By 1955, therefore, little
appeal could be made against German rearmament on the
grounds of international socialist 'solidarity'.

A difference in emphasis between Right and Left about the
importance of foreign agreement to Labour policy also emerged
during the German rearmament debates. Although the Leadership was anxious to have international socialist thinking behind
them on this question, the original Attlee conditions for German rearmament had referred to agreement with the German
'people' as opposed to the German Social Democratic Party.
This resulted from the view that it was false to equate the
German electorate with only one party, albeit a socialist party.
Also, the Right held to the view that foreign policy should be
conducted between *governments* rather than between international *movements*. The Socialist International, although regularly attended by Labour leaders, especially Hugh Gaitskell,
was never considered by the right-wing of the Party as an
important agency for solving international problems. The
Labour Leadership remained constitutionally orthodox in
adhering to the principle of governmentally-conducted foreign
policy.

A less important, though not insignificant, view expressed
was that Labour should refuse to act as an accomplice in re-
arming a 'capitalist' power.[3] This is an extreme (and naïve)
example of an ideological view, based upon the 'capitalist–
socialist' division, of foreign powers. An acceptance of this
criterion of foreign policy decision-making would have entailed
the worsening of relations with many nations whose goodwill
the Leadership felt it was in Britain's national interest to main-

---

1. An account of this meeting is given in *Report of the NEC 1954–5* (1955).

2. See resolution passed on the international situation, including a section on
German and European security, at the Fourth Congress of the Socialist International, held in London, 12–16 Jul 1955, appendix 1, *LPACR 1955*, p. 224.

3. E.g. 'Bred and born in this movement, educated in it, I cannot understand
why the Labour Party, always expressing socialist ideas, claiming to be socialist,
should be prepared to arm capitalism. . . .' R. W. Casasola, *LPACR 1954*,
p. 95.

tain. Nevertheless, to be fair, the Right also did not totally reject this ideological approach because, as has been seen, its own relationship to the United States and its distrust of the Soviet Union contained in part ideological commitments and preferences.

The Right, however, did not argue in ideological terms, no matter how significant in an emotional sense for any Labour Conference, when refuting the contentions of the Left over German rearmament. In fact they often stressed the impotence of the Labour Movement, regardless of its political sympathies, in controlling future events in Europe. It was argued that German rearmament was inevitable because the only guarantee of a disarmed Germany in the long run was a full-scale military occupation by outside powers of what was already a sovereign state.

These, therefore, were the issues involved in the differing approaches to the German rearmament controversy. The victory for the Leadership was yet another stage in the rejection of a distinctive socialist approach to foreign policy – if indeed this was ever a viable concept.[1]

The degree to which the Leadership was responding to American pressure is unknown, but it is doubtful if this was an important factor particularly as Labour was the Opposition Party at the time. It is reasonable to conclude that, as in the case of British rearmament and British support for American Far Eastern policy, the Leadership, and the revisionists who supported it, saw German rearmament not only as inevitable but as vital to the strength of the Western alliance. As we have seen, the health and unity of this alliance was the overriding and almost obsessive concern of revisionists in the 1950s and the early 1960s.

1. An interesting question is posed in the following quotation from an official Labour Party publication: 'Is this [support for German rearmament] a socialist policy? How can it be if the Tory Government supports it? If Labour's foreign policy had at all costs to be different from the Tories, there would be some very strange results. The Labour Government helped to bring about NATO. The Conservative Government has followed Labour's policy of support for NATO. Does this mean that Labour should reverse its policy with regard to NATO? The position of EDC is similar. It was begun with the approval of the Labour Government subject to certain conditions.' *In Defence of Europe*, a Labour Party pamphlet (1954).

THE HYDROGEN BOMB AND DEFENCE, 1955–7

German rearmament was the last major challenge to the ascendancy of right-wing foreign policy until 1960. Even following the Conservative Government's announcement that Britain was to manufacture the hydrogen thermo-nuclear weapon, the Labour Party Leadership managed to keep in existence a bipartisan approach to foreign affairs and defence policy without splitting its own ranks.

On 1 March 1955, the Party tabled an amendment in the House of Commons to a Government motion approving the annual statement on defence. This amendment questioned the Government's efficiency in the conduct of the nation's defence system but accepted British manufacture of the hydrogen bomb.[1] Although 62 back-bench Labour MPs abstained from voting on the Opposition's amendment, this challenge to the bipartisan approach was not followed through at the Party Conference in the autumn.[2] Following a year that was mainly taken up with the Suez crisis, by April 1957 official policy on the bomb remained virtually the same, although the Party tabled an amendment which included a passage regretting the 'undue dependence on the ultimate deterrent'.[3] This was the first public declaration of the need to increase the conventional aspect of NATO forces – a point that revisionist defence thinkers were later to elaborate on at length.[4] Nevertheless, those in the Party who wished to commit Labour against the manufacture of Britain's own nuclear weapons had an even greater setback in 1957 than they had received in 1955. At the

1. The key passage from the Opposition amendment was: 'while recognising that thermo-nuclear weapons have effected a revolution in the character of warfare, and that until effective world disarmament has been achieved it is necessary as a deterrent to aggression to rely on the threat of using thermo-nuclear weapons. . . .' *Hansard* (1 Mar 1955) col. 1,917.

2. Composite Resolution No. 21 stated 'This Conference places on record its opposition to the manufacture of the hydrogen bomb and all nuclear weapons by Great Britain . . .' It was defeated by 5,300,000 votes to 1,174,000. *LPACR 1955*, p. 151.

3. *Hansard* (16 Apr 1957) col. 1,795. For Brown's speech in support of the amendment see ibid. cols 1,774–95.

4. See Mulley, *Politics of Western Defence*, ch. 10; and Strachey, *On the Prevention of War*, ch. 7.

Brighton Conference of 1957 a massive majority of 5,055,000 was recorded against a proposal that Britain should cease manufacturing the nuclear weapon. This huge majority was a crushing defeat for the unilateralists, but then this was the year of Bevan's reconciliation to Gaitskell's leadership. The Left, yet again, had no leader and consequently little support. What had always looked like an impending revolt had evaporated in less than two years.

There are two interesting aspects of these early years of the independent-deterrent dispute. First, not one of the Gaitskellites questioned the assumption that Britain should attempt to remain an independent nuclear power. They did not accept the view that there was any change 'in principle' between the hydrogen weapon and the atomic weapon. Therefore, the need to scrutinise anew fundamental defence assumptions was unnecessary.

Secondly, for the sake of its disillusioned liberal middle-class supporters, a consistent attempt was made by the Leadership to differentiate, albeit within the general framework of bipartisanship, Labour defence policy from that of the Conservative Government. This took the form of disagreement over particular aspects of the Government's defence policy but, in broad terms, too often looked like quibbling.

The testing of thermo-nuclear weapons was one example of this rather forced and pretentious opposition to Conservative defence policy. In 1955 Labour proposed in Parliament that a conference of scientists of all the nuclear powers should be convened to advise their governments on the 'dangers facing mankind'.[1] By 1956 Labour was committed to opposing 'the continuing of nuclear explosions' and expressed its fear of the 'continuing radioactive contamination of the world's atmosphere',[2] and in April 1957 asked the Government:

> to make an immediate initiative in putting forward effective proposals for the abolition of hydrogen bomb tests through international agreement, meanwhile postponing the United Kingdom tests for a limited period so that the response to this initiative of the other Governments concerned may first be considered.[3]

1. *NEC Report* (1954–5) p. 57.
2. *LPACR 1956*, p. 142.   3. *Hansard* (16 Apr 1957) col. 1,795.

Also, the official Labour Party position went so far as to accept Soviet Union proposals for ending nuclear testing as a basis for East–West negotiations on the matter.[1] But this radical posture on nuclear testing was no more than a tactical move to keep Party unity as the Leadership, for the sake of that unity, accepted arguments that were alien to its basic defence thinking. For instance, it never seriously believed that unilateral actions could produce a favourable response from other powers by sheer force of example! Labour was genuinely worried about the harmful effects of radiation, but the Leadership's slide into unilateral posturing was out of keeping with its traditions and can best be explained in terms of an internal unifying gesture.

Labour attempted to trump up a disagreement with the Conservative Government on the more general question of East–West relations and the desirability of summit conferences. On 14 March 1955 Attlee moved a vote of censure on the Government in the House of Commons for failing to convene a meeting between the heads of Governments of the U.S.A., the U.S.S.R. and the United Kingdom and stressed that the separation of the two world power-blocs was the greatest danger to world peace.[2] This was just one example of many such requests made from the Labour front bench in the months following the announcement of the hydrogen weapon. It smacked of a 'sweetening the pill operation' for the benefit of the Left, even though it was, no doubt, genuinely believed. In fact, although firmly wedded to NATO, right-wing Labour was never averse to the need to improve diplomatic relations between East and West. After all it was central to the argument for co-existence and stabilisation between the opposing cold-war forces. Gaitskell himself was a powerful supporter of this view[3] but then so was the whole of the Conservative front bench. In reality, it was hard to outbid Eden and Macmillan in 'summitry' even though on some occasions, and 1955 was one of them, Labour appeared so to do.

A more real division between the two front benches was the

1. See *LPACR 1957*, p. 180.
2. *Hansard* (14 Mar 1955) cols 951–6.
3. See Gaitskell's pamphlet *The Challenge of Co-existence* (1957), particularly part I.

question of national service. The Opposition called for a review of the length of service in 1955[1] and a reduction in length and eventual abolition the following year.[2] The reason for this change in policy was not, on this occasion, a desire to help Party unity, but rather an attempt to gain some electoral popularity. This policy-switch led Labour into a trap, which the Conservatives, although later to be guilty of the same manœuvre, did not fail to exploit. Labour's official defence policy contained a glaring contradiction. By April 1957 the Party was advocating less reliance upon the nuclear response to deter aggression in Europe. This obviously would result in the need for greater conventional strength yet the abolition of conscription ran directly counter to that need. Yet again, niggling attempts to differentiate Labour from Tory defence policy landed the Party in trouble.

Labour was without doubt in a delicate situation in the early years of British thermo-nuclear independence but the Labour Leadership managed to maintain the traditional bipartisan approach to foreign policy between the two major Parties. The period also illustrates how both the Leadership and the revisionist defence thinkers accepted in principle the independent nuclear posture; although they were anxious to oppose the Government on technical questions falling within the broad and agreed framework. Similarly, revisionist socialists did not see this continuing nuclear independence as either a threat to, or a divisive influence within, the Western alliance system, which remained the cornerstone of their foreign policy. This nuclear independence, however, caused the birth of a movement pledged to unilateralism which had its first stirrings in 1957 and which severely challenged the traditional defence attitudes of the Party. This challenge, and the right-wing response to it, is discussed in Part Two of this work.

1. *Hansard* (28 Apr 1955) col. 1,074.
2. Ibid. By February 1957 the PLP was committed to the abolition of national service and in March of that year advocated a postponement of the call-up. See *Hansard* (4 Mar 1957) cols 135–52.

Part Two: 1957–64

CHAPTER SEVEN

Revisionist Leadership

In many respects 1957 was a watershed in post-war Labour Party history. This was the year that witnessed both the publication and acceptance of *Industry and Society* and the overwhelming rejection of unilateralism. It was also the year that saw the reconciliation between Gaitskell and Bevan or, more precisely, the abdication by the latter from the challenge to Gaitskell's leadership of the Party.

This ascendancy of the Right in power terms and revisionism in policy terms was not seriously threatened until after the 1959 General Election. The Left contented itself with extra-party means of gathering support on defence questions. The year 1957 saw the first Aldermaston march[1] and little resistance was offered to Gaitskell's leadership either in the PLP or in the Movement as a whole. Also, the political consequences of the new left-wing leadership of the TGWU were not felt until the 1960 Labour Party Conference, although at the 1959 Biennial Delegate Conference of that union the Party received a taste of what was to come when an ominously ambiguous defence posture was adopted.[2]

The defeat of the Party in 1959, however, produced a totally new situation. This was the third successive defeat for Labour in a general election, and the traditional 'post-mortem' took on a bitterness and an intensity that had been absent since the 'Bevanite' years. The Party not only engaged in a policy debate

1. For a detailed account of these first 'stirrings' of the Campaign for Nuclear Disarmament see C. P. Driver, *The Disarmers: a study in protest* (1964).

2. Frank Cousins succeeded Jack Tiffin as General Secretary of the TGWU in 1956. At the 1959 BDC a motion on defence policy was passed that contradicted official policy on many questions although remaining in the general framework of multilateralism. See *TGWU Record*, xxxix (Aug 1959) 43.

but also witnessed, as in the earlier 'Bevanite' period, a power struggle with the Leadership itself at stake.

The revisionist-wing took the initiative after the election not only with a series of essays and articles by many prominent intellectuals[1] but also at Leadership level by a direct challenge to some of the more entrenched aspects of Socialist and Labour doctrine. The fundamentalist-wing of the Party responded to this challenge most successfully; first, they managed, with the assistance of large trade union elements, to defeat the Clause IV[2] proposals of the revisionists, and secondly they achieved a reversal of traditional Party defence policy (these two issues are discussed at length in the following two chapters).

The Clause IV and defence controversies were but part of a rigorous analysis which at times almost bordered on self-destruction. Labour loves to analyse itself, not only out of egotistic fascination but also because, in the wider world, it is genuinely humble and unsure. This self-doubt reached its highest intensity in the years following the loss of the 1959 General Election and the whole character of radical and working-class politics came under review. Policies were important, but only as symptoms of something deeper and more enduring. The whole nature of the British Labour Party was at stake and its traditions and history were dragged into the market place and squabbled over. It was at times an unseemly debate, but it also rose to great heights where political courage and skill were displayed. It produced a certain political mobility that has often been absent in more entrenched and contented political institutions.

There was a less elevated side to the struggle, however, for the nature of the Party and its policies were inextricably bound up with the role of political leadership and in practical terms with Hugh Gaitskell's highly distinctive political character. The power struggle for the top job tended to obscure the loftier debate but the fact that Gaitskell, in the end, won, had lasting results for Labour's role in British politics. It also significantly affected what the psephologists call its 'image'.

1. The ideas incorporated in these articles are discussed below, in this and the following chapter.
2. See p. 170 below.

THE PARTY IMAGE

The Gaitskellites seemed content with the ideas and policies expressed in the 1959 General Election Manifesto *Britain Belongs to You*, and also with the three more detailed documents that formed the basis of that manifesto.[1] Indeed Crosland said in the *Spectator* as early as 1958:

> The new emphasis, though still encountering some psychological resistance among the local activists, is accepted not merely by the party leadership but by most left intellectuals. . . . I may add that the party has been given insufficient credit for this major re-alignment of its outlook.[2]

Nevertheless, the electorate did not form their judgement of the Party by a process of sophisticated analysis of these policy documents. Labour lost the election, and indeed appeared to be in steady decline, because of less tangible phenomena. Many revisionists argued that the image[3] of the Party was inadequate and irrelevant and that the Labour Party had failed both to project and to interpret their principles in accordance with the changing aspirations of mid-twentieth-century Britain.

Emphasis was placed upon the need for Labour to engage in modern public relations techniques as a means of lessening, where it applied, the divorce between the image and the reality of Party policy and aims. Crosland advocated this in a Fabian pamphlet which he wrote in the spring of 1960.[4] These views were echoed by an NEC document, *Labour in the Sixties*, prepared by the then General Secretary of the Party, Morgan Phillips, and published in July. It stated that 'The National Executive Committee will consult with affiliated Unions on . . . effective means of getting the ideals, policies and activities of the

1. *Towards Equality*; *Public Enterprise* and *Industry and Society*.
2. *Spectator* (24 Oct 1958) p. 555.
3. This is a term used to explain the general personality of a party as seen by the voter. It does not refer to any specific issue of policy but rather to the impression created by an amalgam of them. For an interesting account of the idea of 'image' see J. Trenaman and A. McQuail, *Television and the Political Image: a study of the impact of television on the 1959 General Election* (1957).
4. C. A. R. Crosland, *Can Labour Win?*, Fabian Tract No. 324 (1960) pp. 21–2.

Labour movement over to the public. . . .' This was the first time that Labour, at official level, had even considered that improved methods of electorate communication were needed. It eventually resulted in Party headquarters engaging a firm of public relations experts, a traditional socialist heresy.[1]

Public relations techniques alone were not considered capable of changing the image of the Party with the electorate. Politicians themselves had responsibility for changing certain identification patterns that had resulted in an unsympathetic image. Three broad categories of this unsympathetic 'imagery' were identified by revisionist thinkers.

First, and the most often stressed, was the unfavourable image of Labour as a one-class party composed of, and supported by, the working class. This image was obviously an exaggeration of the real position, especially as far as membership was concerned, but surveys and polls carried out at that time verified this image as a representative one. The most comprehensive survey carried out into Labours' image was that of Research Services Ltd under the direction of Mark Abrams.[2] This survey concluded that:

> The image of the Labour Party, held both by its supporters and its non-supporters, is one that is increasingly obsolete in terms of contemporary Britain. Both groups see Labour as identified with the working-class – especially the poor and the labouring working-class; and at the same time, many workers, irrespective of their politics, no longer regard themselves as working-class. Conversely, the electorate sees the Conservative Party as the Party of middle-class people and young people. . . .[3]

Even before this survey appeared many Gaitskellites had formulated their ideas on the danger to Labour of its exclusively working-class, 'cloth-cap' association in the public mind. They

---

1. Although the Party's television appeals were generally considered to be adequate, it spent only £20,000 on poster advertising for the 1959 General Election. (*Statement of Receipts and Payments, Labour Party, year ending 31 Dec 1959*.)

2. Rita Hinden (editor of *Socialist Commentary*) and Michael Young (ex-head of the research department at Transport House) asked Research Services Ltd to engage on an independent survey, not on the then current political issues, but on the underlying social and political values of the electorate. The results were published in *Socialist Commentary* (May–Jul 1960).

3. Ibid. (May 1960) p. 9. Further information on this subject from opinion polls is analysed in Chapter Eight.

took the view that Labour would be damaged electorally if it continued to be 'working class only' in image because the working class as such was rapidly falling as a percentage of the electorate. Figures that became available about the increasing percentage of workers employed in financial, professional and local and national government services[1] confirmed this trend against Labour.

Another aspect of the class issue was not of such recent origin. Revisionist thinkers from Bernstein, through Durbin, to the post-war writers had emphatically rejected the theory of the class struggle. They had placed great emphasis upon class 'harmonisation' as opposed to 'conflict', and they believed that the 'classless society' should be achieved by breaking class barriers rather than by the enforced supremacy of one class over another. The Socialist Union perhaps expressed this idea best in 1952:

> The class struggle is no more a fixed pattern of action for the achievement of socialism than socialism itself is a fixed set of institutions. It is true that those who suffer from the class structure are more likely to fight against it than those to whom it brings advantages. But members of the privileged classes have also played an important part in the struggle for a better society; and some of the underprivileged have, at times, rebelled only in order to gain new privileges for themselves. Classes cannot be divided off into sheep and goats. Even if they could, to pit class against class in the end leads to a naked struggle for power and advantage, destroying the very values which socialists wish to uphold.[2]

Therefore the attack upon Labour's working-class image was in part based upon electoral considerations but was also a natural expression of a non-Marxist, social-democratic philosophy; the commitment to social harmony and stability.

A further problem involved in the class image of the Labour Party was the general unpopularity of certain aspects of British trade unionism. A number of national polls pointed to growing public annoyance at unofficial strikes, which surprisingly were associated with trade union action, demarcation disputes and

---

1. See Turner, 'Labour's Diminishing Vote', the *Guardian* (20 Oct 1959). This article had an important influence on Crosland's thinking.
2. *Socialism: A New Statement of Principles*, p. 43.

F

other labour practices. This led some leading members of the Party to call for an end to trade union participation in Labour Party decision-making.[1] Although critical of both trade-union organisational structure and restrictive practices, most revisionists were content with Gaitskell's view that no new alignment between the Party and the unions was necessary and that malpractices should be rectified by the trade unions themselves rather than by any outside body.[2]

The second aspect of Labour's image that came in for criticism was the lack of appeal it generated for young people. The Research Service's study concentrated mainly on the political attitudes of the age group eighteen to twenty-four in an attempt to project likely 'Y' voter[3] habits at the following election (although of the sample interviewed just under half had already exercised their vote in the 1959 election). The most important conclusion from the survey was that 'If we ignore the 10 per cent whose political views were so unformed that they could not be described even as "leaning" towards any party, then it appears that 52 per cent of young people today are Conservatives, 43 per cent are Labour supporters and 5 per cent are Liberals.'[4] This was devastating news for a so-called radical Party of the Left.

A reading of the 1959 'post-mortem' Conference shows the concern expressed by all wings of the Party about Labour's lack of appeal to youth, and Gaitskell, as Leader, was ready to admit the Party's shortcomings in this direction.[5] Also, it was argued that changing social patterns, especially in the younger age group, were not being taken into account by the Party, but that there was a genuine radical movement among the young that the Labour Party should channel into political action.[6]

---

1. Dalton records (unpublished diaries) that Jay was privately in favour of a formal break with the trade unions following the 1959 election.

2. *LPACR 1959*, p. 109.

3. An elector who, for reasons of age, is entitled to vote for the first time.

4. M. Abrams, 'Why Labour has Lost Elections', in *Socialist Commentary* (Jul 1960) p. 5.

5. *LPACR 1959*, p. 109.

6. 'Fortunately, the spirit of radical reform is not altogether dead in our society. It shows itself in the vigour of the Campaign for Nuclear Disarmament and in the interest young people have taken in the "new Left" clubs; in the outspoken opposition of many disinterested groups . . . to the policies of white governments in

Nevertheless it was mainly because of the association of the Conservative Party with the consumer boom, with the enlargement of opportunity and, above all, with a keen interest in the young[1] that Labour lost votes among this age group in the election. Although Labour did succeed in the following years in broadening its appeal to include many of the new middle-class elements – scientists and technologists particularly[2] – its policy towards 'Y' voters remained unimaginative. *Labour in the Sixties* simply asked Constituency Parties to concentrate upon a 'further expansion of Young Socialist Groups'.

The image that revisionists found most damaging, however, was the association of the Party with large-scale increases in public ownership. Extensions of nationalisation were undoubtedly unpopular with a majority of the electorate[3] but the Gaitskellites considered that this aspect of Labour's image was both unfair and damaging. It was unfair because, as we have seen earlier, Labour was not a wholesale nationalisation party; indeed, under its new Leader, it had become sophisticated and moderate. Two reasons were advanced to explain this 'unfair' association. First, many of Labour's policy proposals on public ownership were ambiguous and open to various interpretations.[4] Secondly, Clause IV remained part of the Constitution of the Party! It is doubtful whether Clause IV, the theoretical commitment to the public ownership of the means of production,

---

Africa; in the outcry about bad town planning and the destruction of amenities. Here are the dry bones of socialism, wanting only a spirit of purposive development. . . .', 'Socialism for Tomorrow: a manifesto by a group of young people in their twenties', in *Socialist Commentary* (Oct 1960) p. 24. All the 10 signatories were individual members of the Labour Party.

1. The Abrams Survey asked its sample (in the age group 18–25) why certain aspects of the two parties' policies would benefit young people. Thirty per cent of replies stated that the Conservatives were 'genuinely interested' in the young, whereas only 10 per cent of replies gave this as a reason for voting Labour.

2. *Signposts for the Sixties* (1961), the policy document of 1961, was the first ever to talk in terms of the 'scientific revolution'.

3. The Abrams Survey concluded that out of their total sample of respondents only 11 per cent were in favour of more publicly owned industries, whereas 75 per cent were against and 14 per cent were categorised as 'Don't Knows'. Table 18, republished in M. Abrams and R. Rose, *Must Labour Lose?* (1960) p. 35. Further survey information on nationalisation is provided in Chapter Eight under the heading, 'The Politics of Electoral Considerations'.

4. Particularly the sections in post-war Labour's manifestos that referred to possible public ownership when an industry or firm 'fails the nation'.

distribution and exchange, was in any way damaging. It is not unreasonable to assume that only a very small minority of the electorate knew of the existence of the clause or realised that Labour was constitutionally committed in this way. Therefore the publicity Gaitskell gave to this aspect of Labour's Constitution was unnecessary and even possibly harmful in terms of electoral appeal.

Nevertheless in the aftermath of the 1959 defeat, Gaitskell was determined to erase the nationalisation image. There was little he could do in terms of practical policy because Labour was already moderate in its proposals. He was therefore forced to turn to Clause IV, as this was the only written and specific example of the image he wished to eradicate.

Gaitskell's determination to change Labour's image, irrespective of short-term damage to the Party, raises the question as to whether or not the image of an opposition party is important in its quest to regain power. Crossman suggested that there was very little an opposition party could do by itself to regain power; instead it should await the collapse of the government party's popularity. He argued with considerable evidence to back him up[1] that Labour, whatever its policy or image, would have lost the 1959 election because of the association of the Conservatives with the post-war prosperity boom.[2] This view is reinforced by later events. Labour won the 1964 election even though its policy towards nationalisation and public ownership had not changed. Also, Clause IV was still part of the Constitution of the Party. Labour had not changed, in real terms, between 1959 and 1964, but its image was automatically improved by the disintegration of Conservative popularity following Selwyn Lloyd's credit squeeze in 1961. The Tories lost favour with the people and the Opposition Party's image rose accordingly – irrespective of its policies and its Constitution.

Revisionists, however, saw the 1959 defeat not as a temporary

---

1. All the opinion pollsters agreed that the Conservatives' favourable image was conditioned by their association with prosperity. Abrams, however, had reservations regarding the extent to which traditional Labour supporters were affected by increasing material wealth. Abrams, 'Why Labour has Lost Elections', p. 5.
2. R. H. S. Crossman, *Labour in the Affluent Society*, Fabian Tract No. 325 (1960).

débâcle that could be overcome by later Conservative inadequacy, but rather as part of what Albu called a 'steady
decline'.[1] Drastic and divisive measures were therefore needed
in order to halt this trend and a change in image was considered
one of them.

This Gaitskellite preoccupation with image was only one
aspect of the Labour Right's electorally based political philosophy.[2] The Left, too, shared this concern for Labour's image but
reached fundamentally different conclusions. It considered that
the electorate were at fault – they were not sufficiently socialist.
Labour had to educate them! This produced a somewhat
evangelical approach to the function of the Labour Movement;
for instance, Barbara Castle said that instead of reviewing the
relevance of socialism, Labour should 'go out and make
socialists'.[3]

The Gaitskellite wing believed that this process should be
reversed and that Labour should adapt to the electorate
rather than attempting to make the electorate, by persuasion
and propaganda, adapt to Labour. This electoral consciousness
of the revisionists was further illustrated by their attitude to
the question of sovereignty in the Party. Whether Labour
should be essentially a parliamentary force, responsible to and
moulded by the electorate, or whether it should be a 'mass
movement' became a vital question. The debate was between
those who saw Labour as essentially wedded to the existing
system and those who saw it as an agent of revolutionary
change.

PARLIAMENTARY PARTY OR MOVEMENT? – THE
QUESTION OF SOVEREIGNTY

There were certain intrinsic revisionist-socialist reasons that
militated in favour of the 'parliamentary' as opposed to the
'movement' concept. The most important of these was the
constitutionalist theory that MPs in particular and the PLP in
general were responsible to the electorate and not to the mass-

1. A. Albu, 'Comment on Crossman', in *Socialist Commentary* (Aug 1960) p. 12.
2. See Chapter Eight, the section dealing with the 'Politics of Electoral Considerations'.
3. *LPACR 1959*, p. 86.

party, either in the form of Conference or the NEC. Also, the PLP, being elected by the Labour voters as distinct from Labour Party members, was more representative of Labour opinion in the nation.[1] It was vital for revisionists that ultimate sovereignty in the Party should be located in a body which remained sensitive to electoral opinion. This was not only democratic but also sensible. Revolutions were not on in Britain and Labour could only win power through the ballot box. The electorate was the fundamental power base in the country and a party of power, rather than protest, could not afford to ignore it.

To the revisionists the views of Labour voters took precedence over those of the Party activists. It was a common feature of the right-wing case that whereas the Party activists often felt that the Labour Leadership was not representing their views, this was invariably because the mass of Labour voters, quite rightly, had priority over Party workers in influencing the Leaders of the Party. Many survey examples exist to show this close relationship between the Leadership and its mass following in the electorate on questions of policy. One such was on the question of British possession of nuclear weapons. A Gallup Poll survey, the fieldwork for which was carried out from 30 September to 4 October 1960, showed that 34 per cent of Labour voters wanted Britain to continue to make her own nuclear weapons, 26 per cent wanted Britain to pool her nuclear weapons within the NATO system and rely upon American protection in the future, and 31 per cent wanted Britain to 'give up entirely' her nuclear weapons (9 per cent 'didn't know').[2]

This information suggests that twice as many Labour voters were against unilateral nuclear disarmament as were in favour of it and also that a good third of the total, and the largest single category, wanted Britain to remain an independent nuclear power. This particular survey, taken as it was at the zenith of popular support for unilateralism, further underscores the point that there is often an inverse relationship between electoral appeal and party-activist support.

1. Crosland argued that the PLP was also the 'most broadly based in terms of class and occupation'. Crosland, *Can Labour Win?*, p. 20.
2. *Gallup Political Index* (Oct 1960), Report No. 10.

It is not implausible to deduce from this, and from other information already cited, a general theory regarding the relationship between Labour voters and the Party. A conventional theory, and one often implicitly used on the Left, is best expressed in the form of a 'pyramid' or triangular structure in which the Leadership forms the apex and the Labour voters the base. In between the apex and the base are ranged from top to bottom other Party institutions in reverse order of numerical strength. This can best be expressed by a diagram.

	12	PLP Leadership (Shadow Cabinet)
c. 250–350		PLP
c. 1 million		Annual Conference (Constituency Section)
c. 5 million		Annual Conference (Trade Union Section)
c. 12–13 million		Labour Voters

This diagram has a simple numerical basis and tends to suggest that the larger the numerical strength of a particular section of the Party the nearer that section is to the views and aspirations of the Labour voter. This view is obviously open to serious criticism, especially with regard to the representative nature of the votes cast in the name of the five million or so trade union members of the Party at Annual Conference. The fundamental error in the above structure, however, is that the true relationship between the voter and the Leadership is masked. Indeed the apex and the base are often in agreement on policy questions and it is the constituency section of the Annual Conference that is often 'out on a limb'.

The constituency section of the Annual Conference, far from representing the Labour voter, tends to assume distinct attitudes of its own. Indeed the constituency section and the voter often represent the rival pressures exerted upon the decision-making centres of the Party; the Leadership, the PLP and the NEC. The constituency section rarely wins such a conflict.

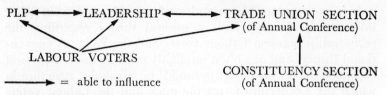

The above diagram attempts to explain the influence relationship between the Labour voters and the Party decision centres. It also shows that the constituency section, being powerless to influence either the PLP or the Leadership, one being largely a function of the other, can only make a significant breakthrough by influencing the trade union section. When it does so, as was the case in 1960, it effectively cuts it off from the mass of Labour voters.

The frustrations caused in 1960 and 1961 by the conflict between Party Conference and the PLP made the academic debate about sovereignty a practical issue. Two views emerged on the Right of the Party as to the best method of achieving freedom of action for the PLP. Dr Saul Rose suggested that subordination of the PLP to the Annual Conference was 'perilous' and that a better arrangement would be a division of function.[1] He suggested that the NEC should remain in charge of the administrative functions of the Party and that the PLP should deal with policy. He pointed to Clause VIII of the Party Constitution to show that this was already the legal position. Clause VIII states that 'The National Executive Committee of the Party shall, subject to the control and directions of the Party Conference, be the Administrative Authority of the Party.'[2]

This view of the division of functions between the PLP and the Annual Conference (and the NEC) was put forward in

1. S. Rose, 'Back to Clause VIII' and 'Thoughts on the Constitution', in *Socialist Commentary* (May and Sep 1960).

2. It was established in 1945, by correspondence between Attlee and Churchill, that the NEC could not give directions to the PLP. Also, the NEC statement on the Constitution (14 Jul 1960) said that 'Annual Conference does not instruct the Parliamentary Party'. Nevertheless the exact relationship between the Annual Conference and the PLP remains vague, although Gaitskell, in an interview on 17 Jul 1959, had intimated that major decisions of principle taken by Conference would bind future Labour Governments. (This interview is reproduced, in part only, in the *Observer*, 8 Oct 1961.)

May 1960. The Party Conference of that year implicitly rejected it by passing a resolution moved by John Stonehouse MP in the following terms:

> This Conference reaffirms that the policy of the Labour Party to be pursued nationally and in Parliament on questions of principle should be determined by Annual Conference. While acknowledging that the day-to-day tactics in Parliament must be the job of the Parliamentary Labour Party, this Conference declares that Labour policy is decided by the Party Conference, which is the final authority.[1]

Another proposal was that 'the Party Constitution should be altered in such a way as to give direct representation to the Parliamentary Party on the National Executive'.[2] Rather than a separation of function, this represented an 'infiltration' process by the parliamentary wing into the mass-movement. This, too, was implicitly rejected by the passing of the Stonehouse resolution.

Although we have seen that there were certain revisionist first principles involved in the elevation of the PLP over Annual Conference and the NEC, the debate on the sovereignty issue was not basically an objective search for a sensible Party structure. Instead, it was an instrument, used by both opposing wings of the Party, in the power struggle.

Both Right and Left were guilty of using the sovereignty question only when it suited them. The Right, for instance, cared little about the issue until 1960 when Conference went unilateralist. Only once before was it thought possible that Conference would oppose the PLP on a major issue of policy, and on that occasion, before the vote was taken, Morrison warned of the dangers involved in a clash between the two bodies.[3]

1. Composite Resolution No. 14, *LPACR 1960*, p. 159.

2. Crosland, *Can Labour Win?*, p. 20.

3. 'If the Executive motion were lost today we should be in a chaotic situation in the House of Commons. We shall be in a muddle if a Labour Government – [interruptions]. . . . Supposing a Labour Government is returned, which is quite possible, are we going to be faced as a Government, as Mr Attlee said, with a situation in which we are tied and fettered and cannot think in relation to the facts of a changing situation?', *LPACR 1954*, p. 108. The issue was German rearmament.

*

Similarly the spokesmen of the Left raised the issue of sovereignty only when it was convenient or necessary for them to do so; for instance in the period 1960–1, following their victory at the Scarborough Conference. They did not argue in the same terms when Conference reverted to its traditional defence policies after October 1961. Obviously, therefore, the sovereignty issue was convenient for them to use as a weapon following the Scarborough Conference, though not so following the Blackpool Conference. It was dropped like a hot potato.

There is little evidence to show that any of the political wings of the PLP took the sovereignty issue seriously. In the autumn of 1960 Wilson opposed Gaitskell for Leader on the specific question of Gaitskell's refusal to abide by Conference decisions. Nevertheless the voting figures for each candidate were virtually identical with the normal left-right divisions of the PLP, although on this occasion some of the centralists voted with the Left.[1] MPs had obviously cast their votes according to their views on defence and the Leadership, rather than with reference to the niceties of the sovereignty issue.

Therefore, neither the Right nor the Left was seriously interested in the academic debate over where power should lie. Although there were important revisionist and fundamentalist principles involved in the sovereignty issue, the basic clash remained over the question of the Leadership with the Left attempting to wrest power from the PLP where Gaitskell was heavily supported. In doing so they hoped to topple the real enemy, Hugh Gaitskell.

THE LEADERSHIP OF HUGH GAITSKELL

Michael Foot has suggested that a Leader of the Labour Party 'must strive to weld all the varying elements of the Party into a cohesive, enthusiastic force'.[2] Attlee's leadership was based upon this formula, for he continually attempted to balance the varying factions rather than give preference to any one of them.

1. The result of the PLP ballot for Leader of the Party announced on 3 Nov 1960 was: Gaitskell 166, Wilson 81 (247 out of 254 Labour MPs cast their vote). This fairly accurately represented the 'Left–Right' power situation in the PLP at the time.
2. M. Foot, 'The Party and the Leadership', in *Tribune* (21 Oct 1960) p. 4.

The history of Gaitskell's leadership, however, provides ample evidence of a new conception of the function of the Leadership. This new style of leadership was not apparent, however, until after the 1959 election. Until then Gaitskell used the Leadership in a way similar to that of his predecessor, for at times the composition and portfolios of his Shadow Cabinet represented all sections and shades of opinion in the Party.[1] He seemed determined to heal past divisions by a conciliatory attitude to Bevan and appointed him spokesman on Foreign Affairs. During the period 1956 to 1959 Gaitskell, although resolute on the need for a moderate Party, engaged in no dramatic initiatives of a divisive character.

All this changed following the election defeat. Gaitskell on the eve of the General Election thought Labour would just win and was stunned by the size of the eventual defeat. After a short period of silence he reversed his strategy and attempted to mould the Party into the shape of his own revisionism. He consequently came to be identified with a 'sectional' or 'factional' interest group. This identification was not illusory.

Gaitskell made no attempt to dispel the growing impression that he was directly influenced by a small group of his close personal friends who often used to meet at his house in Frognal Gardens, Hampstead. Informal meetings were held between The Leader of the Party and many of the revisionist 'intellectuals', notably Crosland, Jenkins, Jay and Gordon Walker. On these occasions political decisions affecting the whole Party were taken.[2] Such meetings were symptomatic of the developing style of highly 'personalised' leadership. His personal, as well as political, loyalty to his colleagues naturally caused resentment on the Left of the Party.

Another aspect of Gaitskell's 'rightist' leadership was his attempt to alter the *status quo* regarding Clause IV of the Party

1. Labour's Central Leadership, under Gaitskell, in 1957 consisted of Griffiths (Deputy Leader), Wilson (spokesman on Treasury matters), Bevan (spokesman on Foreign Affairs) and Brown (spokesman on Defence). Although the 'Shadow Cabinet' (Parliamentary Committee) is elected by the whole PLP, the Leader determines the distribution of offices within it.

2. One such meeting held on 11 Oct 1959 (at Gaitskell's home) co-ordinated much of the 'new thinking' regarding public ownership and the Party name later expounded by Jay and Dalton.

Constitution. On the question of unilateralism, however, he was attempting to restore the *status quo ante* and return to traditional defence policies. Nevertheless, his ruthless adherence to the 'Gaitskell–Healey draft'[1] on defence policy was not an act of conciliation.

A further aspect of this 'rightist' leadership of Hugh Gaitskell is less tangible. He used socialist rhetoric much less than both his predecessor and successor as Leader of the Party. His speeches lacked reference to much of the visionary aspects of socialist doctrine and when he departed from practical issues his political sentiments were often expressed more in terms of human values than the quasi-religious idealism many wanted to hear. Gaitskell also guarded himself against 'affirmationism'[2] as a political reflex and was more concerned with the possible implementation of his political ideas.

The question arises as to whether this particular 'extremist'[3] style of leadership was responsible for dividing the Party after 1959. Following Labour's third successive electoral defeat an atmosphere of gloom and frustration prevailed which, on precedent, would have led in any case to a reappraisal of policy and aims. Divisions were bound to occur. Nevertheless, there is considerable evidence to suggest that, but for Gaitskell's leadership, the Party would have been more united than it was. For instance, even in *Socialist Commentary*'s view, Gaitskell's raising of the Clause IV issue was a mistake: 'He chose the wrong issue at the wrong time.'[4] Also, Gaitskell could easily have worked for a compromise formula over defence, albeit with a resultant ambiguity! He chose instead to split the Party. By using his high office as an instrument of one side in the dispute he purposely led the Gaitskellites on to a collision course with the Left.

To many revisionists this kind of 'collision politics' was necessary and indeed welcome. Crosland suggested that a defeat for the NEC at Party Conference in 1960 would produce

---

1. See Chapter Nine of this work.
2. I.e. he was not content simply to affirm his political creed. He was suspicious of those in the Party who proposed what he considered self-evident truths as though it were their own subjective evaluation, e.g. the statement that 'nuclear weapons are evil'.
3. 'Extremist' in Labour Party terms.
4. Editorial in *Socialist Commentary* (Jul 1960).

a crisis which, far from harming Gaitskell's leadership, would help it:

> We should then have, for the first time in the party's history, a direct confrontation of the Parliamentary group and the Conference.
>
> What the final outcome would be no one can predict. The atmosphere would certainly be explosive. . . . Even if some face-saving compromise were found, things would never be quite the same again. The Parliamentary leadership would have asserted at least some degree of independence and the policy-making role of Conference would be to some extent devalued.
>
> Thus, however partial, an important object would be achieved: the Labour party would be seen by the country to be dominated neither by the bloc votes of the trade unions nor by an unrepresentative minority of left-wing activists.[1]

Thus an important part of the revisionist case for operating on the patient immediately was that surgery, although harmful in the short run, was necessary for the long-run health of the Party.

It is impossible to measure the effect of Labour's internal dissensions and Gaitskell's eventual triumph upon public opinion. Whether the upturn in Labour's electoral fortunes was due to Gaitskell's leadership or was because of Conservative unpopularity is at this point in time and without sufficient evidence a subject for conjecture only.

What is certain is the fact that Gaitskell's headlong assault upon Clause IV, the principal article of faith since 1918, was so traumatic that its effects are still with us. It remains one of the most explosive episodes in Labour's long search for its true identity.

---

1. C. A. R. Crosland, 'British Labour's Crucial Meeting', in *The New Leader* (3 Oct 1960) p. 8.

CHAPTER EIGHT

The Clause IV Debate

Labour went into the 1959 election with a moderate series of proposals for nationalisation. It pledged itself to restore public ownership to the Steel industry and to Road Haulage. Perhaps its most fundamentalist proposal was to take into local-council ownership all existing private housing that had been rent-controlled before 1 January 1956.[1] Apart from this, no further specific extension of public ownership was called for, although there was a generalised statement to the effect that 'where an industry is shown, after thorough enquiry, to be failing the nation we reserve the right to take all or any part of it into public ownership if this is necessary'.[2]

The loss of the election by 100 seats set in train the usual re-appraisal of policy. In the past the right-wing of the Party was usually placed in the position of having to respond to an attempt by the Left to increase the *specific* proposals for public ownership in the Party programme. The aftermath of the 1959 election defeat, however, presented the Party with two, hitherto unknown, initiatives. First, it was not the Left, but the revisionists, who took the first step. Secondly, the Leader himself became actively involved and threw the prestige and power of his office wholeheartedly behind the revisionist initiative.

Another difference between the aftermath of 1959 and that of 1955 and 1951 was that the debate over public ownership assumed constitutional proportions. Until 1959 no section of the Party had attempted to revise or amend the fundamental

---

1. This was based upon an NEC recommendation in *Homes for the Future* that was passed at the 1956 Annual Conference and reaffirmed at the 1957 Conference. See *LPACR 1957*, Composite Resolution No. 31, pp. 95–6.
2. *Britain Belongs to You!*, Labour Party Manifesto (1959) p. 3.

long-term aim of the Party – Clause IV of the Constitution. This clause read as follows:

> To secure for the workers by hand or by brain the full fruits of their industry and the most equitable distribution thereof that may be possible, upon the basis of the common ownership of the means of production, distribution and exchange, and the best obtainable system of popular administration and control of each industry or service.

For a year following the election defeat the issue was not the usual one; whether the specific public-ownership proposals should be increased or decreased. Rather it was whether this constitutionally enshrined long-term aim was relevant to the mid-twentieth century and to the coming decades.

In a sense the debate was more than this. It assumed the proportions of a power struggle between the Leadership and the Left. As we have seen in Chapter Four, the intellectual and theoretical debate over public ownership raged in the mid-1950s but no attempt was made to remove or enlarge the constitutional, theoretical and ultimate aspiration. Once Gaitskell brought it out into the open he was asking for trouble, for the Left were presented with an issue that they could turn to their advantage. He challenged their most cherished belief and the Left responded with a two-year campaign to rob him of the Leadership itself.

Gaitskell's challenge to the Party was the product of a dedicated and considered conviction. He had fought the battles of the fifties alongside Crosland, Strachey and the other revisionists. Indeed, he had been an active participant in the 'new thinking' process and had become personally involved in it. He saw, as they did, the Left's confusion over 'ends' and 'means' but it was only after the election defeat that he enumerated publicly, in a speech to the 'post-mortem' Conference of 1959, what he considered to be his own brand of democratic socialism.

Uppermost in his priorities was a concern for the less fortunate: 'Thus, at home, our concern is naturally for the less fortunate – the old, the sick, the widowed, the unemployed, the disabled and the badly housed ... all those in need or hard-

"BROTHER HUGH, BROTHER HUGH, YOU'VE WRITTEN THAT SINFUL WORD AGAIN . . . !"

ship.'[1] From this premise sprung his belief in social welfare as a major socialist goal. This view was embodied in Gaitskell's *Amplification of Aims*, a modern testament that was placed alongside Clause IV and passed by the National Executive Committee of the Party in 1960.[2]

This aspect of his political philosophy was part of his deep commitment to equality and the 'classless society'. Like the other revisionists, however, he saw the 'classless society' not so much in economic as in social terms: 'we believe in a classless society – a society without the snobbery, the privilege, the restrictive social barriers which are still far too prevalent in Britain today'.[3] A similar statement was incorporated in the seventh item of the *Amplification of Aims* of 1960.

Further socialist ideals, according to Gaitskell, were fellowship and co-operation. His 1959 Conference speech was virtually a potted version of all the revisionist tracts of the fifties:

> Fifthly, British Socialism has always contained an essential element of personal idealism – the belief that the pursuit of material satisfaction by itself without spiritual values is empty and barren and that our relations with one another should be based not on ruthless self-regarding rivalry but on fellowship and cooperation.[4]

This idea, too, found its way into the *Amplification of Aims*.[5]

Gaitskell also shared with the revisionists a deep commitment to freedom. In its political context Gaitskell adhered rigidly to the democratic process, as section (e) of the *Amplification of Aims*, largely his own work, illustrates:

> As a democratic party believing that there is no true Socialism without political freedom, it seeks to obtain and to hold power only through free democratic institutions whose existence it has resolved always to strengthen and defend from threats from any quarter.

Conspicuous by its absence from Gaitskell's socialist 'ends' was public ownership. He saw it as only one of many 'means' to

1. Gaitskell, *LPACR 1959*, p. 111, col. 2.
2. *NEC Statement* (Mar 1960) para. (e).
3. Gaitskell, *LPACR 1959*, p. 111.   4. Ibid.
5. *NEC Statement* (Mar 1960) para. (f).

his own particular socialist 'end', and this entailed the acceptance of the mixed economy for all time:

> Common Ownership takes varying forms, including state-owned industries and firms, producer and consumer cooperatives, municipal ownership and public participation in private concerns. *Recognizing that both public and private enterprise have a place in the economy it believes that further extensions of common ownership should be decided from time to time.* . . .[1]

Both Gaitskell's 1959 speech and his personal influence on the *Amplification of Aims* illustrates his orthodox intellectual revisionism. He was more than a theoretician, however, and it was not merely the intricacies of the intellectual appraisal that led him to point out the inadequacy of Clause IV. As Party Leader he was desperately concerned with the question of power and was determined that Labour should not continue to remain out of office. He considered that the decline of Labour since 1951 was due mainly to its loss of the 'middle ground' of British politics. In order to win elections that 'middle ground' had to be re-captured and Clause IV was seen as an obstacle to this attempt.

THE POLITICS OF ELECTORAL CONSIDERATIONS

It would be inaccurate to credit only the Right with an awareness of the limitations that electoral popularity impose upon the formulation of policy. Indeed, virtually every member of the Party, except those on its lunatic fringes, was opposed to the *immediate* implementation of Clause IV. Also, all wings of the Party agreed with the democratic process – some giving it greater emphasis than others.

Both sides agreed that Labour had insufficient electoral appeal – they could hardly do otherwise – but they differed on how to remedy the situation. Only a few attempted to argue that a more left-wing policy would have won Labour more votes, for the fallacy of this view was apparent to anyone who had contacts with the working class and especially to sensible men on the Left. It was obvious to most that Labour's own traditional supporters in elections were more conservative

---

1. *NEC Statement* (Mar. 1960) para. (j). (Italics mine.)

than many sections of the 'liberal' middle classes who voted overwhelmingly Tory. Labour's voters contained some of the most nationalist and illiberal elements in the political community, and on such questions as capital punishment, homosexual and divorce-law liberalisation they were worlds apart from the average Labour MP. Perhaps it is a tribute to Labour's maturity and political skill that it has managed both to dampen down these feelings and to persuade those that hold them that their wider interests lie in the direction of a Labour Government. This job would obviously be made more difficult if the Party were to adopt leftist policies. Nevertheless, both Aneurin Bevan and Barbara Castle thought the 1959 election defeat a symptom not of wrong policies but rather of bad propaganda. 'The problem is one of education, not surrender,' said Bevan, who also displayed a surprising degree of optimism that this educative process would work.

The Right, on the other hand, treated the electorates' dismissal of Labour in 1959 with a degree of humility bordering on reverence. Labour was wrong; the people were right! This view had interesting consequences for future action. Douglas Jay, in an article in *Forward*,[1] just eight days after the election suggested that the Labour Party had become too rigidly associated with the working class. In a rather over-simplified passage he warned the Party that 'we are in danger of fighting under the label of a class that no longer exists'. He suggested that instead Labour should be 'vigorous, radical, reforming, open-minded' and even advocated a change in the Party's name.[2] On top of all this Jay bluntly called for a total and complete ban on further nationalisation. In his *Forward* article, and also in the November edition of *Encounter*, he argued that the British people associated public monopoly with social ownership as a whole and that therefore 'we should say that we accept the decision of the electorate and would in future propose no further nationalisation'. The importance of these views lies not only in their forthright and uncompromising tone but also because they were echoed, virtually intact, by Gaitskell

1. *Forward* (16 Oct 1959).
2. He suggested either 'Labour and Radical' or 'Labour and Reform' as suitable titles.

himself. *The Times* of 17 October was not engaging in journalistic imagination when it said: 'The first authoritative statement which may fairly be taken as representing Mr Gaitskell's views on the reshaping of Labour party policy was given in an article by Mr Douglas Jay'. Gaitskell refused to go as far as Jay on the question of a change in the Party's name, and decisively ruled it out at the post-election Conference in November 1959. Nevertheless, both on the 'class-image' issue and also on the 'nationalisation' question he sided firmly with Jay.[1] He did not make a specific plea against the inclusion of *any* further nationalisation in Labour's future programme – the Conference was not meant to deal with specifics anyway – but his attitude to nationalisation was made clear by his continual references to extending the frontiers of the 'public sector': 'we may be more concerned in the future with other forms of public ownership – and there are many other forms'. Similarly, he agreed with Jay on the 'class question'. Future electoral popularity was important in this connection, and he made a special appeal to the Party to identify itself with the new social groupings emerging in the nation. Equally as important as the electoral motive as a reason for rejecting the 'class image' of the Party was Gaitskell's philosophic predilection for 'class harmony' as opposed to 'class division' or 'class war'. This partly explains his desire to make Labour a 'classless party' and his intense emotional reaction against the Conservative Party's claim that they represented all social classes whereas Labour was tied to a single class.

From the earliest days of the Party, and with only few exceptions, the Labour Leaders have been sensitive to public opinion – no bad thing for parliamentarians. Nevertheless, only in the late 1950s have they been able to benefit from detailed data about the attitudes of the electorate; until then they had had to rely upon an intuitive understanding. Gaitskell, and other revisionists, were deeply affected by the results of Gallup Poll enquiries into the Labour Party 'image',[2] but of particular

1. See *LPACR 1959*, pp. 105–14.
2. A Social Surveys (Gallup Poll) Ltd survey (carried out between 28 Feb and 6 Mar 1959) presented the following data: when the sample was asked 'What do you think the Labour Party stands for?' 33% replied, 'The working class, the under-dog' and 17% replied, 'nationalisation'. Although the connection of

importance were the results of the Mark Abrams Surveys carried out on behalf of *Socialist Commentary* immediately following the 1959 election.[1]

As we have seen earlier one issue raised by these surveys was the question of the role of the trade unions in the Labour Party. Social Surveys (Gallup Poll) Ltd published a Poll on the trade unions, undertaken for the *News Chronicle*, in September 1959. Two broad conclusions were reached by the pollsters. First, that 'in 22 years of polling the British public we have never found higher acclaim for trade unionism amongst union members themselves than exists today'.[2] Secondly, 'Nor, in that period, have we found a greater criticism of the trade unions with the rest of the population – non-unionists – than exists today'.[3] Another interesting conclusion from the survey was that 43 per cent of the electorate thought that the unions had too much power whereas only 35 per cent of the electorate considered that the financiers and the bankers had too much power.[4]

The Gaitskellites considered that the growing unpopularity of the trade unions was having a commensurate effect upon the Labour Party but nobody of substance advocated the disaffiliation of the unions from the Party. As usual the most radical suggestion came from Jay, who wanted a change in the Constitution of the Party so that sovereignty would reside more firmly in its parliamentary wing.[5] Gaitskell again rejected the

---

Labour in the public mind with the 'working class' had slightly fallen throughout the decade (39% in 1951, 37% in 1955), the connection with 'nationalisation' had risen (6% in 1951, 9% in 1955).

1. Abrams, 'Why Labour Loses Elections'. Abrams also produced some important work on working-class political behaviour in 'The Roots of Working Class Conservatism', in *Encounter* (May 1960).

2. *Gallup Poll on the Trade Unions* (C 53058). This conclusion did not find its way into any of the newspapers of the period and remains in an unpublished form in Social Surveys (Gallup Poll) Ltd's files.

3. Ibid. Non-unionist respondents were asked, 'Generally speaking, and thinking of Britain as a whole, do you think that trade unions are a good or a bad thing?' 53% replied 'a good thing', 30% replied 'a bad thing' and 17% 'don't know'.

4. Ibid.

5. See Jay, *Forward* (16 Oct 1959). He suggested that the NEC should become a 'federal' body and that the PLP should have representatives on it. The result of this would have been to lessen the sovereignty of the Annual Party Conference

views of his adventurous lieutenant; he firmly renounced any change in the structure of the Party which involved lessening union importance. The unions held the purse-strings and they were safe. However, both Gaitskell and Crosland wanted the trade union movement to encompass many more 'white-collar' workers than it then did and also to engage in more public relations techniques.[1]

The changed nature of capitalism; the new approach to 'means' and 'ends'; the deep commitment to the democratic process and a sensitivity to public opinion; and, on a philosophical level, a distrust of the ethic of ultimate ends – all portray the fundamental revisionist approach to the future direction of the Labour Party, as they crystallised in the autumn of 1959. This was, and was seen as, an attack on many of the traditional values and beliefs of large sections of the Party. This division had always existed in the Party, but 1959 saw the first positive attempt to lift the debate out of the policy arena and into one of fundamentals. It became a question of theology.

As well as elevating the debate to a theological level, Gaitskell was attempting to alter the *status quo*. The British Labour Party, for all its talk of radical change, is at heart a conservative institution and this, historically, has been the inherent strength of the Leadership in its resistance to extremism. On this occasion, however, the Leadership itself was advocating change. Gaitskell failed over Clause IV because he was unable to shift the most conservative element in Labour politics: the trade union movement.

THE FIGHT FOR THE AMPLIFICATION AND CLARIFICATION OF CLAUSE IV

At no time during the whole Clause IV controversy did Gaitskell ask for the removal of Clause IV from the Party

---

(dominated as it was, and is, by the trade unions). The question of where sovereignty resides in the Labour Party, when it is in opposition, is a contentious one. See McKenzie, *British Political Parties*, 2nd (revised) ed., and Beer, *Modern British Politics*, for opposing views.

1. Crosland, *Can Labour Win?*

Constitution. The key part of his speech at the 1959 Conference suggested that the clause 'be brought up to date' and he added that 'standing *on its own* this cannot possibly be regarded as adequate'.[1] The obvious conclusion to be drawn from this is that Gaitskell wanted Clause IV to stay, but felt an addition should be made which would make it applicable in modern terms. This interpretation is important in view of the claims that were to be made later that Gaitskell, and those near to him,[2] received a serious rebuff as early as March 1960.

It can be argued that the logic of Gaitskell's position would lead him to reject Clause IV, for a belief in a mixed economy and also in Clause IV were ultimately incompatible. But on the narrower level of Party tactics he did not feel it was necessary to demand the deletion of the clause. What he did ask for, however, was a new declaration of aims to be placed alongside that of Clause IV.[3] This, together with an earlier speech at Nottingham in which he advocated the retention of Steel nationalisation in the Party programme, was taken as a reversal of his previous 'hard-line' policy. In fact, he was simply repeating, almost verbatim, what he had said at the Blackpool Conference in November 1959 about the frontiers of the public and the private sector.[4] *Tribune*, nevertheless, ran the story of the speech under a heading, 'Mr Gaitskell changes his tune' and *The Times* of Monday, 15 February interpreted the speech as 'Mr Gaitskell calls for more public ownership'. Yet Gaitskell was calling for precisely the same amount of public ownership as he had previously advocated before the election.[5]

Between his November speech and March 1960 Gaitskell remained consistent, but the Left, who had previously feared the worse, saw this as an act of conciliation. Those who had bitterly opposed what they had considered his attack on Clause

1. *LPACR 1959*, p. 112, col. 2. (Italics mine.)

2. Neither did Douglas Jay, at any time, call for the removal of Clause IV. His controversial position hinged upon his advocation of no more nationalisation proposals in the next manifesto.

3. See *The Times* (23 Feb 1960) *re* Gaitskell speech to Ruskin Fellowship. Also *The Times* (27 Feb 1960) *re* Gaitskell speech at Cambridge.

4. For a full account of the Nottingham speech, see *Tribune* (19 Jul 1960) p. 1.

5. He reiterated the public-ownership proposals of the 1959 Labour Party Manifesto: Steel, Road Haulage and Water.

IV began to move from their rigid positions. Anthony Greenwood, a member of the NEC, who found himself in opposition
to Gaitskell at this juncture, made a conciliatory gesture in a
speech at the week-end of 22 February: 'If it will make for
peace in the Party . . . most of us would . . . be able to add
anything within reason to the constitution.' Opinion in the
spring of 1960 seemed to be solidifying around the view that
an addition to Clause IV would be acceptable as long as the
1918 statement remained intact in the Constitution. This view
was held by an overwhelming number of trade union leaders
and delegates to the NEC of the Labour Party.[1] However, the
degree of emotional commitment to Clause IV by the unions
was already apparent, and especially among trade union members of the PLP who normally would be associated with the
Right wing.

In a speech in his constituency of Belper, George Brown said:
'Let us accept, on the one hand, that the present constitution
and statement of objects adopted long ago has a place in our
hearts . . . that makes it quite impossible to delete or rewrite
it.'[2] This sentiment was echoed by Edwin Gooch, elected top
of the trade union section of the NEC in 1959 and not considered to be on the Left, in a speech on 13 March.[3] Although
Gaitskell had never advocated the removal of Clause IV, he
had also never directly called for its retention. An obvious
difference of emphasis therefore arose between the Leader and
his intellectual political allies on the one hand and the trade
union Right of the Party on the other.

The NEC meeting of 13 March, however, illustrated the
broad, but temporary, unity that had been forged on the constitutional issue. A twelve-point Gaitskell draft,[4] with the retention of Clause IV *intact*, was adopted as part of the Constitution
of the Party by all the NEC members save one.[5] Nevertheless

1. All the T.U. delegates, save one, voted for this idea at the NEC meeting of
16 March 1960. See *The Times* (17 Mar 1960).

2. See *The Times* (7 Mar 1960). Also, Frank McCleavey MP, not usually associated with the Left wing of the Party, supported Brown's position in a letter to
The Times (7 Mar 1960).

3. See *The Times* (14 Mar 1960).   4. See *NEC Report* (1960) pp. 10–11.

5. According to *The Times* (17 Mar 1960) Harry Nicholas, the TGWU delegate,
voted against the 12 points being included in the Constitution. Nicholas is now
General Secretary of the Labour Party.

there was some debate within the NEC on the controversial tenth point of the Gaitskell draft, namely:

> Recognising that both public and private enterprise have a place in the economy it believes that further extension of common ownership should be decided from time to time in the light of these objectives [the previous 9 points] ... with due regard to the views of the workers and consumers concerned.

But even this clear assertion of the acceptance of the mixed economy was passed by a 'substantial majority'.[1]

March 1960, therefore, saw all sections of the Party satisfied with the outcome of the public-ownership dispute. The Left, mainly through the medium of *Tribune*, claimed that they were satisfied on three major counts. First, that Clause IV itself was still part of the Constitution; secondly, because the new Gaitskell declaration of aims carried in its preamble the word 'reaffirms' when referring to Clause IV; and thirdly, because in the vital Clause X of the new declaration the phrase 'commanding heights of the economy' was included and became the criterion for an expansion of common ownership. Similarly, the Gaitskell wing of the Party seemed to be satisfied with the result because the new statement had actually been accepted as part of the Constitution. Most Gaitskellites did not go so far as Woodrow Wyatt when he claimed that as a result of the new decision 'Clause IV henceforth will have no authority. It is completely superseded by the new and modern expression of what Socialism really stands for in the second half of the twentieth century.'[2] But there was a considerable amount of interpretation of the new decision by the 'intellectual' wing of the Right which claimed that this was an outright victory. For instance, Jay stated that the acceptance of the phrase 'the commanding heights of the economy' meant that no further public ownership should be advocated as the 'commanding heights' were already either publicly owned or controlled.

As usual with a compromise both sides claimed victory.

Despite the claims of both sides the Party in March 1960 had opted for a statement which placed it in a contradictory

---

1. See Morgan Phillips's Press Conference, reported in *The Times* (17 Mar 1960).
2. See *Tribune* (25 Mar 1960) p. 5.

position. Clause IV of the old Constitution, and Clause X of
the Gaitskell draft cannot, within any reasonable interpretation,
be wholly reconciled. It was this lack of reconciliation that
enabled both sides in the argument to claim, in legalistic and
pedantic terms, victory over the other. In fact the issue had
become one of semantics. Nevertheless, as far as Gaitskell was
concerned, by March of 1960 he had gained all that he set out
to achieve. The trade union delegates to the NEC had provided him with the necessary support, but they had acted
individually and without reference to their unions. The union
conferences in the spring and summer of 1960 refused to ratify
the decisions of their delegates, and what in March had
appeared as an agreed solution had by the autumn turned into
a defeat for Gaitskell.

HOW THE UNIONS DEFEATED THE REVISIONISTS

In the end only two of the six major trade unions affiliated to
the Labour Party supported the proposed amendment to
Clause IV of the Party Constitution. The first of these was the
USDAW, which, on 25 April 1960, voted by a two to one majority
to accept the change only after its President, Walter Padley,
had emphasised the importance of the 'commanding heights'
section of Clause X and devalued the 'mixed economy' section.[1] The only other union to follow the USDAW example
was, predictably, the 'loyalist' NUGMW, which passed the
following resolution by 204 votes to 132: 'Congress declares its
support for the revised declaration of Labour Party objects . . .
as agreed by the NEC of the Labour Party on 16 March 1960.'[2]
More significant than this was the defeat of a resolution, at the
same Conference, reaffirming a belief in the public ownership
of the basic industries of the country.[3] The NUGMW, as usual,
remained the most trusted of Gaitskell's friends.

Apart from the NUGMW and USDAW no further support
was forthcoming for Gaitskell and the NEC. On 4 May the

---

1. *USDAW Annual Delegate Meeting Report* (1960) pp. 73–5.
2. *NUGMW Conference Report* (1960), p. 325.
3. A motion asking Congress to 'reaffirm its belief in the public ownership of
the basic industries of this country . . .' was lost. Ibid. pp. 329–33.

National Committee of the AEU (the Annual Conference of the union) passed unanimously a resolution recording its 'complete opposition' to any change in the Party Constitution as well as advocating the public ownership of Steel, Road Transport, Aircraft, Shipbuilding, Chemicals, Motors and Machine Tools, among others. On 3 June the Executive Committee of the TGWU joined the AEU in outright opposition to any change in the Constitution. Any last hopes that the NEC could carry the 1960 Conference on its constitutional proposals were lost on 6 July, when both the NUM and the NUR Annual Conferences[1] rejected the official position. In one day, therefore, 914,000 votes were added to the 2,352,000 already registered by union conferences against the NEC of the Labour Party.[2] By 11 July, only two days before the NEC was due to meet, the vote *for* the proposed constitutional amendment so far registered amounted to only 1,355,000, whereas the vote *against* had risen to 3,033,000. It was still technically possible for the NEC to muster enough votes to win, as the number recorded against them did not, as yet, amount to a majority. However, this would have meant relying on virtually every constituency Labour Party vote and also on the overwhelming support of the minor unions that had not yet mandated their delegates. In real terms it was almost certain that the NEC would be defeated if it continued to press for a constitutional amendment. This was the major factor that caused Gaitskell not to proceed with his new declaration of aims in the form of a constitutional change. Instead he supported an NEC resolution that decided:

> not to proceed with any amendments of an addition to Clause 4 but declares the statement which it adopted on 16 March is a valuable expression of the aims of the Labour party in the second half of the twentieth century and commends it to conference accordingly.[3]

This July meeting of the NEC brought to an end the ten-month debate over Labour's Constitution. The result was a blow for

1. Resolution opposing the constitutional amendment was carried by 66 votes to 11 at the NUR Annual Conference.
2. See *Tribune* (17 Jun 1960) p. 3. The NUM possessed 642,000 votes and the NUR 272,000 votes.
3. See *The Times* (14 Jul 1960).

Gaitskell and his revisionist colleagues as the Constitution was to remain totally unchanged. Although Conference passed the Gaitskell draft as a 'valuable expression of the aims of the Party' this was not what Gaitskell had set out to achieve. Although it was a set-back it was not a defeat. In the 1960s practical policy proposals were to be no less revisionist or moderate than they had been before. Although the Constitution remained exactly as it was in 1918, the debate that had been initiated by Gaitskell had shown clearly that the Party was attached to Clause IV in a sentimental way rather than as a basis for future policy proposals.

This set-back for Gaitskell was caused by a 'rank-and-file' trade union revolt against their leaders' acceptance of the NEC proposal of 16 March. At their Annual Conferences the AEU, the NUR and the NUM executives had supported, and indeed argued for, the NEC March proposal. That they were defeated shows the 'grass roots' attachment to Clause IV that existed in the unions. A decision by these three unions to support their executives' stand would have added 1,609,000 votes to the NEC proposal and would have assured, albeit narrowly, a victory for Gaitskell at the Party Conference. This fact underlines an important aspect of the power situation within the Labour Party.

To be assured of victory at the Labour Party Conference the Leadership needs roughly $3\frac{1}{2}$ million votes. Most of these must come from the unions, as there are only about 1 million votes allocated to constituency parties and other organisations.[1] Let us assume that at the very worst the Leadership (NEC) can count on 24 per cent of the votes cast by the constituency parties,[2] and roughly 500,000 votes from the small unions.

[1]. The 58th Annual Conference of the Labour Party (1959) allocated the following votes to affiliated organisations:

Trade Unions	5,665,000
Socialist Societies	8,000
Co-operative Society	20,000
Labour Parties	1,017,000
Federations	16,000.

[2]. This was the percentage of constituency votes that the NEC achieved in the German Rearmament debate of 1954. The percentage achieved in the Defence debates of 1960 and 1961 was considerably higher. For more details see Hindell and Williams, 'Scarborough and Blackpool', pp. 306-20.

This latter figure is probably an underestimate of minimum leadership strength in the smaller unions, as in the 1960 Defence debate over 1 million votes from this quarter went in support of the multilateralist resolution. Therefore, from these two figures a total of about 750,000 votes are certain, in any Conference, for an NEC motion. Over $2\frac{1}{2}$ million votes are then needed from the 'big 6' in order to guarantee a 'platform' victory. This is guaranteed if any four of the six major unions support the NEC. Usually, however, the breakdown of the 'big 6' is not as simple as this. For instance, the Leadership relied during the early fifties, in its struggle with the 'Bevanites', upon the TGWU–NUM–NUGMW axis which held steady even during the crisis over German rearmament. The late fifties and early sixties, however, have shown greater fluidity in voting habits within the 'big 6', as Table 4 shows.

It is obvious that the TGWU–NUM–NUGMW axis saved the NEC from defeat in the two major debates in the early fifties. The small margin gained for the German rearmament proposal was the result of the overwhelming opposition of the constituency parties. However, two major points are important when comparing the figures of the 1950s and the 1960s. First, the TGWU, mainly because of the influence of its new General Secretary, Frank Cousins,[1] continually opposed the NEC in the debates of 1960 and 1961, and hence removed one million votes from the 'loyalist' axis. There is little doubt that if the TGWU–NUM–NUGMW voting pattern had been repeated in 1960 over defence, unilateralism would have been defeated! Secondly, with the overwhelming majority received for the NEC defence policy in 1961, the 1960 result can be seen as a temporary aberration from traditional union support for the Leadership on questions of defence and foreign policy. Indeed, by 1961 only the TGWU, of the major six unions, was opposed to the 'platform'. By 1961 USDAW, AEU and NUR, traditionally left wing and 'Bevanite' unions, were backing official

1. Harrison, *Trade Unions and the Labour Party Since 1945*, writes on pages 132–5: 'The public image of the TGWU is essentially the impression made by its General Secretary on opinion. In Deakin's time the "T & G" stood for militant anti-communism and an only slightly diminished hostility to left-wing policies. . . . The problem Mr Cousins set the Party was that their support could no longer be depended on as it was in Deakin's day.'

Table 4. NEC Proposals 1952–61

For		Against
(A)	*Rearmament* (1952) Passed	
TGWU		AEU
NUGMW		USDAW
NUM		NUR
(B)	*German Rearmament* (1954) Passed	
TGWU		AEU
NUGMW		USDAW
NUM		NUR
(C)	*'Industry and Society'* (1957) Passed	
TGWU		NUR
NUGMW		
USDAW		
AEU		
NUM		
(D)	*Clause IV* (1960) Defeated[1]	
NUGMW		TGWU
USDAW		AEU
		NUR
		NUM
(E)	*Defence Policy* (1960) (multilateralist) Defeated	
NUGMW		AEU
NUM		USDAW
		NUR
		TGWU
(F)	*Defence Policy* (1961) (multilateralist) Passed	
NUGMW		TGWU
NUM		
AEU		
USDAW		
NUR		

1. This did not come to a vote at Party Conference, but the unions had, in the spring and summer of 1960, mandated their delegates.

policy and by so doing departed from the position they had held in the early 1950s.

Trade union support for the NEC on defence, although substantial, was less resounding than traditional trade union support for the NEC in matters relating to public ownership. Whenever in the 'Bevanite' period the NEC opposed an extension of the 'shopping-list' principle[1] they were supported overwhelmingly by the 'big 6'. Also, in the debate on the revisionist document *Industry and Society* only the NUR opposed the NEC statement. Therefore the overwhelming decision of the unions to oppose Clause IV was out of keeping with their traditional support for NEC public-ownership proposals. The thesis that the unions support the Leadership on foreign policy and defence, out of 'patriotic' working-class sentiments, whereas they are more sceptical on the issue of public ownership cannot be maintained.

Three points emerge that may help to explain trade union reluctance to accept the Clause IV constitutional change. First, the Clause IV controversy can be distinguished from all the other crises that the Labour Party faced since the time it left office in 1951. This was the only time when the Leader of the Party, through the NEC, took the initiative and proposed a fundamental *revision* of attitude and policy. All other home-policy issues arose out of an attempt by the 'Bevanite' and left-wing section of the Party to institute change. The NEC remained consistent in resisting this change and in keeping the Party on a moderate and electorally conscious public-ownership platform. It gathered trade union support not only because its policy towards public ownership was moderate but also because this was in keeping with *traditional* Labour Party policy. A revision of Clause IV, however, was an attack on perhaps the most sacred *traditional* element of the Party – its Constitution.

Another factor that isolates the Clause IV issue from other major controversies, and thus may help to explain trade union

1. E.g. the debate on *Challenge to Britain* 1953 – amendments were lost by 3–4 million votes which advocated outright nationalisation of Machine Tools, Mining Machinery, Aircraft, Electrical Equipment, Shipbuilding, Motor Vehicles, etc.

reaction against it, is its central position in Labour Party dogma. The 'shopping-list' controversies and *Industry and Society* were concerned mainly with Labour's next election manifestos. They were essentially debates about practical political proposals for the coming few years. Clause IV, however, belonged to the dimension of sentiment and aspiration.[1] This alliance of sentimental attachment to Clause IV by the normally right-wing trade union movement and the more practical support for it by the left-wing unions and constituency parties defeated and isolated the revisionist 'intellectuals'.[2]

Possibly a third reason for trade union rejection of Gaitskell's proposed constitutional amendment was the fact that many of the individual unions contained a clause in their own constitutions similar to Clause IV. The NUM Constitution called for 'the complete abolition of capitalism' and the National Union of Vehicle Builders' Constitution demanded 'the transfer of the means of production to the people'. Both these unions voted against the constitutional amendment. However, a reading of their Conference reports shows that this was a relatively unimportant factor in their decision – and in other unions' decisions. For instance, the NUGMW had a clause in its own constitution almost identical to Clause IV itself. This, naturally, did not preclude the NUGMW from acting out its usual loyalist role.

There is little doubt that the revisionists met with defeat in formal terms by elevating the debate to the 'constitutional' level. Nevertheless, the slow erosion of public ownership, both as an end in itself and as a practical socialist weapon in economic policy-making continued. On balance it seems that Gaitskell and his immediate advisers made a tactical error in publicly exposing themselves to defeat. His victory on the defence issue, however, more than compensated for the defeat on Clause IV and established his unrivalled ascendancy over the Party. The consequent growing identification of the Labour Party with Gaitskell meant that his known views on the future of public

---

1. E.g. my earlier quotations of Brown and Gooch (p. 168 above).

2. The NUGMW and USDAW did, however, support the Clause IV constitutional revision.

ownership assumed a new importance. Although the Party had reaffirmed its faith in Clause IV of its Constitution, Gaitskell's personal authority minimised its impact upon the electorate. The defence controversy was the key factor in establishing this authority.

CHAPTER NINE

The Alliance and the Bomb

Attlee's narrow victory on German rearmament spelt the end of one era of controversy. The decision of the Churchill Government in 1955 to manufacture the H-bomb heralded in another. The whole nuclear debate reached its zenith in 1960 at the Scarborough Conference, but, paradoxically, virtually the whole Party by then supported, in one form or another, the ending of British nuclear independence.

It is not the aim of this chapter to trace the complicated intra-party disputes of this period but rather to look at the attitudes of the major Gaitskellite thinkers – those who basically rejected the concept of a 'socialist foreign policy' – to nuclear weapons, strategy and tactics and the other related issues. The chronology of Labour's in-fighting will evolve from a discussion of these issues.

Throughout the whole debate very little effort was made to define the various issues that arose. This was obviously a difficult task mainly because the complex nature of the subject intertwined many areas of policy and made them dependent upon each other. Nevertheless, four differing components of the debate can be isolated. First, the question of the independent nuclear deterrent; secondly, the whole issue of the Western military alliance and neutralism; thirdly, the policy towards foreign bases on British soil; and fourthly, the question of nuclear testing. Underlying these specifics, and often responsible for shaping them, were the more general issues concerning the foreign policies, and indeed the whole political nature, of the U.S.A. and the U.S.S.R. Also important was the German question – the relationship of West Germany to the alliance and the training of German troops in Britain.

THE BRITISH BOMB

Before 1960 and the cancellation of Blue Streak – our last hope for an independent delivery system – Britain's own nuclear weapon was the major issue within the Party. But it could hardly be called a controversial issue in terms of voting at Party Conferences. In 1957 a motion calling for unilateral nuclear disarmament was defeated by 781,000 to 5,836,000 votes.[1] In 1958 a similar motion was also defeated, but by a slightly smaller margin: 890,000 to 5,611,000.[2] Unilateralism counted for little in the late fifties. Nevertheless, the debates on the nuclear question became a yearly ritual at Labour Party Conferences and forced the Right wing of the Party to analyse and defend its position in public. In fact a dialogue was set in motion that gathered momentum steadily until the 'crunch' of 1960 and 1961.

Before Blue Streak's cancellation one of the major arguments of the Right in favour of Britain remaining an independent nuclear power was that it would continue to give the country a degree of independence from the United States. It is interesting to note that until 1960 those in the Party who supported an independent nuclear role did not associate unilateralism with leaving NATO. Obviously, therefore, if Britain were to remain in NATO, the abandonment of the deterrent would have a deleterious effect on British independence. Strachey, who throughout this period was in the forefront of the debate on defence, made this point in 1958:

> we must retain the ability to take a different course, even though doing so might deeply alienate America and even drive her towards isolationism. How can it possibly be maintained that a Labour government's ability to do that would not have been gravely impaired if by depriving ourselves of defences, including nuclear weapons of our own, we had made ourselves wholly dependent on American protection?[3]

In fact, Liberal Party policy, which at that time was based upon abandoning Britain's independent contribution to the

1. *LPACR 1957*, Composite Motion No. 24, p. 165.
2. *LPACR 1958*, Composite Motion No. 27, p. 191.
3. J. Strachey, *Scrap ALL the H-Bombs* (1958) p. 15. Issued by the NEC (not as a statement of policy but as a useful contribution to the debate).

"... AND MAY I SAY TO HON. MEMBERS OPPOSITE ME ..."

defence of the West, was often ridiculed and attacked for being dependent upon the United States.[1] Gaitskell, too, was frightened of dependence upon the United States. This fear was the product of a suspicion about American resolve which he publicly stated as late as 1 March 1960:

> The real case for our having our own independent nuclear weapons is fear of excessive dependence on the United States. It springs from doubts about the readiness of the United States government ... to wish the destruction of their cities on behalf of Europe. It depends also, I think, on fear that an excessive dependence on the United States might force upon us policies with which we did not agree.[2]

Here was, from hindsight, an almost Gaullist interpretation of Western international relations; a lack of trust in the Americans to defend Europe in a crisis (could we really envisage an American President devastating the United States for the sake of Europe?) and the consequent need for independent policies as a reinsurance. This nuclear Gaullism of the Labour Right soon vanished following the cancellation of Blue Streak. It lost its logic when it became obvious that Britain could no longer afford a delivery system that was truly independent. The roles were then reversed; Gaitskell became the main advocate of interdependence whereas the unilateralists adopted more and more 'pacifist Gaullist' postures.

Before 1960, however, the Right hammered away at the need to maintain the British bomb. Without it, it was argued, Britain would lose her influence in the councils of the world and her bargaining power would be diminished. Michael Stewart, for instance, suggested that Britain needed her bomb in order to strengthen her voice so as to achieve desirable ends:

> If we make the latter choice (abandoning our bomb) we abandon any hope of being able to influence American policy. . . . Any proposals we make for Disarmament or for the control of Atomic

1. Ibid. p. 17. See Strachey's speech to Labour Party Conference 1957, p. 177.
2. *Hansard* (1 Mar 1960) col. 1,136. Also in 1957, in a Harvard Lecture, Gaitskell gave another reason for maintaining British nuclear independence: 'Precisely because the decision on this remains a matter for the United States, precisely because there are inevitable doubts as to when and whether the decision to threaten the use of the bomb would be taken, the United Kingdom felt obliged at vast expenditure to manufacture the hydrogen bomb herself.' Gaitskell, *The Challenge of Co-existence*, p. 43.

Energy will be regarded ... as no more than an interested attempt to deprive others of a power we do not possess.[1]

This idea of the loss of effective power was taken up by Bevan in his famous speech to the Labour Party Conference of 1957:

> But if you carry this resolution [a unilateral resolution] and follow out all its implications ... you will send a British Foreign Secretary, whoever he may be, naked into the conference chamber ... able to preach sermons of course. ....[2]

Bevan's conversion to the politics of power was, of course, a major factor in the negligible size of the unilateralist vote at Annual Conferences in the late fifties.

Bevan and the Right were never intrinsically concerned with British power. The extent to which Labour politicians can ever publicly declare in Britain's interest is limited by considerations of Party unity; instead they argued that Britain needed negotiating power in order to work for multilateral disarmament.[3] The British bomb, they suggested, helped the cause of peace. This, of course, was a basic difference in outlook from many in the Conservative Party. They argued that British power was good in itself and helped effectively to maintain British interests abroad.

Multilateral, as opposed to unilateral, disarmament was a key theme of those who supported the continuance of British nuclear weapons. Philip Noel-Baker, later to play a significant part in the Socialist Campaign for Multilateral Disarmament,[4] was the most dedicated champion of general and complete disarmament and considered that nuclear unilateralism must be considered in this context. He bluntly stated that 'unilateral disarmament would mean surrendering Britain's influence in the world-wide struggle to de-militarise the world'. Noel-Baker consistently opposed unilateralism from its birth in 1957 to its death in 1961. He represented a strand of socialist thinking on foreign policy which has its roots in a collectivist approach to world problems. He maintained that adequate collective

1. Stewart, *Policy and Weapons in the Nuclear Age*, p. 16.
2. *LPACR 1957*, p. 181.
3. For instance, see George Brown's speech, *LPACR 1958*, p. 213.
4. Noel-Baker was President of the Socialist Campaign for Multilateral Disarmament. This was mainly a Parliamentary organisation with the aim of ensuring that adequate speakers on defence were available when needed.

security in the thirties would have saved the world from war and consequently he doubted the validity of unilateral declarations and enforcements.[1]

Multilateral disarmament was, of course, the official policy of the Party right up until 1960. This was reaffirmed annually in policy debates at Conference,[2] and in Joint Statements from the NEC and the Trades Union Congress. At the Party Conference of 1957 a motion calling upon the British Government to 'seek support' for a ban on all nuclear weapons[3] was passed. Also, in the 1958 Joint TUC–NEC Declaration, multilateral disarmament was again suggested as the key to further progress. The major theoretical exposition of this case came in a pamphlet written by John Strachey in 1958, entitled *Scrap ALL the H-Bombs*. This was not originally to be an official publication but rather an independent effort by a member of the Party. Gaitskell later legitimised it by providing an introduction which described it as a 'useful contribution' to the debate. In this pamphlet Strachey put powerfully and cogently the basic multilateral case:

> the essential thing to grasp is that there is no safety whatever for us in trying to contract out of a world war. The only way in which we can save ourselves is to prevent another war from ever happening . . . nothing can remove the nightmare which hangs not only over Britain but over the whole world except general all-round disarmament on the part of all the major nations. There are no short cuts [i.e. unilateral disarmament] by means of which Britain can save herself alone. But she can and must take the lead in world disarmament.[4]

Sometimes this argument was quite unfairly used against the unilateralists to suggest that they were unconcerned about American or Russian nuclear weapons, but simply wanted an affirmationist posture by Britain:

> Are we, at the next election, to go and give the country the impression that the only hydrogen bombs we are concerned about

---

1. This view is developed in his major work: *The Arms Race: a programme for world disarmament* (1958).
2. E.g. 1957, 1958. There was no debate in 1959; instead there was a Special Conference on the loss of the General Election.
3. *LPACR 1957*, Composite Resolution No. 23, p. 163.
4. Strachey, *Scrap ALL the H-Bombs*, p. 17.

abolishing are the British hydrogen bombs and that we are not concerned about getting rid of American and Russian hydrogen bombs?[1]

Indeed this was part of the emotionally-based charge and counter-charge that was to disfigure the debate at a later stage. The unilateralists often claimed, just as unjustifiably, that multilateralists were against peace!

Part of the reason why the Gaitskellites stressed multilateralism so emphatically was their conviction that British unilateral renunciation would have no effect on other powers. Strachey, Gordon Walker and Gaitskell stressed this point continually throughout the debate.[2] Many defence thinkers were of the opinion that those who advocated the abandonment of British nuclear weapons were contributing nothing to the real problem, having no effect upon the other major powers and simply engaging in moralistic arguments with which all men of good will agreed. One who was unafraid to say this was Emanuel Shinwell, who, as an ex-Minister of Defence, carried some weight in the Party. His exchange of letters with Bertrand Russell in *The Times* of March 1958 contained this retort from Shinwell:

> Bertrand Russell is mistaken in thinking that I fail to grasp the dangers inherent in nuclear war. . . . This is common ground, so don't let us waste any more time on this issue. I invite Russell to address himself to the question: 'Would British renunciation of nuclear weapons encourage the Russians and the Americans to do the same?' . . . of course we shall ascend to a high moral plane, but if Russell believes that will impress either of the principals in this affair, he deceives himself.[3]

Before leaving the debate on the single question of British independent deterrence some mention must be made of another important, though less aired, argument of the non-unilateralists. Both Aneurin Bevan and Michael Stewart used the British position as head of the Commonwealth as a reason, an added reason, for her retention of the bomb. Speaking of

---

1. Strachey, *LPACR 1959*, p. 177.
2. See Strachey's speech, *LPACR 1959*, p. 177; Gordon Walker's speech, *LPACR 1958*, p. 204; Gaitskell's speech, *LPACR 1958*, p. 221.
3. *The Times* (7 Mar 1958).

the British bomb in 1955, Stewart said, 'This is a matter on which the Commonwealth nations cannot escape their responsibility. Britain's defence is their defence. . . .'[1] Aneurin Bevan on the other hand, at the 1957 Conference, used the Commonwealth argument to instil what he called a 'responsible attitude' into the delegates. The commitments and obligations that Britain had assumed in the world, and especially the Commonwealth, precluded unilateral action; any action which would weaken British defences should only be taken after consultation with our allies, and with the members of the Commonwealth. Commonwealth idealism was always a bonus at gatherings of the Labour faithful.

Very much a part of the multilateralist position was the brief, and unsuccessful, flirtation with the concept of a 'non-nuclear club'. This became the official policy of the Party in July 1959, with the publication of the TUC–NEC statement *The Next Step*. It was in keeping with the overall framework in which multilateralism operated, for it rejected any unilateral action by a British government. Nothing should be done without agreement with other nations, except this time the United States and the Soviet Union were discounted. Britain, as a sort of twentieth-century pied-piper, would lead all the other nations, if they would agree, to a non-nuclear paradise.

The ideas in *The Next Step* were not original. A year previously *Socialist Commentary* had put some of them forward; as it was not averse to reminding its readers in August 1959:

> By offering to renounce it [H-bomb] if all others do likewise (apart from the two giants) she is excellently placed to take a powerful initiative. . . . We take pleasure in remembering that *Socialist Commentary* advocated precisely this policy as long ago as April 1958.

The 'non-nuclear club' idea had a prolonged airing in fairly influential newspapers during the middle and latter part of 1958 and, indeed, was touched upon by Gaitskell himself in October 1958:

> But if you can really get agreement among all the other countries of the world to establish international controls over abolishing

---

1. Stewart, *Policy and Weapons in the Nuclear Age*, p. 17.

nuclear weapons, I should be astonished and deeply depressed if it were not possible at the same time to get America and Russia to agree as well. *However I recognise the force of the idea.*[1]

Anthony Greenwood advocated a rather more dramatic form of non-nuclear alliance a year or so before it became, in more timid form, official Party policy.[2] However, this sort of policy certainly had much more of a 'left-wing' flavour than any previous official pronouncement. The idea that a British initiative to form a non-nuclear club would somehow have some effect on other powers was decidedly 'affirmationist' in character. It was part of the 'let Britain lead and the others will follow' syndrome. On the other hand it had become a natural argument for the Right that British initiatives achieved very little.

Nevertheless, by July 1959, on this specific issue of unilateral initiatives and their usefulness, the Leadership had engaged in a volte-face: a volte-face that nevertheless did not satisfy the Left. The Left was suspicious of what it considered a loophole in the now official policy, namely the insistence on *all* other powers, save the U.S.A. and the U.S.S.R., agreeing to the plan before Britain acted. On this crucial point the document read:

> The objective which the Government should set itself is an agreement, preferably under the auspices of the UN, signed by *every* nation with the exception of the U.S.A. and U.S.S.R. Under this agreement each nation would pledge itself not to test, manufacture or to possess nuclear weapons.... The Government should be prepared to announce *now* that, if such an agreement could be successfully negotiated, Great Britain would not only cease the manufacture of nuclear weapons but also deprive herself of their possession.[3]

Tribune quite properly pointed out[4] that the conditional offer falls down unless all nations accept the undertaking. As the Leadership had on many occasions scornfully attacked the usefulness of British initiatives, this particular aspect of policy was seen by many to be simply a ploy. If it was not, then right-wing thinking on defence had suddenly become strangely

1. *LPACR 1958*, p. 222. (Italics mine.)
2. *Tribune* (3 Jul 1959) p. 9.
3. *Disarmament and Nuclear War – The Next Step* (24 Jun 1959) p. 7. (Italics mine.)
4. *Tribune* (3 Jul 1959) p. 9.

utopian. The Leadership, on the other hand, claimed that there was a realistic basis to the policy in that this sort of non-nuclear agreement was in the interest, the national interests, of the two major powers. Whether or not this factor would have any bearing on the other nations of the world was left open to doubt.

The Left rightly mistrusted this document because it went no further along the road to unilateralism, in the sense of abandoning the independent deterrent, than any previous statement. Under no circumstances was Britain to commit herself independently of other powers. On NATO, also, the document remained unequivocal and firm: 'In present circumstances we regard it as essential that the NATO alliance should be maintained. . . . As members of the alliance we should play a full part.'[1]

If, therefore, *The Next Step* gave nothing to the unilateralists, why did the Leadership find it necessary to add this extra element of a non-nuclear club? The Left saw it as a shameless attempt to win them over at a time of growing support for unilateralism. *Tribune* adopted a highly cynical attitude towards the new document in the week following its publication:

> Everyone knows the real reasons. . . . The success of Aldermaston . . . plus the vote of the NUGMW . . . plus the known views of Frank Cousins and the imminence of the three union conferences taking place this coming week.[2]

It is certainly true that in the early months of 1959 the Leadership had been under increasing pressure to take a new stance – and a different one from the 1958 document. Indeed, the sensitivity of the Leadership to this new pressure was shown in April 1959 when Bevan, in the House of Commons, made a pledge that a Labour government would stop all H- and A-bomb tests.[3] This, in itself, was not a new declaration of policy[4] but *The Times* of 29 April seemed to read something else into the statement:

> The deliberation with which he uttered it and his statement that 'we shall not be influenced by the technical and political situ-

---

1. *The Next Step*, p. 6.   2. *Tribune* (3 Jul 1959) p. 9.
3. *Hansard* (27 Apr 1959) col. 915.
4. The 1958 policy document had advocated a suspension of tests for a limited period.

ation ... when we assume office' goes some way to suggest that Labour leaders are becoming rather more sensitive to party pressure upon them to take a firmer line on the nuclear question.

This pressure built up even further when the 'loyalist' trade union NUGMW voted in favour of an outright unilateralist resolution, albeit by a minority vote of all those entitled to be delegates.[1] There can be little doubt that this surprising resolution from a 'safe' union, plus the likely vote of other major unions, would place the Right at the forthcoming Labour Party Conference in jeopardy. Therefore the fear of a unilateralist victory in the autumn was obviously a factor in determining the need for some form of new initiative from the Leadership.

It is always difficult to determine motives in political action, but, together with the clear and compelling need to forestall the unilateralist advance, *The Next Step* could also have been motivated by the newly developing concern about proliferation which the document itself emphasised. The 1958 statement, although concerned with multilateral disarmament, made no reference to the danger of proliferation of nuclear weapons. This danger became the *raison d'être* for the new policy. Indeed, *The Next Step* quoted the 1958 Conference speech of Gaitskell:

> It is a terrible prospect that nuclear weapons should come into the hands of more and more ... governments. If it were really a choice, if we in government knew for certain that only our contriving to manufacture these weapons stopped this agreement which would finally freeze ... the distribution of nuclear weapons to the U.S.A. and U.S.S.R. ... I would regard it as a very powerful argument indeed. ...[2]

Here then is foreshadowed the idea of the non-nuclear club and real concern on the question of proliferation. It is open to doubt, however, whether it was this concern, or the more 'political' arguments, that caused the new initiative embodied in *The Next Step*.

There is much evidence to suggest that there was a significant movement building up in the Party against an independent British deterrent in 1959. The decision of the NUGMW meant

1. *NUGMW 44th Congress Report* (1959), Motion 233, p. 337. Motion passed by 150 votes to 126 with 75 delegates absent or abstaining.
2. *The Next Step*, pp. 6–7.

that if a Party Conference had been held in 1959, then the votes cast on the issue would have been fairly evenly divided; although it is probable that the Leadership would still have won. The official response to this growing clamour for uni-lateralism was to reaffirm the concept of multilateralism but to add the idea of the 'non-nuclear club'. All this was firmly placed within the framework of British membership of NATO.

Therefore, right up until July 1960 the official Labour position, supported by the revisionists led by Gaitskell, was based upon support for an independent nuclear policy. The political furore caused by the cancellation of Blue Streak, however, throws some doubt upon whether this support was one of principle or simply a question of military and economic strategy and tactics. Did Gaitskell and the Right want a British bomb at almost any cost? Not really; from 1958 on-wards Gaitskell made it plain that nuclear independence was negotiable, but that, on balance, it was in our interest to main-tain it. The cancellation of Blue Streak tilted the balance the other way.

THE CANCELLATION OF BLUE STREAK

The cancellation of the Blue Streak rocket programme by the Conservative Government in 1960 was a major watershed in the debate on nuclear weapons in the Labour Party. The whole question of the maintenance of an independent British contri-bution to the nuclear power of the West was thrown open and became a major point at issue between the parties as well as within the Labour Party. It also caught Gaitskell and the Right off balance as it seemed at first that the defence of British nuclear independence was now academic. Without a delivery system the defence of the British bomb seemed absurd and unrealistic.

The question immediately arose whether Labour would still cling to the idea of Britain as a nuclear power. Surprisingly, there was total unanimity in the Shadow Cabinet, and on the Right, that this decision of the Government had created a totally new situation; one that called for a thorough review of

Labour's official policy. This review sparked off a debate within the central leadership itself which was fought out in the public arena. The issue at stake was the Party's policy towards the *existing* nuclear weapons and whether Labour should announce its intention of abandoning British independent nuclear power *now* or *later*.[1] George Brown and Harold Wilson seemed to present Gaitskell, who was out of the country at the time, with a *fait accompli* when they spoke in the Commons in the defence debate of 27 April 1960. Brown declared his opposition to Britain's remaining an independent nuclear power from then on:

> The argument for maintaining the independent British deterrent for political reasons is one thing when you have it. The argument for going back into the business when you are out of it is an altogether different thing. . . . Even I cannot be expected to go on supporting a policy which has no chance of ever existing.[2]

Wilson put it rather more succinctly – 'What we have seen today . . . is the end of the independent nuclear deterrent.'[3] Wilson had always been willing to take opportunities that would lead to an area of agreement with the unilateralists and therefore his statement was no surprise. Brown's speech was a different matter. It obviously called for comment when Gaitskell arrived back from his period abroad.[4] In a speech at Leeds he felt it necessary to put the record straight. Referring to the House of Commons debate he said:

> Nothing said by Labour's official spokesmen could possibly mean they wanted Britain to disarm unilaterally, give up NATO and become neutralist. They did not say we should give up our existing nuclear weapons. They were concerned solely with the future – *what our position would be in five years' time*.[5]

Without engaging in undue pedantry, Gaitskell's interpretation may have been fair as regards Brown, but it was certainly not in keeping with the spirit of Wilson's Commons speech. Here indeed were the seeds of a further disagreement, which extended across the Right wing of the Party, as to *when* exactly

---

1. The V-bomber force was still operational and effective at this time.
2. *Hansard* (27 Apr 1960) col. 228.   3. Ibid. col. 329.
4. He was at an International Socialist gathering in Haifa, Israel.
5. *The Times* (2 May 1962) p. 12d. (Italics mine.)

Britain should cease to be an independent nuclear power. The issue was not settled finally until 1961, when Denis Healey was instrumental in changing official policy in favour of the 'as of now' principle. However, the official policy statement debated at the 1960 Conference remained vague on this issue; 'We believe that *in future* our British contribution to the Western Armoury will be in conventional terms, leaving to the Americans the provision of the Western strategic deterrent.'[1] The new policy was imprecise and in a Fabian Tract as late as December 1960 John Strachey seemed to feel that some form of independent nuclear deterrent was still Gaitskellite policy: 'Its [the 1960 official policy] main innovation is to express a conviction that Britain can no longer sustain a *fully* independent nuclear deterrent force.'[2]

Official indecision was a product of Gaitskell's insistence that the existing V-bombers, then still operational, should not be scrapped. This was a surprisingly rigid position for one who had never as a matter of *principle* supported the British bomb. Indeed, he said in his Leeds speech:

> We have never committed ourselves to going on indefinitely with our own independent deterrent. In the Defence debate last year I said that the issue of whether Britain, within NATO, should have nuclear weapons under her own control was one of balance.

This was not a case of Gaitskellite back-pedalling in the face of changed circumstances. Informed opinion had for some time been aware of the Leader's true position. *The Times* of 25 April 1960 said: 'But Mr Gaitskell has already conceded that there is a powerful case against Britain's independent nuclear weapon – on the grounds of cost and the risk that nuclear weapons will spread to other countries.' Gaitskell returned to this question again in his 1960 speech to Conference: 'It is not, in my opinion, a matter of principle but a matter of balance of arguments, economic, military and technical, on which a cool re-examination and reappraisal was necessary from time to

---

1. *Joint Statement on Defence and Foreign Policy (1960) by NEC/TUC*, reproduced in *Report of the NEC* 1959–60, pp. 13–16.
2. J. Strachey, *The Pursuit of Peace*, Fabian Tract No. 329 (1960) p. 22. (Italics mine.)

time.'[1] Therefore, it was the economic argument of the cost of producing missiles rather than any principled opposition to the British bomb that caused Gaitskell to change his mind. This, of course, left him open to two charges. First, that he had given up the British bomb reluctantly, and secondly, that in a possible future situation, given the economic, military and technical ability, Britain could, with Gaitskell's blessing, start afresh as a nuclear power. On the first charge – that of reluctance – there was a grain of truth. All his life Gaitskell had been concerned with power. He was certainly reluctant, as a possible future Prime Minister, to see the power of the office to which he aspired diminished. Nevertheless he was also a realist and accepted, as he saw them, the realities of the situation. Secondly, the contention that Gaitskell left open the door for Britain to return to nuclear status at a later date was valid, especially in view of later developments.[2] But by the spring of 1961 this was a submerged issue. The Party was publicly committed to ending the British bomb.

Healey had forced the issue on the question of ending British nuclear independence, whereas Gaitskell had preferred a looser commitment on the lines of the 1960 official document. In the end however Healey had his way and Gaitskell's concurrence brought to an end the four-year debate over the British bomb. This enabled Gaitskell to change the issue dividing Right from Left from one of independence to one of neutralism. By raising the spectre of neutralism he put the Left on the defensive.

THE NEUTRALIST ISSUE

With the cancellation of Blue Streak, and after the initial confusion that followed it, the main defence issue was no longer the British bomb but the question of Britain's relationship with

---

1. *LPACR 1960*, p. 197. Virtually an identical point was made by Gaitskell as early as March 1960 – before Blue Streak was cancelled. See *Hansard* (1 Mar 1960) col. 1,135.

2. I.e. the Nassau Agreement of November 1962 between Macmillan and Kennedy, whereby the Americans agreed to supply Britain with Polaris nuclear missiles, has not yet been 'de-negotiated' by the Labour Government.

the NATO alliance. There were many and varied strands of opinion stretching from wholesale neutralism through 'critical, conditional membership of NATO' to a firm and unequivocal support of the alliance and all the duties that that support entailed. It is interesting to note that before 1960 NATO was hardly mentioned by the Leadership in defending its nuclear policies. Loyalty to NATO was never brought into question *as an issue to be discussed* in Bevan's 1957 and 1958 speeches to Conference. Gaitskell did mention the consequences of leaving NATO in the Conference debate of 1958 but he did not tar his opponents, then unilateralists, with any neutralist brush. As late as the March 1960 defence debate in the House of Commons he was drawing distinctions between the vast majority of unilateralists and the neutralists. But Gaitskell's precise distinction between unilateralism and neutralism was only a temporary phenomena. He, quite rightly, saw that neutralism was the Left's Achilles heel and he prodded it for all he was worth.

Was it reasonable of the Gaitskellites to see the clash of 1960 and 1961 as the challenge of neutralism to the Party? Of course there were large segments of the unilateral disarmers who thought that Britain ought to opt out of 'cold war' politics. The 'New Left' was instrumental in searching for a third-force role for Britain. Nevertheless, the unilateralist motions that appeared at Scarborough in 1960, and were narrowly carried by the Party,[1] did not specifically or openly advocate a neutralist posture for Britain. The AEU resolution demanded 'the unilateral renunciation of the testing, manufacture, stockpiling and basing of all nuclear weapons in Great Britain'. This was not a clarion-call for a neutral Britain although arguments were used that suggested that the elimination of bases from our shores was incompatible with a full and meaningful membership of the alliance.[2] The other resolution, that of the TGWU, made no reference to Britain's membership of NATO but called for 'a complete rejection of any defence policy based

---

1. AEU Resolution: for – 3,303,000; against – 2,896,000. TGWU Resolution: for – 3,282,000; against – 3,239,000. (The NEC defence policy was defeated by 297,000 votes.) The story of the defence row is told, through the eyes of the Campaign for Democratic Socialism, in Chapter Ten.

2. See *LPACR 1960*, p. 195.

on the threat of the use of strategic or tactical nuclear weapons'.[1] This had a rather more neutralist slant to it in that Britain was being asked to withdraw from a defence organisation based upon the threat of nuclear power. Surely this could only mean NATO? There were some on the Right and within the central leadership itself who did not see the TGWU resolution in this light. George Brown, until now a Gaitskell loyalist, decided at the last minute that as well as supporting the official line he would also support the TGWU motion. His reasoning for this rather paradoxical pose can be found in an eve of Conference issue of the *New Statesman*:

> Its [the TGWU resolution] terms are *not* a flat contradiction of the official statement. . . . Its major point is the rejection of a defence policy *based* on the threat to use nuclear weapons – an attitude which is fully in harmony with the official policy statement. No thoughtful man today believes that a national defence policy can be *based* on the threat to use nuclear weapons. It is absolutely clear that the only *effective* defence policy today is complete and general disarmament.[2]

Brown's article was in a great tradition of Labour leadership. It was pure semantics; an attempt to unite irreconcilables on the eve of an Annual Conference. Gaitskell, on this occasion, refused to abide by the traditions. It was part of his case that neutralism was implicit in both the AEU and the TGWU motions. As such he asked the Party to have no truck with them.

One way in which Gaitskell attempted to widen the debate to include neutralism was to pay careful attention to those elements of the Party, individual members and groups, that supported the two union resolutions. A close examination of the speeches in support of these resolutions confirms Gaitskell's view that many of their supporters were openly neutralist. Indeed, the whole 'atmosphere' of the speech of the mover of the AEU resolution was one of hostility to NATO: 'The whole question is this: if we really believe in world peace can NATO provide the answer? If you think it can, you are not with me.'[3]

1. *LPACR 1960*, p. 178. Resolution No. 60, sub-section (a).
2. *New Statesman* (1 Oct 1960) p. 461. (Italics mine.)
3. *LPACR 1960*, p. 177.

Also, in proposing the TGWU resolution, Cousins ended his speech with this curious and confused argument:

> When I am asked if it means getting out of NATO, if the question is posed to me as simply saying, am I prepared to go on remaining in an organisation over which I have no control, but which can destroy us instantly, my answer is Yes, if the choice is that. But it is not that.[1]

Although Gaitskell was exaggerating when he suggested that these unilateralist resolutions, if implemented, would lead to a neutralist Britain, he certainly had ample reason for suspicion. Allied to his attack upon the neutralist intentions of the backers of the two motions was his challenge to the Party to scrutinise the official policy of the Campaign for Nuclear Disarmament towards the Western alliance; he suggested it was openly and unashamedly neutralist.[2]

Having branded CND as openly neutralist Gaitskell concentrated upon exposing the 'hidden neutralism' of the two union motions:

> The implication is that we go to NATO, to the Western Alliance and say, 'Give up your weapons unilaterally, even if the Soviet Union retain theirs; and if you do not, we withdraw from the Alliance.' True is it not?[3]

Another method by which Gaitskell attempted to isolate the neutralists was by drawing a distinction between those who believed in giving up the independent deterrent on principle, before and after the cancellation of Blue Streak, and those who simply saw it as a matter of balance; as a practical consideration. He posed the problem thus:

> Those who advocate unilateral nuclear disarmament by Britain on grounds of principle are bound to ask themselves this question: are they then taking the line that all they want to do is to get rid of what they regard as the moral discredit attaching to Britain's having these weapons, while they can get the security they want because America has them?[4]

Therefore, whether or not neutralism was a major motive behind the unilateralists in 1960, Gaitskell certainly made it

1. Ibid. p. 180.   2. Ibid. p. 197.   3. Ibid.   4. Ibid.

appear so. This was important in weakening the Left for it drove a wedge between those who were neutralists and those who felt uneasy over Britain's leaving NATO. Whether Gaitskell actually believed this or used it as a tactical weapon in his battle with the Left is open to doubt. Nevertheless, this ₁widening of the debate easily solidified behind him those elements in the Party which, over many years, had been opposed to a neutralist Britain.

Since the war Labour's 'anti-neutralism' has had two main ideas behind it. The first was an overriding concern with Soviet foreign policy as an aggressive force in the world and as a threat to all non-Communist elements. This was an essentially negative attitude as it involved no particular enthusiasm for the social or political system of the United States *or* any basic commitment to the West as such. It implied that the danger of world communism necessitated alliances, albeit of countries with differing political traditions and systems. Denis Healey was perhaps the greatest exponent of this type of anti-neutralism. In 1955 he wrote:

> Neutralism based upon the belief that Socialists should stand midway between Communist Russia and Capitalist America is faulty not only in its vision of the Soviet System as in some way Socialist. . . . Indeed this type of Neutralism depends essentially on the argument that there is nothing to choose between a little of a bad thing and a great deal of a bad thing.[1]

Healey obviously was not over-pleased with 'capitalist' America, but his emotional and intellectual antagonism towards the Soviet system produced extreme denunciations of neutralism: 'Refusal to commit oneself in the struggle against Communist expansion in fact means an abdication of responsibility to play an active role in progressing beyond power politics towards International Society.'[2] In fact, throughout the 1950s Healey was the most extreme anti-Communist in the Party. It was a position based upon his revulsion from Soviet policy in Eastern Europe immediately after the war.[3] Michael Stewart was another example of a 'negative anti-neutralist' in

---

1. Healey, *Neutralism*, p. 19.   2. Ibid. p. 57.
3. See *The Curtain Falls*. Healey edited this booklet, which described, often emotively, the establishment of communist regimes in Eastern Europe.

that, although he remained fairly Left in the British domestic political spectrum, he became very cynical about Soviet intentions, as he showed in his Fabian Tract of 1955: 'The Soviet Union has repeatedly shown that she will snatch anything that is within her grasp, and which she believes can be snatched without starting a World War.'[1] He went on to argue that the withdrawal of Britain from the NATO alliance would encourage Communist expansion by weakening the West.

Stewart's attitude differs from what, for want of a better expression, can be called 'positive anti-neutralism'. This particular form of anti-neutralism springs not solely from an aggressive anti-communism but also from a certain sense of kinship with the foremost Western power, the United States of America. Crosland, for instance, saw virtues in American society; virtues that he readily admitted were in keeping with certain of his revisionist socialist principles (equality, social justice and freedom). To many revisionists it was good in itself to ally Britain to the United States; it was not an 'unhealthy but necessary' alliance. The Presidency of John Kennedy, for whom Gaitskell particularly had a high regard, revived and renewed this faith.

In fact, the general debate on neutralism went into greater specifics than these general attitudes shown above. Six basic arguments for remaining in the alliance were given by the Right. First, it was argued that if Britain left NATO, then Germany would become the main ally of the United States in Europe.[2] Secondly, if this did not happen it would only be because the United States, rebuffed by British neutralism, had gone isolationist.[3] A third argument used was that Britain's departure from NATO would so weaken the West in terms of political power that the Soviet Union would gain an immense advantage. This was the view that both Stewart and Strachey advanced consistently. Not only would the weakening of the West be an undesirable thing in itself, but, as Strachey pointed out, the weakening of the Western alliance *vis-à-vis* the Soviet bloc would have some very grave short-term consequences for

---

1. Stewart, *Policy and Weapons in the Nuclear Age*, p. 64.
2. See Gaitskell's speech, *LPACR 1958*, p. 221. Also Strachey, *Pursuit of Peace*.
3. See Gaitskell's speech, *LPACR 1960*, p. 198.

the balance of power and hence, world peace. This was part of the wider case for ensuring a 'stalemate' between the two blocs; anything that led to a change in the *status quo* (for instance, Britain's leaving NATO) would be dangerous. It would be dangerous because it would create a power vacuum which could become a destabilising influence.[1] Also, any war which resulted from this instability would almost certainly include Britain,[2] the very thing neutralists wanted to avoid! In short, Britain could not opt out of the world power political system without damaging itself and the world in the process.

Even before it became clear that Gaitskell would win the Party back from its unilateralism of 1960 the great debate on neutralism lost much of its importance. In early 1961 the NEC set up a 'Committee of 12' to draft a policy document on defence. The results of this drafting process showed that neutralism had ceased to be a divisive factor. Three major drafts were submitted to the NEC and none of them advocated British withdrawal from NATO. The Gaitskell–Healey draft was naturally the most committed to the Atlantic alliance: 'Britain must remain a member of NATO and seek to reform it from inside.'[3] The Crossman document differed hardly at all from this line: 'A repudiation of NATO and an attempt to commit the next Labour Government to withdraw from it would not be a contribution to world peace. Our job is not to get out of NATO, but to reform it.' A slight difference, however, arose between the two previous documents and that presented by Frank Cousins to the 'Committee of 12'. Cousins suggested that NATO membership, although accepted, should not be considered an overriding necessity. Also, whereas the Crossman document rejected 'repudiation' of NATO, the Cousins document simply rejected 'unqualified repudiation' of NATO.[4] These differences amounted to very little indeed and serve to show that the

1. For a longer exposition of this case, see Strachey, *On the Prevention of War*, particularly part 1. See also Strachey, *Pursuit of Peace*, pp. 6–7.
2. See Strachey, ibid., p. 5.
3. Gaitskell–Healey draft, clause 5. This draft later became the official document, *Policy for Peace*, that was presented to Annual Conference.
4. A thorough analysis of the three documents presented to the 'Committee of 12' appears in *Tribune* (31 Mar 1961).

question of whether Britain should or should not remain in the alliance had become redundant.

The defeat of neutralism can be interpreted in two ways: either as a victory for Gaitskell in his struggle to keep the Party wedded to the alliance or alternatively as a vindication of the theory that the Left never really intended to leave NATO. There is little doubt, however, that the Cousins document of March 1961 was less neutralist in its implications than either the TGWU motion or his speech at Party Conference of October 1960 would suggest. Gaitskell had stood firm; it was Cousins who had moved.

FROM NEUTRALISM TO NATO STRATEGY

By October 1961 the real differences among the three sections of the Party[1] had become centred upon the question of NATO strategy. There were still many members of the Party and of the Parliamentary Party who advocated unilateral nuclear disarmament for Britain. Nevertheless, by the spring and summer of 1961 it had ceased to be a central issue for debate. The new Gaitskell–Healey document, which became 'official' NEC policy, pledged the Party to 'cease to attempt to remain an independent nuclear power, since this neither strengthens the alliance nor is it now a sensible use of our limited resources.'[2] This was *unilateral* action. Although there was obviously a wide gulf between this view and that of the TGWU or AEU motion at the 1960 Conference, the whole Party was, by the spring of 1961, unilateralist in one sense or another.

Unilateralism had been accepted, but neutralism had been defeated! All that was left was NATO strategy.

Cousins was willing to vote for the Crossman draft in the 'Committee of 12', although nowhere in Crossman's document was there a reference to a 'rejection of an alliance or defence policy based on the threat or use of nuclear weapons'.[3] In fact the major differences between the Crossman draft and the

1. 'Crossman–Padleyism' here is treated as a 'section' – although their declared aim was to secure Party unity and bring the other two sections to a compromise solution.
2. Gaitskell–Healey draft, clause 8.
3. The main point of the 1960 TGWU resolution.

Gaitskell–Healey draft dealt with NATO nuclear strategy; not with whether or not there *should* be a NATO nuclear strategy. The fact that Cousins allied himself with Crossman shows that the debate had become much narrower and more precise. The issues in 1961 were the question of first-use of nuclear weapons by the West, the use of tactical nuclear weapons and the question of second-strike capacity. Allied to these questions were the issues of vulnerability of nuclear installations and the need to strengthen Britain's and NATO's conventional capacity. These questions were certainly not as fundamental as the debate over the alliance and the independent deterrent and a strong argument can be made for the thesis that the debate was no longer one of basic philosophy; it had degenerated into quibbles over military tactics.

Over-reliance upon Nuclear Weapons

The Gaitskell–Healey draft presented to the 'Committee of 12' emphasised the need to strengthen conventional forces in Europe:

> The NATO armies, however, are at present perilously dependent upon nuclear weapons. . . . Britain should press urgently . . . to make it possible for NATO to halt a local conflict with conventional weapons alone.

Indeed the major official case against the Conservative Government's defence policy from 1957 – the inception of the Sandys massive-retaliation policy – to 1961 was the over-emphasis on nuclear weapons at the expense of a conventional-response capability. In the 1958 defence debate in the House of Commons the Opposition moved an amendment specifically rejecting a defence policy that relied *predominantly* upon the threat of thermo-nuclear warfare.[1] George Brown put the official Labour argument thus:

> What is shocking people is that the Right Hon. Gentleman [Minister of Defence] seems to have no other idea for dealing with any conflict other than the merest, smallest border incident except the thermo-nuclear weapon.[2]

Strachey, in the same debate, shows that his thinking was

1. *Hansard* (28 Feb 1958) col. 417.   2. *Hansard* (26 Feb 1958) col. 398.

moving towards 'graduated' or 'flexible' response theory, and quoted the American nuclear theorist Kissinger in defence of his argument against over-reliance on nuclear weapons.[1] (indeed the new school of American military theorists was to become compulsory reading for Labour's official defence spokesmen over the next few years).

In the next three defence debates in the House of Commons (1959, 1960 and 1961) the official Labour defence spokesmen continued to attack Government policy in this way, and Hugh Gaitskell himself was in the forefront of this attack.[2] At the 1960 Labour Party Conference Gaitskell used this issue as an example of a genuine agreement, albeit limited, between all wings of the Party: 'We are agreed that the strategy of NATO is at present far too strongly based upon the use of nuclear weapons should a conflict of any kind break out.' At the NATO Council in 1961 General Norstadt, Supreme Allied Commander in Europe, proposed further reliance upon nuclear weapons in case of war and Denis Healey, official spokesman on defence, led a united Party in attacking him.[3]

But during the long debate on over-reliance on nuclear weapons official Labour policy never once advocated a return to conscription. Although conscription was a delicate issue with significant electoral overtones, it was taken up forcibly by a group of centralist MPs headed by Crossman and Wigg. Crossman raised the issue in February 1958:

> I say quite frankly that the Sandys plan of abolishing conscription is making this country totally dependent upon nuclear weapons and simultaneously impotent, and that I would rather postpone the abolition of conscription than condemn us to that.[4]

The first use of nuclear weapons

Crossman was forced into this position by his refusal to countenance the first use of nuclear weapons (strategic or tactical)

1. *Hansard* (27 Feb 1958) col. 652.
2. See *Hansard* (1 Mar 1960) col. 1,145.
3. See *Hansard* (27 Feb 1961) cols 1,227–8. For a detailed account of the 'official' position regarding over-reliance on nuclear weapons in NATO see Strachey, *On the Prevention of War*, ch. 7 – 'A Reversal of NATO's Nuclear Strategy'.
4. *Hansard* (27 Feb 1958) col. 638.

by the West. Gaitskell, as Leader of the Party, had less freedom of manœuvre. He refused to contemplate a reintroduction of conscription and this led him to accept the first use of *tactical* nuclear weapons by NATO in Europe. He made an honest decision between two very clear alternatives and chose what he considered to be the lesser of two evils. Yet until 1960[1] the first use of nuclear weapons by the West was a hidden issue, submerged beneath the larger questions of nuclear morality, unilateralism and neutralism. However, Michael Stewart, a member of the Shadow Cabinet during the Sandys era, had previously said:

> It can hardly be contended that the West is bound by some rule of chivalry to keep war on the conventional level. The guilt of war lies on the aggressor and its wickedness lies in the fact that it is an appeal to physical force ... the power that makes this appeal cannot then claim that the conflict shall be conducted with only those weapons that suit it best.[2]

This was bold stuff and, not surprisingly, he did not repeat it, nor did his colleagues, in the defence debates of the later fifties. Michael Foot interpreted the silence of the Party leaders on the first use of *strategic* nuclear weapons as proof of their guilt:

> For some years the official leaders of the party resisted the demand that any reference to the use of nuclear weapons first should be included in official party declarations. Mr Gaitskell was especially adamant in this respect. Presumably ... he must have thought that such a pledge might injure the general credibility of the deterrent theory.[3]

There could be no doubt, however, regarding the official position on the first use of *tactical* nuclear weapons. In the House of Commons defence debate of 1958 George Brown, the official Labour spokesman, said: 'Tactical nuclear weapons are not strategic nuclear weapons, but are the weapons we always understood were to be used on the battlefield to make up for our shortage of manpower.'[4] Strachey defended the

---

1. It was urged by the official policy of 1960 that the West must never be the first to use nuclear weapons. This was repeated in the 'Gaitskell–Healey draft' in 1961. This, it later turned out, referred only to strategic nuclear weapons!
2. Stewart, *Policy and Weapons in the Nuclear Age*, p. 6.
3. *Tribune* (3 Mar 1961) p. 7.   4. *Hansard* (26 Feb 1958) col. 412.

first use of nuclear weapons by his theory of staged response.[1]
He pointed to a theoretical Russian attack on West Berlin
and stated that if the Soviet Union attacked with *either* tactical
nuclear weapons *or* with overwhelming conventional strength
then the West should use tactical nuclear weapons in response.
This obviously implied, in given situations, that the West
should use *tactical* weapons first.

This approach of the Leadership appalled Crossman, who
argued that we should concentrate on building up our conventional forces[2] (he did not answer, however, how the West was
to contain an invasion while its conventional forces were being
built up). Nevertheless, in the following year's defence debate
Strachey stated that it was an 'absolute necessity'[3] for the
army to have tactical nuclear weapons. Gaitskell and Healey
were not so adamant. Although they never openly repudiated
the 'first use' policy the two architects of the 1961 draft were
noticeably less enthusiastic about it than either Brown or
Strachey. In the defence debate of 1960 in the House of
Commons Gaitskell showed his apprehension over the growing
lack of identity between strategic and tactical nuclear weapons:

> What makes us much more anxious is the fact that the so-called
> tactical nuclear weapons are now no longer tactical at all. . . . We
> are getting away from the idea of battlefield weapons. It is ex-
> tremely doubtful whether the West would be prepared to use
> nuclear weapons in these circumstances and, if so, the deterrent
> effect of them is lost.[4]

But Gaitskell believed in the deterrent theory! Logic dictated
to him the need for a first-use posture even though it was hard
to distinguish between strategic and tactical nuclear weapons.
Even though he agreed with his Leader, Healey was worried:
'Most of us have tremendous doubts as to whether, once
atomic weapons are used, even on the battlefield, there is much
chance of halting the progress of events before it leads to all-out
total global thermo-nuclear war.'[5]

1. See his speech in *Hansard* (27 Feb 1958) col. 655.
2. *Hansard* (27 Feb. 1958) col. 639.   3. *Hansard* (26 Feb. 1959) col. 1,410.
4. *Hansard* (1 Mar 1960) col. 1,145.
5. It must be made clear that the 1960 official policy agreed to the manufacture
of tactical nuclear weapons only if they were deployed under 'strict NATO
control'.

All this illustrates the complex and often paradoxical nature of Labour's military policy in the nuclear age. With Gaitskell and Healey locked in intellectual contortions about the definitions of strategic, tactical and battleground nuclear weapons, George Brown, in the same Commons debate, attempted to clarify the position:

> at this time the forces have been so run down that we cannot take the atomic fire power out, but it must be our purpose, as we say in our new document [the Healey–Gaitskell draft], to get back as quickly as we can to a situation in which we can say that NATO does not need to react nuclearly to an attack which itself is conventional.[1]

It is clear then that Gaitskell, Healey, Brown and Strachey were not totally convinced that 'the West must never be the first to use the H-bomb'.[2] Yet this was the very policy they proposed to the Party in 1960 and 1961. Such is the measure of confusion that military tactics present to politicians concerned with Party unity.

There was no confusion on the long-term aim to adopt second-strike capacity and thereby lessen vulnerability. This was the reasoning behind Gaitskell's opposition to the Thor missile bases. The original reason for opposing these bases, however, had been that their installation worsened the international atmosphere on the eve of the projected summit talks.[3] By 1960, though, both Gaitskell and Strachey changed their ground. Thor was a fixed, land-based liquid-fuel missile and, as such, was vulnerable to attack.[4] In his Scarborough speech Gaitskell emphasised that the opposition to the Thor missile was one of the vital policies which united the whole Party.

Another aspect of NATO strategy which united all wings of the Party was the question of collective political control.[5] Both Right and Left accepted the need for greater British participation in NATO decision-making. Nevertheless, the contention

1. *Hansard* (28 Feb 1961) cols 1,498–9.

2. Healey–Gaitskell draft, article 9. Reprinted in *Tribune* (31 Mar 1961).

3. See the Opposition amendment to Government motion in the defence debate of 1958: *Hansard* (26 Feb 1958) col. 417.

4. See Gaitskell, *Hansard* (1 Mar 1960) col. 1,144. Strachey, *Pursuit of Peace*.

5. See Mulley, *The Politics of Western Defence*, chs 6 and 7, for the most detailed account of the problems involved in political control of nuclear strategy.

that those who supported increased British participation in NATO planning and strategy had at the same time no idea how this was to be achieved was a very powerful one. The only argument that the Right could muster against it was that a British exit from NATO would destroy any influence she might otherwise have.

American bases in Britain

Although unanimity was secured over the question of Thor and more British participation in NATO, American bases in Britain remained a tricky problem. Gaitskell saw them as part of Britain's alliance responsibility; he also went as far as supporting the training of West German troops in Britain. The Left, Centre and some of the Right could not agree; and in September 1960 the Trades Union Congress passed a TGWU resolution requiring the removal of all bases equipped with nuclear weapons from Britain.[1] Gaitskell was further defeated on the matter at the Scarborough Annual Conference in the autumn of 1960 even though his declaratory policy was vague; NATO bases were simply not mentioned in the official policy of 1960. By 1961 the Leadership had become much less coy on the matter. The Gaitskell–Healey draft read as follows:

> It may well be that in a few years Western defence will not require America to have strategic bases overseas. Meanwhile, as a loyal member of the Alliance, Britain cannot oppose on principle the establishment of allied bases on her territory. But she must remain free to decide according to the circumstances of the case whether or not any particular project should be accepted and under what conditions.

The idea that in the future the whole question of American bases would become redundant was also an element in the Crossman draft. Whereas the Leadership remained passive on this issue, the centralist draft actively sought to create just that situation: 'The Labour movement, therefore, should press for a radical reconstruction of NATO ... and ... to end the need for American nuclear bases in Europe, including Britain.' It must be assumed that in the meantime American bases were

1. *TUC Report* 1960, p. 396.

necessary.[1] In contrast to this, the Cousins draft was quite definite: 'The provision of nuclear bases, including supply and servicing depots for Polaris submarines, is in opposition to our policy of reducing the dependence upon nuclear weapons, and cannot be supported.'[2] Although Gaitskell was victorious at Blackpool in 1961 that same conference went on to pass a resolution calling for the removal of Polaris bases from Britain. This was in direct contradiction to article 6 of the official document and led to some degree of subsequent confusion. From 1961 to the present day both Leaders of the Party, Hugh Gaitskell and Harold Wilson, refused to be bound by this decision.[3] The Polaris decision of the 1961 Conference was a small crumb of comfort for the defeated Frank Cousins but, like most Conference decisions inimical to the PLP, it was ignored.

The major victory of 1961 went to Gaitskell and those in the Leadership who had remained loyal to him.[4] This was not, in a strict sense, a victory over unilateralism. The Gaitskell–Healey draft had conceded unilateralism already and Cousins's decision to accept the Crossman draft showed that he was willing to compromise as well. Gaitskell's view was that as he had already conceded important points in his own draft he could not accept any more. He rejected Crossman's compromise out of hand and decided to risk another head-on clash with the Left and Centre; a clash that was resolved in his favour in October 1961.

If in 1960 at Scarborough Gaitskell had lost an important battle, then in 1961 at Blackpool he had won the war.

THE IMPORTANCE OF THE DEFENCE ISSUE

The rather sophisticated issues involved in the defence debates of the Labour Party in the period following the 1959 General

1. See Silverman's view of the Crossman policy in *Tribune* (5 May 1961).
2. *Tribune* (31 Mar 1961) p. 5.
3. See McKenzie, *British Political Parties*, 2nd (revised) ed., pp. 624–5.
4. The only major figures who never deviated from Gaitskell's position throughout the whole controversy were Callaghan and Strachey. Brown 'tottered' in his *New Statesman* article on the eve of Conference 1960, and Healey engaged in the famous 'switch' of 1961 when he committed the Party to ending the independent nuclear deterrent *immediately*.

Election tended to obscure what was fundamentally a division over less tangible and more general questions of the foreign-policy attitudes of the Party. Indeed, just as the rearmament debates of the early fifties had strong undercurrents of more permanent questions – neutralism, independence, alliance-orientation and attitudes to the United States and the Soviet Union – the post-1959 debates had similar undercurrents. These underlying problems, however, never surfaced as major issues mainly because the Left was reticent to assume the full neutral-ist mantle and to state plainly the consequences that would follow from such a posture. Instead, the debate resolved itself into a tactical battle between Left and Right with the Leader-ship of the Party as the prize for victory. This, therefore, was the reason for the lack of a consistent theme in the dialogue between Right and Left.

Before the cancellation of Blue Streak the arguments were, to some extent at least, fairly clearly based upon the rejection or acceptance of British nuclear independence. Following April 1960, however, they became bogged down in definitions and defence semantics. In a sense the whole Party was uni-lateralist after the July declaration of 1960 – certainly, anyway, by February 1961 – and unilateralism therefore ceased to be an issue. If unilateralism was not the issue at the 1960 and 1961 Annual Conferences, then what was? There is no definite answer in terms of policy. Although Gaitskell suggested that it was neutralism, the bulk of opposition to 'the platform' never explicitly asked for a rejection of NATO. In fact, Gaitskell used the neutralist issue, skilfully and successfully, in order to split the Left; and in formal terms the major division between the forces of the Left and Right by 1961 was simply the question of NATO nuclear strategy.

It is surprising that the Labour Party, which had never been particularly interested in the sophistications of military strategy, should have torn itself apart on this issue. A mass political party is obviously not the ideal institution within which to engage in a detailed debate about questions such as 'first-strike' capacity and distinctions between 'tactical' and other types of nuclear weapons. Indeed very few of the leading members of the Party on the Right and Left were at all interested in these concepts. They were the preserve of a small number of revisionist intellectuals.

All this seems to suggest that the defence debates, although originating in fundamental and principled divisions over policy, were but manifestations of the continuing power and personality struggle in the Party. Conference did not make its mind up according to the merits of the various defence strategies placed before it but rather it voted for or against the then current Leadership.

There is little doubt that it was Gaitskell's leadership that was at stake in 1960 and 1961 rather than any particular defence strategy. The broad direction in which he wished to lead the Party had been made apparent with the Clause IV issue, and the acrimony and vehemence of the defence debate was directed as much at him personally as at the defence policy for which he stood. If Gaitskell had been defeated in October 1961 the defence policy of the Party, in broad terms, would have changed little, but his own personal position as Leader, and the consequent revisionist direction of the Party, would have been in considerable doubt.

As it was, the victory in 1961 was a consolidation of his leadership. It was the trade unions that were primarily responsible for this reversal of 1961, but as important, in terms of revisionist history, was the dedicated effort of the first major revisionist pressure group, the Campaign for Democratic Socialism.

CHAPTER TEN

The Campaign for Democratic Socialism

The Campaign for Democratic Socialism (hereafter referred to as CDS) has a unique place in the history of the Labour Right. It remains to this day the only organisation set up within the Party by revisionists with political power as its ultimate goal. It also attempted to influence political thinking by propagating views that were distinctively revisionist, but its importance, however, lies in its organisational activities; CDS was active at constituency level, in trade union branches and in the PLP.

The Campaign had its first stirrings in April 1960. At this point the Party[1] had already defeated the Clause IV moves of Gaitskell and the coming Party Conference showed all the signs of a defeat for the Leadership on the issue of defence. These events led to a meeting between Bill Rodgers, General Secretary of the Fabian Society, and Anthony Crosland, MP for Grimsby and author of *The Future of Socialism*. They both agreed that there was inadequate contact and co-ordination between those in the Party who wished to preserve both Gaitskell's Leadership on the one hand and multilateralism on the other. It was agreed that an integrated Right, both at Leadership and constituency level, was the only effective way of stemming what was seen as the rising tide of unilateralism.

Soon after this meeting it was decided that a drafting process should be initiated with a view to publishing a manifesto in the autumn. Thirteen Party members, drawn mainly from Parliament and the constituency parties, were instrumental in producing the first draft. The leading figures among 'the 13'

1. This was mainly carried out at NEC level. See Chap. Eight on Clause IV.

H

were: Alfred Robens (MP), Denis Howell (former MP for the All Saints' division of Birmingham), Bill Rodgers, Ivan Yates (political journalist), Dick Taverne (barrister and ex-candidate for Putney), Patrick Gordon Walker (Shadow Foreign Secretary), Philip Williams (Fellow of Nuffield College, Oxford), Frank Pickstock (Oxford local councillor) and Anthony Crosland (MP).[1] The main policy work on the document was completed by Crosland and Williams and then presented to 'the 13' for discussion and amendment. Finally, a completed draft was presented to a meeting of the signatories the week-end following the 1960 Scarborough Conference. None of the signatories of the manifesto were MPs, but the list included candidates, councillors, university fellows and chairmen of local Labour parties – all of them individual members of the Labour Party.[2]

More important than the actual manifesto was the simultaneous formation of the organisational apparatus of the Campaign. At the time of the launching of the policy manifesto certain hints were given by the three leaders of the group, Rodgers, Howell and Pickstock, that they intended to begin operations in constituency parties and trade union branches. Very little commitment was made as to the ultimate, precise intentions of the group but foremost in their minds was the need to counteract the organisation and propaganda work of the Left-wing pressure group 'Victory for Socialism' (VFS).[3]

On 24 November the group announced that its official title was to be the Campaign for Democratic Socialism and that

1. See also Lord Windlesham, *Communication and Political Power* (1966), chs 4 and 5. Windlesham records that in the summer of 1960 'three interconnected groups in London and in Oxford began to coalesce'. (Pp. 95–6.) He states that two groups existed in London. The first consisted of Rodgers, Taverne, Yates and Michael Shanks (Industrial Editor of the *Financial Times*) and the second was exclusively parliamentarian, consisting of Crosland, Gordon Walker, Jay and Jenkins. The Oxford group was composed of Pickstock, Williams, Ron Owen (Oxford City Councillor) and Brian Walden (former Chairman of the National Association of Labour Student Organisations).

2. The signatories were: J. Conway, H. Dickson, A. Dumont, A. Grant, T. H. Hockton, D. Howell, D. Jones, S. Jones, B. Magee, G. Mcquade, D. Matthews, J. H. Matthews, K. May, R. Owen, R. Parker, F. V. Pickstock, F. L. Price, F. V. H. Ramsbottom, W. T. Rodgers, M. Shanks, D. Taverne, B. Walden, Miss H. Walker, R. Waterhouse, H. W. Waterman and P. Williams.

3. *The Times* (19 Oct 1960) p. 12d.

W. T. Rodgers was to be its Chairman. After an initial period in Oxford the CDS set up a permanent headquarters office in Red Lion Street, London, financed by contributions from individual members of the Labour Party. It was from this office that a network of contacts and supporters was established in both local Labour parties and the trade union movement.

Once the headquarters organisation had been set up the specific political motives behind CDS began to emerge. In a letter sent to all supporters on 24 November[1] the *raison d'être* for CDS was explained:

> We must now attempt to provide a continuous voice for rank and file opinion in the centre of the party and a rallying point for the great majority of men and women of good will who want to see the party genuinely united and on the road back to power.

The leaders of the CDS considered that an unrepresentative and well-organised minority had managed, temporarily, to gain control of the Party. In order to reassert moderate opinion a new organising centre was needed to act as a rallying point for what was considered a majority of the Movement.[2]

CDS was of the opinion that there was a real need for an alternative pressure group to the VFS, *Tribune* and the Campaign for Nuclear Disarmament. It was a deeply held view that one of the reasons for the unilateralist victory at Scarborough was that these pressure groups had, up until 1960, been subjected to no organised opposition at 'grass-roots' level. The Left was organised, the Right was not; and it was felt that a day-to-day opposition to these Left-wing pressure groups would raise morale among the more moderate elements in the Party.[3]

Another motive for action was the growing attraction of the centralist 'unity' campaign. Many supporters of Gaitskell felt that certain moderate sections of the Movement, tending to

1. This letter was reproduced in full in *The Times* (15 Nov 1960) p. 15d.

2. W. T. Rodgers said at a press conference to launch the group, 'All of us working in constituencies were conscious that the voices raised were not rank and file voices at all. They were the voices of a loud, persistent and organised minority.' Quote in *The Times* (19 Oct 1960).

3. A bizarre example of the continual scrutiny by CDS of the CND occurred on 15 Feb 1961, when the CDS attempted, and failed, to organise a meeting in Carlisle Cathedral. A protest was sent from Red Lion Street to the Dean because the CND had previously been granted permission to hold such a meeting.

under-estimate their own strength, would be attracted by the compromise policy of Wilson, Crossman and Padley. Certain issues of *Campaign*, the monthly broadsheet of the CDS that was sent to all key supporters, urged the Party to support the new official defence policy, *Policy for Peace*, and to withdraw support from the Crossman–Padley draft.[1] The immediate objective of CDS was therefore solely concerned with the mechanics of Party opinion on the defence issue. After all, Gaitskell's defeat on defence had brought it into being. This, however, was purely a short-term objective.

THE POLICY OF THE CDS

Although 1961 was completely dominated by the defence quarrels, CDS had broader aspirations for the Movement in terms not only of practical policy but also of image and long-term direction. The original manifesto contained seven basic points regarding contemporary democratic socialism, all of which were thoroughly revisionist in nature, but none of which was additional to those already elaborated by the leading revisionist political thinkers. Nevertheless for the first time a concise statement of political principles was circulated and propagated within the Party around which those of similar persuasions could gather. This, combined with the specific campaign to reverse the decisions of the Scarborough Conference and reassert Gaitskell's leadership, was the contribution CDS made to revisionism in the 1960s.

Most of the fundamental aims of CDS were stipulated in the manifesto, but these were elaborated on and defended at greater length in the issues of *Campaign*. The first important aim was concerned with ideology. The manifesto stated that 'The British Labour movement owes its inspiration to British radicals, trade unionists, co-operators, non-conformists and Christian socialists, not to Marx and Lenin', and it emphasised that in its view the Party was a reforming rather than a revolutionary institution. This idea resulted in a strong and militant attitude towards both international and national communism.

1. *Campaign* (Labour Manifesto group), issues 3 and 5. This broadsheet was not placed on sale to the public.

In its attitude to the Soviet Union the CDS was often highly expressive and emotive:

> The easiest way for Krushchev to get his way is to use threats. They cost him nothing. How should we react?
> Let us look at the record. It shows that countries that have stood firm in the face of Soviet blustering have preserved both peace and their own independence. And they have set limits to Soviet expansionism.[1]

CDS campaigned as vigorously against the influence of the British Communist Party in Labour Party affairs,[2] as well as rejecting its political creed. Nevertheless the revisionists of CDS were less concerned with attacking Marxism-Leninism than they were with counteracting the arguments of the affirmationist non-Marxist Left. The question of the exact balance between power and principles in political life became of absorbing interest to those in the campaign who wished to refute the contention that 'rightist Labourism' had divorced itself from action based upon moral and ethical judgements. CDS was adamant that 'the purpose of political activity is to win power and use it to put principles into effect',[3] and derided those who preach principles irrespective of their application as being 'anxious only to save their souls'.[4]

The CDS, like all social-democratic institutions, was not without its own set of first principles and was not loath to parade them. It reiterated earlier revisionist thinking by placing priority upon equality (or, at least, greater equality) of private wealth and it considered that the balance of interests between the private and public sectors in the economy was unevenly distributed in favour of the former. This emphasis on equality was part of a broader scheme of first principles that was summarised in a form reminiscent of Socialist Union eight years earlier:

> We interpret socialism not as an arid economic dogma, but in terms of freedom, equality, social justice and world co-operation.

---

1. *Campaign*, 3 (Mar 1961).
2. *Campaign*, 7 (Jul 1961). In this issue *Campaign* republished a letter regarding Communist activities in the CND.
3. *Campaign*, 8 (Aug/Sep 1961).
4. Ibid.

We believe that the British people, who rightly distrust doctrinaire utopianism, will always respond to an idealistic appeal to remedy real evils by practical and radical reform.[1]

Here, clearly, is a declaration that democratic socialism, as seen by the CDS, should work within the context of the political, economic and social situation in which it finds itsel and not engage in a revolutionary upheaval of that system. CDS also attempted to illustrate not only the futility of, but also the inhumanity of, revolutionary ardour based upon doctrine. It interpreted democratic socialism, and particularly the Labour Movement's role, as a political force concerned with what it considered tangible 'everyday' problems; the social services, the taxation system, the housing problem, the education system and other similar social and economic phenomena. Also, it did not see these social problems as soluble by means of a basic change in economic or political structure. It tended to treat each one as separate, hermetically-sealed compartments with solutions inherent within them. This did not detract, however, from a socialism based upon the principles of equality, freedom and social justice, but the CDS did not lay quite the stress upon general and universal ethics that Socialist Union had done a decade earlier.

These were political attitudes upon which all revisionists could agree and unite. On all the particular issues that emerged from 1961 to 1964, save Britain's entry into the European Economic Community, CDS adopted a position indistinguishable from that of Gaitskell.[2]

The defence issue illustrates this continued identity between the Leader's policy and that of CDS. CDS supported all Gaitskell's arguments during 1960 and 1961, particularly those concerning the first-strike capacity, the need for a greater conventional weapons emphasis in NATO, a more effective political control over nuclear weapons systems, a greater United Kingdom influence in NATO contingency planning, the disengagement proposals and the independent nuclear deterrent issue.[3] The history of the CDS position on the British

---

1. *A Manifesto, Addressed to the Labour Movement*, para. 14. This was the original manifesto published on 18 Oct 1960.
2. *Campaign*, vols 1–12.   3. Ibid.

bomb is an instance of its unswerving loyalty to Gaitskell which was held regardless of official vicissitudes in policy. Until March 1961 the CDS policy had been vague about whether or not Britain should continue as an independent nuclear power. Indeed as late as February of that year *Campaign* was still ambiguous on the question.[1] However, by March of 1961, after the publication of the new NEC policy document on defence and disarmament *Policy for Peace*, *Campaign* fully supported the renunciation of British independent nuclear power.[2] This slight, but significant, change in emphasis further supports the view that in dealing with specific policy issues the CDS was primarily interested in supporting and bolstering Gaitskell than in analysing and prescribing short-term policy.

CDS gave similar unquestioning support to Gaitskell on the question of public ownership. The group had only been conceived at the time of the Clause IV controversy, but at birth it issued the following statement:

> Recognising that public, co-operative and private enterprise all have a part to play in the economy, we regard the public ownership of particular industries or services as a *useful technique* to be justified on its merits.[3]

This was virtually identical with what had appeared six months earlier in Gaitskell's 'statement of aims'.[4] On public ownership, as on defence, CDS was Gaitskellite to the core.

Gaitskell received unqualified backing from CDS on both the National Health Service charges[5] issue and also for his stand on the Conservative Immigration Bill.[6] More important,

---

1. *Campaign*, 2 (Feb 1961) said: 'Because Russian forces in Europe are equipped with nuclear weapons, we cannot do without them. But we possess them, not because we intend to use them aggressively, but to deprive the Russians of any temptation to use theirs.' There was no clarification in any CDS publications at, or before, March 1960 as to whether the 'we' referred to Britain, the United States, or NATO.

2. *Campaign*, 3 (Mar 1961) said: 'The West *as a whole* (italics mine) must remain armed with the same weapons as the East.'

3. *A Manifesto Addressed to the Labour Movement*, para. 11. (Italics mine.)

4. *Labour's Aims* (Labour Party, 1960) stated: 'Recognising that both public and private enterprise have a place in the economy it believes that further extension of common ownership should be decided from time to time in the light of these objectives and according to the circumstances.'

5. *Campaign*, 3 (Mar 1961).   6. Ibid. 11 (Dec 1961).

from a Party viewpoint, was its support for Gaitskell's implicit undermining of the sovereignty of the Labour Party Conference. CDS attempted to illustrate how, in its view, the question of Conference sovereignty was being used as a personal vendetta against the Leader:

> The only real question at issue is the basic constitutional one – over the long-established right of the Parliamentary Labour Party not to accept dictation from Conference. . . . Mr Gaitskell's opponents, in making their attacks narrowly personal, are trying to ignore the right of the Parliamentary party to do this.[1]

This dubiously constitutional assumption[2] that the PLP, by virtue of a 'long-established right', was totally free from Conference dictation was but a function of a need to transfer Party opinion away from an allegiance to Conference towards an allegiance to the PLP – where Gaitskell received much greater support.

CDS policy and philosophy were therefore thoroughly revisionist and its views were identical to those of Hugh Gaitskell. The Party Leader had nothing to do with the formation of the Campaign and at no period formally associated himself with it. Nevertheless it possessed, and was seen to possess, all the qualities of organised Gaitskellism; with the expressed purpose of working for a new-style Labour Party on the lines suggested by the Leader himself.

SUPPORT FOR THE CAMPAIGN

An appraisal of the support that CDS received from the Movement can shed some light on the extent to which Gaitskell's immediate aims, if not his long-term political goals, were representative of all types of 'rank-and-file' opinion. It is important to note that it was not revisionist philosophy as a whole but the specific questions of defence and Gaitskell's leadership that were the issues before the Party in 1961. The Party therefore was not really divided over revisionist or fundamentalist theology, although ingredients of this division

---

1. *Campaign*, 1.
2. For a definitive work on the relationship between Conference and PLP see McKenzie, *British Political Parties*, 2nd (revised) ed., pp. 485–516.

were present. CDS was the only 'grass-roots' organisation func-
tioning on the Right and, as such, attracted to it wider support
than it might have achieved in normal circumstances. The crisis
situation and polarised atmosphere precluded compromise;
Labour had to choose between the Right and the Left in a
stark and immediate manner. A final assessment of support for
CDS must be seen in this light. Many who sided with CDS
may not have done so on grounds of philosophical niceties or
long-run aims. Many of them were certainly not revisionists or
Gaitskellites.

As with any organisation which has no official membership
an estimate of CDS support is a difficult undertaking. One
method is to analyse the various bodies and individuals that
gave support to the organisation; either openly, by the acceptance of office in it or by public declaration, or less openly, by
the pronouncement of policies that were closely akin to the
stand taken by CDS but without any formal association.

The parliamentary backing for the Campaign was the most
impressive and also the most easily ascertainable. In the March
1961 edition of *Campaign* it was announced that a letter had
been received from some 45 MPs pledging support.[1] This
letter not only welcomed the CDS stand on collective security
and multilateral disarmament but also 'applauded the spirit
in which the Manifesto was launched'.[2] Praising multilateralism was one thing; applauding CDS's 'spirit' was another.
This letter identified the 45 MPs as 'hard-core' revisionists,
for the manifesto to which they referred was a broad declaration of revisionist policy which contained only one sentence
on the question of defence. None of the 45 was a member of the
Shadow Cabinet or of the NEC and were, therefore, in a sense,

---

1. The 45 were: J. Ainsley, A. Albu, C. Bence, W. Blyton, J. Boyden, E. Brad-
dock (Mrs), D. Chapman, G. Chetwynd, J. Cronin, C. A. R. Crosland, J. Diamond,
D. Donnelly, A. Fitch, E. Fletcher, G. de Freitas, D. Ginsburg, C. Grey, W. Han-
nan, H. Hayman, J. Hoy, H. Hughes, S. Irving, D. Jay, G. Jeger, R. Jenkins, D.
Jones, H. King, M. Lloyd George (Lady), E. L. Mallalieu, R. Mason, C. Mayhew,
J. McCann, R. Mellish, B. Millan, F. Mulley, R. Paget, R. Prentice, G. W. Reynolds, G. R. Rodgers, G. Strauss, A. Thompson, F. Tomney, P. Wells, C. Wilcock.
Conspicuous by their absence from this list were John Strachey and Philip Noel-
Baker (the Chairman of the Campaign for Multilateral Disarmament). By their
public speeches they were associated with CDS defence policy.
2. *Campaign*, 3.

'grass-roots' parliamentarians affirming 'grass-roots' feelings. The letter was intended to be seen as such.

The following year saw this nucleus of CDS supporters in the House of Commons increased by new MPs elected at by-elections. These included Jeremy Bray (Middlesbrough West), Bill Rodgers (Stockton), Dick Taverne (Lincoln),[1] Tom Bradley (Leicester North-East), Tam Dalyell (West Lothian), Guy Barnett (South Dorset), Niall Macdermot (Derby North) and Denis Howell (Birmingham, Small Heath). Macdermot and Howell were both ex-MPs who had lost narrowly in 1959. All these incoming MPs had associated themselves with CDS either by taking office in the Campaign, before they were elected, or by speaking on CDS platforms. It is significant that during a period when there was keen competition between Left and Right for parliamentary candidatures in by-elections so many successful 'CDS-associated' candidates were selected.[2] CDS was obviously busy at work in the constituencies.

Therefore, in late 1960 and early 1961, before the Scarborough decision had been reversed, one-fifth of the PLP publicly supported an organisation which was attempting to change the whole direction of the Party. On the more limited question of defence this fraction can fairly be said to have increased to roughly two-thirds, as the voting lists from the defence debates in the House of Commons testify;[3] and on the issue of Gaitskell's leadership a similar percentage emerged.[4] The discrepancy between the one-fifth of the PLP who openly supported CDS and the two-thirds who supported both multi-lateralism and Gaitskell illustrates the fact that many MPs,

1. Dick Taverne became Treasurer of the CDS in January 1962, and resigned upon being elected to the House of Commons. The reason for this was the Campaign's preference for non-parliamentary officers, a position in keeping with their determination to represent 'grass-roots' opinion. Also, when Rodgers became an MP he resigned as Secretary of the organisation and Bernard Donoughue (a Lecturer in Government at the London School of Economics) took his place.

2. The number of Labour MPs returned in by-elections in the 1959–64 Parliament was 29, and those who had a close association with CDS amounted to 14. A further 9 were 'loyalist' right-wing members.

3. E.g. on 10 Dec 1960, 50 Labour MPs abstained on a division on an official Opposition motion criticising Government defence policy; 163 Labour MPs supported the Whip. Full voting figures can be seen in *Hansard*, vol. 632 (1960–1) cols 351–4.

4. Gaitskell beat Wilson by 166 to 81 on 3 Nov 1960.

although sympathetic to the Campaign, were worried about associating themselves formally with an organisation seen to be uncompromisingly Right-wing. Trade union MPs particularly were among those who were reticent.

More significant than back-bench support was that of the Shadow Cabinet. In fact the whole Central Leadership of the Party in Parliament, with the single exception of Wilson, were Campaign sympathisers.[1] Gaitskell, of course, had no official contact with the CDS for obvious reasons but, in so far as he never repudiated the organisation and agreed with so much of its policy, his real position was in no doubt. Further credence to this view is given by his close personal and political association with many of the leading members of the group. The other members of the Shadow Cabinet were in a different position and George Brown (Shadow Defence spokesman), Denis Healey (Shadow Colonial spokesman), James Callaghan (Shadow Chancellor of the Exchequer) and Patrick Gordon Walker (Shadow Foreign Secretary) all had firm and open links with the organisation. Gordon Walker was actually involved in the drafting process of the original manifesto and the other three accepted invitations to speak on CDS platforms.

Open backing for the Campaign came from Labour Peers in the House of Lords. The most prominent of whom were: Lord Attlee, whose Presidency of CDS was announced in February 1961, Lord Dalton, who chaired the CDS February demonstration, Lord Pakenham and Lord Listowel.

Support in the trade unions is more difficult to gauge. A distinction must be drawn between those unions, branches and individual trade unionists who supported multilateralism, or who later adopted it, and those who explicitly associated themselves with CDS. Lord Windlesham suggests that certain key trade unionists were closely associated with CDS. He states that 'in November Mr Carron had been one of the prominent trade unionists whose support had been announced by CDS'.[2] Also, 'his principal henchmen on the Executive [of the AEU], J. M. Boyd and W. M. Tallon, representing the AEU on the

1. Jay, Mayhew and Mulley were front-bench spokesmen but not in the Shadow Cabinet.
2. Windlesham, *Communication and Political Power*, p. 121.

NEC and on the General Council of the TUC respectively, were also well disposed towards any activity that would assist their anti-communist crusade'.[1] Windlesham also lists J. Conway (AEU's National Organiser)[2] and F. Hayday (NUGMW's representative on the General Council) as particularly closely associated with the organisational activities of CDS. It is also fairly clear that Jack Cooper (NUGMW), Sam Watson (NUM's representative on the NEC) and Ron Smith (General Secretary of the Post Office Workers' Union) were committed to and involved with the campaign. CDS themselves announced open support from Miss A. Godwin (General Secretary of the Clerical and Administrative Workers' Union), W. J. P. Webber (General Secretary of the Transport Salaried Staffs Association) and Sir Thomas Williamson (President of NUGMW).[3]

Many of the trade union leaders who were reticent about open association with CDS were nevertheless prepared to associate themselves with the nuclear policy of the Leadership. A statement was issued following the 1960 Party Conference by twenty members of the General Council of the TUC which read:

> In view of the controversy conducted in public, on the subject of unilateral disarmament, we as members of the General Council of the TUC should like to make it clear that we firmly adhere to the policy of collective security, multilateral disarmament and the maintenance and strengthening of NATO as set out in the joint statement of the TUC and Labour Party which was overwhelmingly endorsed by the General Council of the TUC and the National Executive, the Parliamentary Committee and the Parliamentary Party of the Labour Party.[4]

The signatories to this statement were: C. Bartlett, W. B. Beard, A. Birch, W. Carron, J. Cooper, J. Crawford, H. Douglass, Anne Godwin, S. Greene, F. Hayday, G. Lowthian, A. Martin, Sir T. O'Brien, J. O'Hagan, S. Robinson, G. F. Smith, W. Webber, Sir T. Williamson, L. T. Wright and Sir T. Yates. All of these signatories held key posts in their unions.

Trade union leaders, in the last resort, reflect the views of

1. Ibid.   2. J. Conway was a signatory of the original manifesto.

3. Ron Smith spoke at a CDS demonstration at the Caxton Hall, Westminster, on 2 Feb 1961.

4. This statement is also quoted in Windlesham, *Communication and Political Power*, p. 124.

their active members but it is almost impossible to estimate the 'rank-and-file' trade union support for CDS. The only information available on this subject comes from *Campaign* of May 1961. This issue analysed union support as being about one thousand active members and 'several hundred' office-holders. It also claimed that every major union was represented and 'all but a few of the minor ones'. Much of this was naturally propagandistic but there is little reason to doubt that CDS had helped to organise moderate union opinion in substantial numbers. CDS was a convenient rallying-point for the small, but significant, trade union activists who were disaffected with their bosses and executive committees.

Whether CDS was instrumental in actually changing the defence policies of the major unions is another matter. Many of the leading officers of CDS were active in lobbying unionists at their annual conferences but the ingredients of a multilateralist victory were already present in many of the unions. The most vital of all the 'big 6' trade union conferences was the first one – the USDAW Annual Delegate Meeting (ADM). Walter Padley, the President of the Union and a centralist in Labour Party terms, had greater personal influence with his own union than any other contemporary trade union leader. He managed to persuade the ADM to vote both for the Crossman–Padley compromise[1] resolution and to reject a unilateralist motion. However, a motion, moved by the Aberdeen delegate, pledging support for *Policy for Peace*, the Gaitskellite policy, was also passed by the ADM by 103,707 votes to 98,888.[2] As the compromise motion was only mandatory *if it could gather enough support from the other major unions*, it soon became clear that USDAW was committed at the Labour Party Conference in the autumn to supporting Gaitskell's defence statement! This was crucial. The USDAW block vote itself was enough to reverse the previous Scarborough decision, provided that the other multilateralist unions held firm.

1. See my chapter on the defence controversy (1960–1), and *USDAW ADM Report*, 1961.
2. *Report of the Proceedings of the Fifteenth Annual Delegate Meeting (USDAW)*, 30 Apr, and 1 and 2 May 1961, p. 108.

There is some evidence to suggest that the CDS played an important role in this decision of the USDAW. Windlesham reports that T. Fyfe, the mover of the pro-Gaitskell Aberdeen resolution, was a CDS supporter and following an attempt to get the Aberdeen motion withdrawn he 'turned to the Campaign for advice. The result was that Fyfe declined to withdraw.'[1] This was without doubt a vital move in securing Gaitskell's victory in the autumn. Equally significant was the role of Padley himself. At the previous year's ADM he had not intervened in the debate and sat silent on the platform. But in 1961 he lent his personal authority to the compromise motion and this was interpreted by many as a move to change the ADM's unilateralist stance. Padley himself was never a unilateralist, and, although he had reservations regarding the question of first use of nuclear weapons, his sympathies lay with the multilateralists,[2] although not with Hugh Gaitskell. Therefore, it was a combination of the influence of CDS and the President of USDAW that contributed to the reversal of this key union's nuclear policy. It is ironical that a leading member of the centralist group in the Party played such a major role in reversing the 1960 decision and thereby consolidating the Leadership of Gaitskell.

CDS was also active at the second trade union conference of the season, that of the AEU. The union voted unilateralist at Scarborough but reversed its decision in 1961.[3] This was a success for CDS, but most of the credit must go to the organising ability of Bill Carron and his like-minded colleagues in the upper reaches of the union hierarchy. The AEU and the USDAW decisions were enough to ensure an NEC victory at Blackpool, and even if their change of policy was not basically due to the organisational activity of CDS it did verify the Campaign's claim that the 1960 decision was but an aberration

1. Windlesham, *Communication and Political Power*, p. 135.

2. Padley's speech at the 1961 ADM, although a plea for unity, was more critical of the unilateralists than the multilateralists, e.g. 'I simply say to the unilateral comrades – and they are my dear friends – is there any point in committing this Movement of ours to a policy which in the heat of international difficulties would collapse like a pack of cards?' *ADM Report*, p. 95.

3. A 'compromise' resolution was passed, but more importantly, a unilateralist resolution was defeated by 28 to 23 votes, with 1 abstention.

and that the 'majority voice' of the Movement would be restored by concerted organisation.

The constituency parties, although wielding far fewer votes at Conference than the unions, were more susceptible to CDS pressure. The active 'Party-worker' backing is difficult to appraise and the only information available on this again comes from *Campaign*. In its first five issues *Campaign* published the number of separate offers of support it had received from what it termed 'key' Party workers. In January the figure was 2,113 and by May it claimed 3,011. This was the last time the organisation published its individual 'grass-roots' support and from May 1961 to the present day no further figures have been available.

3,000 out of 90,000 or so individual Party members does not, in statistical terms, constitute a large percentage, but the Campaign claimed that its support in the constituencies came from the more important sections of the constituency membership. Of the 3,000 it was claimed that over one-third of this total held office in local Party organisations. If as a definition of 'office' the Campaign meant membership of the executive committees of constituency parties, and it did talk in terms of 'key' workers, then it had the impressive support of between one-fifth and one-third of these important members. If it was referring to ward or local Labour parties[1] then the figure would be much lower.

The Campaign also claimed that roughly 1,500 of its supporters were aldermen and councillors and that over 200 had been parliamentary candidates. It also maintained that:

Very few constituencies are without CDS supporters. We are particularly strong in Greater London, the East Midlands, the West Riding, Lancashire and Clydeside. . . . The Campaign is a cross-section of the whole Labour movement.[2]

The fact that many constituencies contained CDS supporters is meaningless in terms of the power struggle in the Party unless most of them were in such 'key' positions that they could influence policy. One proving-ground for their strength was the Party Conference of 1961; CDS had been active for about one year and its claims could be put to the

1. 'Local' in this sense refers to a subdivision of a rural Constituency Labour Party.
2. *Campaign*, 5 (May 1961).

test. However, reservations must be made as to the exact relationship between voting at Conference and CDS influence. First, when voting on the defence issue constituency parties had to take into account other factors than the purely intellectual case for or against unilateralism presented to them by CDS. Secondly, those constituency parties which mandated their delegates in favour of multilateralism may have done so without reference to CDS. Nevertheless, certain interesting conclusions emerge from an analysis of the Conference voting pattern. In 1960 it has been estimated that constituencies split 67 per cent to 33 per cent in favour of the official policy, and in 1961 they divided 63 per cent to 37 per cent.[1]

These figures show a small decline in constituency support for official policy between the two Conferences but leaves us uncertain as to the influence of CDS. What is certain was the solid majority support for Gaitskell even in 1960![2] A large body of multilateralist opinion already existed before CDS got to work and the result of a year's campaigning was, in statistical terms, to decrease constituency support for Gaitskell. However the figures may be somewhat misleading as some constituency delegations broke their mandate in 1960.[3] The 1961 Conference, however, portrayed constituency feeling more accurately as by that time general management committees had tightened up control of their delegates. On this reading it seems that support for Gaitskell in the constituencies remained high and static between the two Annual Conferences. Therefore CDS, although active in the constituencies,[4] just did not have the material for conversions. Surprisingly then, the supposed 'hot-beds of socialism' evidently supported Gaitskell all along.

The CDS was also active in the youth section of the Move-

1. Hindell and Williams, 'Scarborough and Blackpool'.

2. This again, however, substantiates the CDS claim that they represented majority opinion in the Party.

3. Many parties broke their mandate following Gaitskell's speech. This was certainly not because of any last-minute intellectual doubts but because of the emotion of the moment and the fear of a divided Party.

4. CDS sent out to its supporters in every constituency party motions that they should present to their GMCs for the 1961 Party Conference. An interesting example of this is given in Windlesham, *Communication and Political Power*, p. 117. It also organised a Speaker's panel and helped aspiring candidates to get to selection conferences.

ment but, as would be expected, it met with little immediate success. In the autumn of 1961 an organisation was established within the Young Socialists based upon a declaration very similar to that of the original CDS manifesto. 'Counterblast',[1] as the group was called, shunned any official link with the CDS, for in the context of Labour youth politics it would have been the kiss of death. The group tried to rid the Young Socialists of 'Trotskyist' influence as well as fight for multilateralism. The two objectives were not incompatible; but neither was successful.

CDS was at work in all sections of the Party. Its presence was felt in trade union branches, women's organisations, local and ward Labour parties and even in the Young Socialists. But the extent of its operations was not commensurate with its real influence. The Press, however, seemed to think that it was.

THE SUCCESS AND IMPORTANCE OF CDS

The reversal of the USDAW and AEU decisions in the spring of 1961 led to continuous and sustained journalistic comment about the decisive role played by CDS in defeating the unilateralists. For instance the *Guardian* stated:

> It is clear that the defeat suffered by the unilateralists was more crushing than expected. ... In part, this is tribute to the energy and organising skill of the Campaign for Democratic Socialism.[2]

All other major national newspapers and periodicals, with the exception of the *Daily Worker* and *Tribune*, echoed this view. As has been seen above, however, this was an exaggerated conclusion, probably reached because of the success of the political

---

1. *Counterblast – A Declaration for Labour Youth* (1961).
2. The *Guardian* (May 1961), cited in *Campaign*, 6 (Jun 1961). Other press and periodical comment was as follows: 'Mr Gaitskell has been saved ... by a combination of his own courage, the astonishing discovery of an enormous reservoir of fiercely loyal support ... and above all, by the sheer, hard grind of his supporters, particularly the Campaign for Democratic Socialism who have gone out into the field and organised and drilled and persuaded and canvassed and generally put their backs into it.' *Spectator* (12 May 1961) p. 670.
'There is no doubt that at national level the Campaign for Democratic Socialism has played a decisive role in swinging opinion in the unions and in the local parties. ... It has obviously had the most impressive results.' *The Sunday Times* (May 1961), cited in *Campaign*, 6 (Jun 1961).

proposals with which CDS was associated. The 1961 reversal of policy, or rather resumption of traditional policy, was as much a symptom of the inherent rightism of the unions as it was of CDS pressure. This inherent rightism was reinforced on this particular occasion by appeals to loyalty and anti-factionalism. Also crucial was Gaitskell's emotionally persuasive personality.

The contribution of CDS was less obvious, but nevertheless real. The fact that an organisation was at work in the Party at 'grass-roots' level with attendant publicity and propaganda methods no doubt raised the morale of loyalist elements which, following Scarborough, had tended to withdraw from active political life in the constituencies and trade union branches. Also, the Campaign did achieve a phenomenal success in changing the image that the Party presented to the public. It was extremely successful in its promotion of parliamentary candidates, for in the majority of by-elections in the 1961–3 period there was a large influx of the type of MPs that a moderate and revisionist party would call forth. These new MPs, in practice, and also in 'public image' terms, had little in common with unilateralism or fundamentalism.

Two further points underscore the importance of CDS. First, although the Party and Movement have inbuilt safeguards against Left-wing policies, there is a need from time to time to give organisational and intellectual direction to an otherwise inherently strong yet sluggish structure. CDS is a unique example of an attempt to provide this direction. Secondly, CDS was, perhaps, the most representative 'faction' in post-war Labour politics. It was representative not in the sense that it received overwhelming direct involvement but in the sense that its policies and programmes had mass Party support. This is true, although to a much lesser extent, with its ultimate objectives. The vast majority of the Labour Movement has always identified the Labour Party with social-democratic reforming ideals and had never, in practical terms, taken Party rhetoric, including Clause IV, seriously – except in the form of symbolism.

In effect, therefore, it was the representative nature of CDS that limited its influence because the Party did not, in a long-term sense, need to be evangelised into accepting multilateral disarmament. The year 1960 was an aberration from which Labour soon recovered. CDS was therefore a restorative agency rather than an influence for change and it pursued this function with exceptional organising ability.

These short-run objectives met with considerable success because they were also majority objectives. The long-term revisionist objectives of CDS, although popular with Labour voters, were a different matter. The Party could not absorb them too quickly but the process had begun. This process was temporarily suspended when CDS 'wound up' voluntarily following Labour's victory at the 1964 General Election.

The last years of CDS were not as exhilarating as its first. The organisation was caught in the crossfire between its own supporters on the question of British entry into the European Economic Community.

CDS, LABOUR AND THE COMMON MARKET

Britain's proposed entry into the European Economic Community was not an issue that separated Gaitskellites from others in the Movement. It was largely unrelated to ideological differences and the revisionist wing of the Party itself was seriously divided as to what Labour policy towards negotiations with 'the Six' should be. This, therefore, was not a simple 'Left versus Right' question as were many of the debates of the 1950s. The Left had its share of pro-Marketeers[1] just as the Right had its share of anti-Marketeers.[2] This led to some

1. Certain 'Left-wing' MPs were in favour of British entry, e.g. Hugh Delargy (MP for Thurrock), Bob Edwards (an ex-ILP member, MP for Bilston and Member of the Chemical Workers' Union), A. J. Irvine (MP for Edge Hill, Liverpool). W. Padley (MP for Ogmore, President of USDAW and a 'centralist') was also in favour of Britain's entry.

2. The dividing-line between those in favour of Britain's entry and those against is imprecise. For purposes of definition 'pro' will mean: being in favour of entry as soon as possible and with only minor emphasis on the terms to be negotiated. 'Anti' will mean: in favour of entry only after certain rigorous, and almost prohibitive, conditions had been met with, and a belief that if Britain remained outside the EEC she would not suffer economically or politically as a result. Although the question of 'terms for entry' is crucial to any understanding of the 'pro' and 'anti' positions, they were often used as weapons to obscure the real motives that existed for and against Britain's entry.

interesting permutations and combinations. Many leading members of the revisionist and CDS group, some of them high in the hierarchy of the Party, associated themselves, on this issue, with the Centre and Left. Gaitskell was one of them.

CDS, still predominantly pro-Market, was placed in a difficult position. Until 1962 it had been fiercely loyal to the Leadership but nevertheless grew increasingly despondent with Gaitskell's insistence upon rigorous conditions before entry.

The CDS stated plainly, in its manifesto of October 1960, that 'we are convinced Europeans, certain that Britain's destinies are inextricably bound up with those of a resurgent and united Europe'. After Macmillan's announcement of the British application to join the Common Market the debate in the Party became less academic and by October 1962 it was the major political issue. During the fifteen months between the Prime Minister's announcement and the Brighton Conference, CDS, through its main organ *Campaign*, had launched a persistent operation which had as its central aim the commitment of the Party to an enthusiastic Common Market posture. During this period *Campaign* published no less than six leading articles in favour of Britain's entry and also a large number of quotations from leading figures in the Movement who had made statements sympathetic to their stand. By October 1962, having realised that Gaitskell was setting the foundations for opposition to Britain's entry, CDS for the first time openly criticised their erstwhile hero: 'If the leadership continues the process of pulling the Party into an outright anti-European position the result may be irreparable damage to Labour's future.'[1]

Although revisionists found themselves on opposing sides in the dispute the CDS was accurate in contending that a significant majority of them were enthusiastically in favour of British entry. In the PLP those MPs who could be classified as revisionists, and this does not include the majority of 'loyal' trade union MPs, divided roughly in the order of 75 per cent pro-Common Market and 25 per cent anti-Common-Market.

1. *Campaign*, 20 (Oct 1962).

Table 5. COMMON MARKET DIVISION

Pro-Common-Market		Anti-Common-Market	Undecided[1]
L. Abse	C. Grey*	G. Barnet*	J. Boydon*
W. Ainsley*	R. Gunter	W. Blyton*	J. Callaghan
A. Albu*	A. D. Houghton	T. Dalyell*	G. Chetwynd*
S. Allen	D. Howell*	H. Gaitskell	J. Cronin*
C. Bence*	S. Irving*	P. Gordon Walker	W. Hannan*
A. Bottomley	G. Jeger*	D. Healey	H. Hayman*
T. Bradley*	R. Jenkins*	D. Jay*	J. H. Hoy*
J. Bray	C. Johnson	H. Marquand	H. Hughes*
G. Brown	H. King*	F. Peart	J. McCann*
D. Chapman*	E. L. Mallalieu*	M. Stewart	R. Prentice*
C. Crosland*	R. Mason*		G. Rogers*
G. de Freitas*	F. Mulley*		P. Wells*
J. Diamond*	R. Paget*		
D. Donnelly*	G. Reynolds*		
A. Fitch*	W. T. Rodgers*		
E. Fletcher*	J. Strachey		
D. Foot*	C. Strauss*		
M. Lloyd George (Lady)*	D. Taverne*		
D. Ginsburg*	A. Thompson		
	G. Thomson		

* Denotes declared supporters of CDS. It includes both MPs who signed the letter of support to CDS in March 1961 and leading figures in the organisation. Supporters in the Shadow Cabinet are not marked.

Table 5 illustrates this vast pro-Market preponderance among the parliamentary revisionists.[2]

In the PLP as a whole however the pro-Marketeers were not in a majority[3] and far fewer of those listed above carried their opposition to Gaitskell's policy into the open by signing a pro-Market motion placed on the order paper by Jenkins, Diamond and Mason.[4]

The main revisionist support for Gaitskell's highly negative

1. This list includes those revisionist MPs who it appears made no press statements on the issue or whose views were not as decided as those in the first two columns.

2. Information is gathered from speeches and articles in national and local newspapers, personal interviews and Labour Party Conference reports.

3. *The Times* (8 Mar 1963) suggests, in an analysis of the two groups, that the anti-Market group was larger than the pro-Market group.

4. The 'early-day' motion placed on the order paper on 7 Dec 1961, standing in the names of Jenkins, Diamond, Woodburn, Hynd and Mason, was signed by a further 23 MPs only.

approach to British entry, however, was to be found in the Shadow Cabinet. Gaitskell himself, together with Healey, Stewart, Gordon Walker and Callaghan, formed a powerful enough grouping and the addition of Wilson and Lee, both non-revisionists, ensured an adequate vote against those who wanted a more positive approach. Indeed, only Brown, Gunter and Houghton provided any opposition to the Gait-skell line from within the hierarchy of the PLP.

All the major trade unions, and most of the smaller ones,[1] were content to accept the Gaitskell position, based as it was upon the famous five conditions: no entry until safeguards are provided for Commonwealth Trade, Britain's EFTA partners, home agriculture, the freedom to plan the economy, and the freedom to pursue an independent foreign policy. Of the 'big 6' unions only the right-wing NUGMW stepped slightly out of line. It passed the following resolution:

> Congress believes that British membership of the European Economic Community could provide an opportunity for a mutually advantageous increase in trade between Britain and the rapidly expanding European market; that the ultimate removal of intra-European trade barriers on the widest possible scale would contribute to the progressive improvement of living standards and strengthen the economic, social and political ties between the peoples of Europe. . . . In addition it should increase the ability of the industrial nations to aid the less developed parts of the world.[2]

Although the motion, in later passages, made all the right noises about safeguards, its whole tenor and spirit was pro-Market. This was partially a result of the very strongly held pro-European views of the General Secretary, Jack Cooper, whose speech at Party Conference in 1962 was one of the most ardent defences of the pro-Market position.[3]

1. The Association of Supervisory Staffs, Executives and Technicians and the National Union of Tailors and Garment Workers were among those unions who carried their opposition to Gaitskell, from an anti-Market point of view, to a card vote. See *LPACR 1962*, p. 185 and p. 194.

2. *NUGMW Annual Congress Report 1962*, p. 370. The motion also contained passages which insisted upon safeguards for the Commonwealth, the EFTA countries, British agriculture and the right of Britain to plan her own economy. It was moved by the General Secretary, J. Cooper.

3. See *LPACR 1962*, p. 180.

Cooper was not the only example of a right-wing trade union leader, with previous revisionist and CDS connections, who felt strongly on the subject. Bill Carron, President of the AEU, was also an enthusiast for British membership of the Common Market and he maintained his position both at Party Conference and in his own union.[1] Watson, of the Miners, and Birch, General Secretary of USDAW, also shared this view.[2]

As the issue of Britain's entry into the Common Market never required an immediate decision, because of the breakdown of negotiations at governmental level, the strength of feeling in the Party was never adequately tested. There is little doubt, however, that the majority of revisionists, including those in the trade unions who had associated themselves in the past with revisionism, were disappointed at the lack of enthusiasm towards Europe contained in official policy. Many of them thought that Hugh Gaitskell had let them down on a crucial revisionist aspiration.

The Arguments For and Against Entry

Until the emergence of the Common Market as a major political event revisionists had found themselves united on virtually all the practical policy decisions that had faced the Party both as a government and as an opposition since the war. How was it that their agreement on first principles led them to take differing positions when confronted with this practical issue?

Perhaps an adequate answer to this question can be found in the nature of the dispute itself. The Common Market debate was not based upon ideological differences; although many of the left-wing arguments contained ideological elements. The underlying issues of the political debates of the 1950s – NATO, nuclear weapons, attitudes to the foreign policies of the United States of America and the Soviet Union – were not involved in the same degree in the controversy of 1962. Gaitskell himself had always maintained that the arguments for and against Britain's entry were evenly balanced and that a decision

1. See *LPACR 1962*, p. 174; and *Campaign*, 8 (Aug/Sep 1961).
2. *Campaign*, 8 and 11 (Aug/Sep 1961 and Dec 1961).

should be taken only after a careful and pragmatic 'weighing' of the political and economic factors involved. Also, much of the argument, at least among the Gaitskellites, was carried out on the level of a sophisticated economic analysis of the likely effects of British entry.

This was in keeping with the emphasis placed upon economic growth, efficiency and enterprise that had become an important part of the philosophy of revisionism – perhaps too important a part. This concern with economic growth was written into the original CDS manifesto:

> We do not believe our mixed economy to be in serious danger of sudden collapse or massive unemployment. But we resent its lack of enterprise and technical innovation; it is a disgrace that the rate of economic growth in Britain is now the slowest of any advanced industrial country.[1]

Britain's entry into the Common Market was seen, therefore, by many revisionists as being in keeping with this desire to promote efficiency, enterprise and more dynamism in the economy. Those revisionists who opposed Britain's entry, notably Douglas Jay, did not attempt to refute this argument by appealing to any question of principle but based their opposition on the practical grounds that a European protective barrier over imports of food and raw materials would severely damage the U.K's economy. Moreover, it was argued that, far from helping to create a competitive economy at home, entry would severely hinder the ability of British industry to compete at all in certain areas of its home market.[2]

Also the equality and social justice principles of revisionist-socialism were used by those Gaitskellites who opposed Britain's entry to buttress some of their arguments. Jay particularly was insistent that entry would lead to a more regressive tax system and he sustained this by giving examples of the percentage of revenue of the various Common Market countries that was collected from direct taxation.[3] Britain's right to control her

---

1. *A Manifesto*, para. 10.

2. See Jay's pamphlet *The Truth About the Common Market* (a Forward Britain Movement publication) (Aug 1962).

3. He cited the following figures for revenue coming from direct taxation: 47% of U.K., 24% of French, 26% of Italian, 29% of German. ('The Real Choice', in *New Statesman* (25 May 1962).)

own social services was another point made by the anti-Marketeers. In opposition to all this the pro-Market revisionists, instead of denying or devaluing the importance of this equality and social-justice principle, contended that although the direct-taxation point was undeniable, the Treaty of Rome provided for 'social harmonisation' in an upward direction. They also argued that pensions in Germany and family allowances in France were higher than in Britain.

Another revisionist value involved in the debate was internationalism. Indeed, the CDS thought that it would be a betrayal of this concept if Britain remained outside the EEC:

> The concept of socialism is incompatible with insularity. If we could only achieve our goals by cutting ourselves off from the world, there would be something wrong with the goals . . . an inward-looking re-orientation would encourage the conservative and not the progressive forces in Britain. Those who are most suspicious of foreigners are most nervous of change.[1]

The loss of sovereignty, whether economic or political, involved in a British signature to the Rome Treaty was seen by many on the Right of the Party as inherently good in itself as it furthered the concept of the outward-looking, extrovert Britain that they hoped to create. The anti-Marketeers, on the other hand, claimed to possess just as valuable internationalist credentials as the CDS and rejected the view that theirs was an insular attitude. Jay suggested that by joining 'the Six', far from widening and broadening her relations with the world, Britain would be taking the 'biggest step backwards towards protectionism in 100 years'.[2] More important than this view was the proposition by Denis Healey, another anti-Market revisionist, that those who argued for Britain's entry on sovereignty grounds were evading other vital questions. Healey argued that the important issue was not how Britain should settle her relations with Europe, but rather how she could best work for agreement between the U.S.S.R. and the U.S.A. on disarmament and arms control and also integrate the new nations into the international system.[3] As Healey saw it, the

---

1. *Campaign*, 18 (Jul 1962).   2. Jay, 'The Real Choice'.
3. D. Healey, 'Political Objections to British Entry into the Common Market', the *Observer* (25 May 1961).

question was not whether Britain should give up her sovereignty (for all socialists were in agreement that in long-run terms this was essential and desirable) but whether or not this European grouping was the right organisation to receive it. Concerning the prospects for peace and stability Healey considered that the crystallisation of the world into a few super states would not help as much as the proliferation of international groups. He suggested that Britain's joining the Common Market was undesirable, as it would help the former process at the expense of the latter.

Another aspect of revisionist philosophy involved in the debate was the power-political creed. Gaitskellites had always argued that politics was primarily the art of attaining, maintaining and using power. Pro-Marketeers developed this theme when they argued that Britain's interests would be severely damaged if she did not attempt to exert her influence in what was quickly becoming a new power-centre. Also it was suggested that Britain would be able to influence the future direction of the new Europe much better if she were inside the EEC rather than if she were isolated from it.[1] A genuine fear existed that if Britain remained outside of the Common Market she would become an economic and political 'backwater' and thereby lose her world role. Against this view it was propounded that British influence would cease altogether if she joined Europe for she would then be subject to overall control in foreign-policy decisions by 'the Six'. Gaitskell particularly was concerned with this:

> The second possibility is majority decisions on political issues, just as we are to have majority decisions on economic issues. Do we want that? Well, I suppose you might say we would be able somehow or other to outvote those we disagree with. I would like to be very sure of that before I committed myself.[2]

The final issue of principle that acted as a conditioning factor on the arguments within the Gaitskellite camp on the Common Market was the question of the democratic nature of the institutions involved in the EEC. Gaitskell, who admitted

---

1. This view was forcefully stated by Roy Jenkins at the Party Conference of 1962 (see *LPACR 1962*, p. 173); and also *Campaign*, 7 (Jul 1961).
2. *LPACR 1962*, pp. 158–9.

that the economic arguments were balanced fairly evenly, tended to concentrate mainly on the political objections. The question of the representative nature of Common Market institutions was one of his major preoccupations. He was particularly anxious about the powers of the Commission in the Constitution of the EEC, and the importance, in real terms, of the Assembly in dealing with it. This was a crucial point, based upon sound socialist-revisionist value-judgements, and the pro-Market revisionists either ignored it or fell back upon the contention that we should first of all join and then exert our influence to change those aspects that we felt to be undesirable.

These then were the value-judgements brought to bear upon the Common Market debate that raged upon the Right of the Labour Party. It shows that those who agree upon first principles can, and often do, come to totally separate conclusions on matters of policy.

Gaitskell broke politically with many of his friends on this issue. His opposition to the 1962 negotiations was both definite and complete. Some have attempted to suggest that he saw electoral popularity in a hostile attitude to the Common Market. How otherwise, they argue, could he part from his traditional internationalist political philosophy?

Perhaps it was simply a question of the generation gap. While his younger revisionist followers were impressed and excited by the modernisation and technological advance involved in European co-operation, Gaitskell, who had lived through two world wars, was intensely patriotic. His evocation of 'Vimy Ridge' and 'Gallipoli' in his famous speech at Brighton in 1962 was indeed somewhat out of character and it deeply shocked and wounded some of his younger supporters. Here was the strange spectacle of a modernising radical appealing to what many considered to be old-hat sentiment.

Yet Gaitskell's appeal to the British people lay precisely in this direction. He was indeed a moderniser but he rarely got carried away by fashionable and transient modish philosophies. He was careful to keep science, technology, economics and sociology firmly in their places as subordinate to politics and he recognised, and was able to give expression to, the true content of political life, human values and feelings.

His Brighton speech against Britain's entry into the Common Market, although depressing to many of his followers, was a supreme example of his ability to combine logic and emotion in a public performance. It established him as a national leader but at the same time did not cost him the comfort of the friendship of those who, on Europe, bitterly disagreed with him. Roy Jenkins writes: 'For the last few weeks of his active life we were back on terms of the closest friendship.'[1]

1. R. Jenkins in *Hugh Gaitskell*, ed. Rodgers, p. 131.

CHAPTER ELEVEN

The Modern, Revisionist Labour Party

HUGH GAITSKELL'S LEGACY

By the close of 1962 Gaitskell's ascendancy in the Party was complete. His personal victory over unilateralism at the 1961 Annual Conference had established him as a national leader endowed with the politically attractive qualities of courage and determination. His failure to change the Party's constitutional commitment to public ownership was either unknown or largely forgotten in the public mind and the Party as a whole was becoming increasingly identified with his particular brand of reformist, liberal social democracy.

The price of Gaitskell's victory was costly, however. A deep residue of bitterness remained against his policies and his particular style of Leadership. The Left remained suspicious of the new revisionist Labour Party that was emerging and were never totally reconciled to it; although the Common Market debate that raged during the summer and autumn of 1962 served partially to alleviate much of this distrust. Gaitskell's anti-Market speech at the Annual Conference at Brighton in 1962, his last major address, caused consternation among his supporters but was praised by the Left of the Party. The Brighton address, in one fell swoop, mended many of the Leader's broken fences with the Left. This was the first time in his career that Hugh Gaitskell had sided with the Left on a major policy issue and it also established him, in their eyes, as something more than a tool of a handful of revisionist intellectuals. The reaction to the speech by his revisionist friends, particularly Roy Jenkins and William Rodgers, reinforced the impression that a real break was imminent.

The Common Market issue, therefore, restored a good deal of the unity that had been shattered in the 1960–1 period. This new-found unity, together with Gaitskell's increased stature as an alternative Prime Minister, heightened Labour's popularity in the country. But his popularity was more a result of the Conservative Government's inadequacy than of changes in Labour's internal politics. The economic crisis of the summer of 1961 and the restrictive measures taken to cope with it began the long process of Conservative decline and punctured the myth of invulnerability surrounding Prime Minister Harold Macmillan. The drastic reorganisation of the Cabinet undertaken by Macmillan in July 1962 did not succeed in stopping the Conservative decline. Throughout 1962 the Conservatives suffered a disastrous series of by-election defeats and their Gallup Poll ratings, together with those of the Prime Minister, fell to an all-time low. It seemed almost inevitable that Labour would form the next Government and that Hugh Gaitskell would, at last, become Prime Minister of England.

Hugh Gaitskell died on 18 January 1963. In a sense, his death ended an era in British Labour politics. Together with Aneurin Bevan, who had died two and a half years earlier, he had been a prominent figure in British and European left-wing politics for almost two decades. More significantly, he had become the embodiment of an attitude and a philosophy. He had succeeded in merging political power and high principle in a way rarely seen in British politics and had inspired intense loyalty among his followers because of it. His name has been given to a school of political thinkers and to a group of political practitioners.

'The Gaitskellites' did not cease as an entity with his death and 'Gaitskellism' will continue to have a place while social democracy remains a force in political life. In immediate terms, perhaps, his greatest achievement was to prepare Labour for government and to give it clear and definite leadership during the long years in opposition. Gaitskell's actual skill as a party politician remains arguable and his ability as a national leader was never tested, yet his Leadership of the Party from 1956 until his death was an important factor in its return to office in 1964. The failure of the Conservatives, together with the skill of the new Labour Leader, Harold Wilson, were no doubt important also, but Labour's credibility as a responsible and non-doctrinaire alternative government in the election of 1964 rested largely upon Gaitskell's legacy.

An important element in this legacy to the Party was the re-establishment of parliamentarianism. The concept of Labour as a 'Movement' was roundly defeated under his Leadership and the Party was firmly wedded to a constitutional and electorally respectable path. It is highly doubtful that the Party would have strayed from the parliamentary road, but it was possible that it might have lapsed into an extremism from which it would have been hard to recover. The very vehemence of Gaitskell's constitutionalism put the issue beyond doubt.

Part of his legacy, too, was the eradication of even the last vestiges of doubt in the public mind about Labour's patriotism.

Since its inception Labour has been tainted with public suspicion about its commitment to British interests. This has not only been due to its neutralist, pacifist and nuclear-pacifist factions, but also to its socialist internationalism. Gaitskell, how-ever, managed to marry a firmly held commitment to inter-nationalism, in the form of support for the United Nations and collective security, to a deeply felt patriotism. His victory over the unilateralists assured the electorate, albeit in simple terms, that Labour was not going to leave the country 'defenceless and alone' and remarks in the Brighton speech of 1962 about Britain's 'thousand years of history' illustrated the simple and emotional nature of his patriotism. Gaitskell's leadership effectively destroyed the 'old bogy' of Zinoviev.

The establishment of Labour as both a constitutional and a patriotic party was an essential prerequisite for its success in the British political system; Gaitskell managed to achieve this in its final and irrevocable form. He re-established the Party as a responsible 'alternative government' in a period in which one such was desperately needed.

Constitutionalism, patriotism and responsible government was only one side of Gaitskell's legacy to the Party. The other was his liberal, social conscience, which formed the basis of his revisionist philosophy. His resentment of snobbery, class-consciousness, inefficiency and the lack of equal opportunity in British twentieth-century society appealed to many young middle-class voters and this appeal helped Labour. He gathered under Labour's wing the scientists, technologists, computer-programmers, teachers and other middle-class elements that were to help put Labour in power in 1964. Many of those sections of the community in business and the professions who felt their talents were ill-used and whose ambitions were frustrated by old-fashioned ideas and out of date structures were attracted to a Labour Party which they had previously shunned because of its dogma and class-consciousness.

Gaitskell's greatest achievement, however, did not lie solely in his appeal to middle-class, egalitarian aspirations. Neither did it lie in his more traditional constitutionalism and patriotism – for which there has always been much working-class support in Britain. Instead it lay in his ability to combine the two. He was certainly middle class in his upbringing and intellectual in his method but his deep emotional empathy with the working class and its conditions made him a far broader and richer person than the 'Hampstead intellectual' caricature given him by certain political commentators.

This dual appeal was Gaitskell's legacy. A legacy which both the Party and his successor as Leader would rely heavily upon in the pre-election atmosphere of 1963.

HAROLD WILSON AS LEADER

The battle for the succession, although softened by both the grave sense of loss felt throughout the Party and the need for unity before the impending General Election, displayed many of the personal and ideological characteristics of earlier times. The Party was basically still split three ways between the Right, the Centre and the Left and although the new Leader, whoever he was to be, would inevitably follow closely the lines laid down by Gaitskell, the various wings of the Party took up their positions almost as of old.

The contest did not develop into the straight 'Right–Left' battle that might have been predicted. The Party was aware that, with a General Election pending and a chance for office after thirteen years, the best man should be chosen with as little regard as was possible to old feuds and rivalries. It was obvious that the main contenders were to be Harold Wilson, the Shadow Foreign Secretary, and George Brown, the Deputy Leader.

Many MPs on the Right, both revisionists and trade unionists, were attracted to Brown because of his history of loyalty to Gaitskell, but, for personal reasons, found it difficult to give him their vote. Harold Wilson, on the other hand, was still distrusted by large sections of the Right both for his motives in standing against Gaitskell for the Leadership in 1961 and for what many considered his disguised left-wing views. For these MPs the candidacy of James Callaghan, then the Shadow Chancellor of the Exchequer, was attractive. He combined a flawless loyalty to Gaitskell (he was the only member of the Party's central Leadership who wholeheartedly supported the Leader at the Scarborough Conference of 1960) with an attractive political personality.

In order to win a candidate must achieve an absolute majority of the votes cast, and on the first ballot, announced on 7 February 1963, the figures were as follows: Wilson 115, Brown 88, Callaghan 41. The PLP rules for election of the Leader stipulate that if no candidate receives an absolute majority on the first ballot then the bottom man must retire from the contest, and accordingly the final ballot was between Brown and Wilson. It was apparent that Wilson, just short by 8 votes on the first ballot, would be the new Leader of the Party. On the second ballot, announced a week later, Wilson secured 144 votes to Brown's 103. Assuming that those who voted for the leading contenders on the first ballot remained with their original choice on the second, then Wilson gained the majority of Callaghan's original supporters. The final vote suggests that Wilson's appeal was much wider than simply to the Left. In fact, a majority of those who supported him on the second ballot were from the Right and Centre of the Party.

Brown's second ballot vote remained impressive, however, but was almost exclusively from one source – the right-wing trade union MPs. Most of the middle-class, revisionist intellectuals voted either for Wilson or Callaghan on the first ballot

I

and for Wilson on the second. Wilson's support was broader than Brown's not only in the negative sense that Brown was felt to be personally inadequate for the job but also because of qualities already manifest in the Shadow Foreign Secretary.

Wilson was the only serious contender who had previously held high office (President of the Board of Trade in the Attlee administration) and had Cabinet experience.[1] He was also a proven parliamentarian whose wit and bite in debate, particularly as Shadow Chancellor during the Selwyn Lloyd economic restrictions, had made him a formidable despatch-box figure. Wilson also possessed a power-base outside the PLP, as he was regularly voted high in the poll for the constituency section of the NEC. He had also been Chairman of the Party from 1961 to 1962. There was, perhaps, another element that accounted for Wilson's success; he had been formally educated to a high level. The three Leaders of the Labour Party since the war had all gone to Oxford, as had every post-war British Prime Minister with the exception of Sir Winston Churchill. It was perhaps this factor, not important in itself, that gave Wilson the extra dimension of intellectual polish that Brown lacked.

The division of the right-wing vote between Brown and Callaghan on the first ballot was crucial for Wilson. Had Callaghan been the sole contender against Wilson on the first ballot the outcome might have been different. In the eyes of many right-wing MPs Callaghan possessed the personal qualities which Brown lacked. His considerable 'shadow' experience, together with his polished parliamentary manner, would have made him a formidable focus of right-wing opposition to Wilson and could have united both the trade union MPs, released from their commitment to Brown, and the younger middle-class revisionist intellectuals. This would have been an unstoppable combination, indeed one which has traditionally been the basis of power in the PLP since the war. Whether this coalition was split by Wilson's skill and moderation in the weeks following Gaitskell's death or simply by Brown's candidacy remains a matter for speculation.

Wilson's election as Leader of the Labour Party in 1963

1. Wilson had been the youngest member of the Cabinet since Pitt the Younger.

was a turning-point in the method and style of Labour Leadership, although the policy and 'image' of the Party remained the same. The modernisation of Labour that had begun under Gaitskell was both consolidated and expanded under Harold Wilson. He added the further dimension of science and technology to Labour's existing revisionism and elevated it into a major election plank in the Party's platform for the 1964 General Election.

The emergence of science as a serious political issue in the Labour Party dated from 1960. In that year Morgan Phillips, the General Secretary of the Labour Party, produced a blueprint of the framework for policy in the coming decade in which he stressed the relevance of the scientific revolution to modern social and political development. The debate on this document at the 1960 Scarborough Annual Conference, submerged at the time in the welter of publicity over unilateralism, illustrates Wilson's early commitment to science as an economic and electoral weapon. He stated quite bluntly: 'We have to appeal to the scientists'[1] and went on to wed science to socialism in the distinctive style that was later to be projected to the nation in the election campaign:

> This is our message for the 60's – a Socialist-inspired scientific and technological revolution releasing energy on an enormous scale and deployed not for the destruction of mankind but for enriching mankind beyond our wildest dreams.[2]

In the same Scarborough hall three years later Wilson, now Leader of the Party, elaborated his thesis in a major speech devoted solely to *Labour and the Scientific Revolution*, a policy document published by the NEC earlier in the year. As in his 1960 speech he continually alluded to the Soviet challenge in the field of science and technology and to the need for greater scientific research in industry. He advocated the setting-up of a separate Ministry of Science and the expansion of the National Research Development Council in order to promote state-sponsored research and consequently state-controlled industries. It was by this route that, in his words of 1960, 'Socialism must be harnessed to science and science to Socialism'.[3] Wilson's use

1. *LPACR 1960*, p. 151.   2. Ibid.   3. Ibid.

of the language and rhetoric of Socialism kept faith with the Party activists while his emphasis upon science continued the process of modernisation, with its consequent electoral appeal, initiated by Gaitskell.

It was this dual appeal both to his Party activists and to the middle ground of the electorate that made Wilson's leadership of the Party unique. The policy of the Party remained thoroughly revisionist, more so with the addition of science, but its leadership was from the Centre. Wilson's style was in marked contrast to that of Gaitskell. He avoided head-on clashes with any section of the Party and was content to balance forces and conciliate differences in a way that Gaitskell's political philosophy and temperament would never allow him to do. Gaitskell was a leader whereas Wilson was a party manager.

This contrast in the style and method of political leadership is especially interesting in the light of the two men's supposed internal political leanings. Gaitskell was a politician of the so-called Right, steeped in the parliamentary tradition of conciliation and compromise, yet at the same time wanting to give a firm, and sometimes stubborn, directional lead to his followers. On the other hand, Harold Wilson, a man of the so-called Left, saw political leadership from an inverse angle; as the art of the management of men and ideas. Henry Fairlie, with some truth, has suggested that 'for the student of politics, he [Harold Wilson] will for a long time remain a model of the complete politician, seeking and finding the point of contact between different ideas and attitudes, the common ground which makes government possible'.[1]

Wilson's first task as Leader was to bring the Left back into the fold from which he felt they had been excluded during the 'Gaitskell years'. In attempting this healing operation Wilson's history in the Party was an advantage. He had resigned with Bevan in 1951 and although he broke with the 'Bevanites' later he was never associated with the Gaitskellites in the controversies of the late fifties or early sixties. Indeed he had challenged Gaitskell for the Leadership in 1960 and was supported by the Left in the contest of 1963.

Even after his victory in 1963, and with the full glare of

1. H. Fairlie, *The Life of Politics* (1968) p. 27.

national publicity upon him, Wilson refused to ignore the needs of the Left. He continued to use the language and rhetoric of traditional socialism even though, in the process, he was modernising the Party and its policies and appealing to a wider electorate. Not once during his seven years as Leader did Gaitskell, when referring to Labour, use the term 'Socialist Party' in a public performance, whereas Wilson, on the other hand, was continually using this label. Also, Wilson refused to be defensive about Clause IV of the Party Constitution and on one memorable occasion in the House of Commons he interrupted a speech by Gerald Nabarro, the Conservative MP for Kidderminster, to declare that it remained the policy of the *whole* party.[1]

Another aspect of Wilson's style, as opposed to substance, that was appreciated by the Left was his refusal to become personally identified with any particular group in the Party. He had no personal clique of political friends around him and no political 'set' in which he confided. Apart from Richard Crossman, who had arranged his campaign for Leader in 1963, and George Wigg there was no particular grouping to which he owed allegiance. Consequently the left wing of the Party felt less isolated than it had been under Gaitskell's Leadership and was therefore less prone to wrecking tactics. Those crumbs of comfort that were thrown to the Left during Wilson's Leadership cost him very little in terms of popular support but further cemented a real unity the like of which had not been seen since 1945.

The coalition nature of the Labour Party, however, precludes its ever becoming monolithic and although the Campaign for Democratic Socialism was formally wound up following Wilson's election to the Leadership, the revisionist and Gaitskellite elements in the Party retained informal, personal contacts even after the structure of organisation was disbanded. However, a centralist or 'left of centre' Leader need never expect as much trouble from the revisionist and right wing of the Party as a 'right of centre' Leader can expect from the

1. Wilson said: 'I heard the Hon. Gentleman muttering something about Clause IV. I am glad he understands it because it is the position of the whole Party.' *Hansard* (18 Feb 1963) col. 106.

Left. The Right's instinctive loyalty and lack of rigid ideology precludes the sacrifice of unity for the sake of purity of principle. With consummate skill Wilson relied upon the loyalty of the Right when indulging in socialist rhetoric but used the Left's faith in his socialist past when modernising the Party. Unity, Wilson's lifelong ambition, was real and, for the foreseeable future, guaranteed.

THE MODERN, REVISIONIST LABOUR PARTY

Labour went into and won the General Election of 1964 as a united, progressive, modernising, energetic, reforming party. Its public image was that of a moderate revisionist social-democratic party; the type of party that Gaitskell and the revisionists had worked so hard to create.

Although the Party was led and unified by a centralist Leader the revisionist Gaitskellites had won the post-war battle for the soul of the Labour Party. The mark of this victory was the new image and appeal of the Party exemplified by the speeches of its leaders and particularly by the manifesto for the 1964 General Election, *The New Britain*. Unlike previous Labour propaganda appeals this manifesto did not attack the Conservatives for their private-enterprise philosophy or for the business interests that supported them, but rather for their fustiness, incompetence and out-of-date attitudes. Labour attempted to paint a picture of a weak, vacillating and inefficient Conservative Government – a government that had lost its will to govern.

The manifesto promised 'fresh and virile leadership', an overhaul of the machinery of government and a strengthening of Britain's conventional military position. In short the appeal was to strong, yet just, government.

Planning and social welfare, for many years revisionist tools for changing society, had pride of place in the mechanism whereby Labour would restructure the nation. The key to future expansion, which was to replace the 'stop-go' policies of the Conservatives, was to be planning. Labour had a plan for everything: a National Plan for the economy and economic growth, a plan for the regions, a plan for transport and a plan for tax reform. In its economic policy Labour was therefore thoroughly revisionist. Emphasis was put upon growth and planning, whereas public ownership, particularly old-fashioned 'Morrisonian nationalisation', was played down.

The radical and egalitarian elements in Labour's programme consisted largely of its proposals for social welfare. National Insurance benefits were to be raised, an incomes guarantee for the retired and for widows established and wage-related retirement, sickness and unemployment benefits introduced. These and other social-security provisions were to be paid for out of the fruits of a higher growth-rate and by taxation reforms. The most spectacular tax change proposed by the Party was a capital gains tax, an example of the revisionist redistributive theory that had been advocated in the late fifties and early sixties. Yet another feather in the revisionists' cap in the social-policy field was Labour's commitment to reorganise secondary education on comprehensive lines, a measure pioneered in the political field by Crosland in his work *The Future of Socialism.*

Labour's approach to British foreign policy in the 1964 General Election also kept faith with the traditional liberal sentiments of the Party. Emphasis was placed upon the 'war on want' and the ultimate aim of world government was restated within the context of greater support for the United Nations, 'the chosen instrument by which the world can move away from the anarchy of power politics towards the creation of a genuine world community and the rule of law'.[1] This, however, was an internationalism that did not involve an attack upon British national interest. Pacifist and neutralist sentiments were notably absent. All that had been decided in 1961! Consequently Sir Alec Douglas-Home's campaign against Labour's commitment to abolish the independent nuclear deterrent had little effect on the Party in electoral terms. It never got off the ground as an issue.

The Gaitskellite influence on the modernisation of Labour in the period leading up to the 1964 General Election cannot, however, be measured simply by the extent to which its ideas found their way into official documents and policy pronouncements, particularly election manifestos. More important than the

1. *The New Britain: The Labour Party's Manifesto for the 1964 General Election*, p. 22.

particulars of an election manifesto as a measure of revisionist success was the changed context of political debate and argument within the Movement. No longer did the political debate centre around the issue of public ownership and in particular nationalisation. The new thinking of the fifties had not only introduced novel methods of public ownership which made nationalisation seem almost Victorian in style, but also had shifted the ground for debate from *ownership* to *control* of the private sector. Furthermore, as we have seen, the whole question of public ownership became increasingly redundant with its supersession by controversies about economic growth and the application of science to industry. No longer did the debate revolve around futile 'Socialist versus Capitalist' controversies but instead became concerned with how best to manage and work the mixed economy and to use the new technology in the interests of social justice. Also, no longer was foreign policy dominated by 'NATO versus Neutralism' but rather by how to find a new role for Britain within the Western Alliance.

This changed context of political debate was not solely a function of Gaitskellite influence. The world was changing; new issues appeared and new problems had to be solved. The social and economic fabric of the nation itself was in flux, in part as a consequence of decisions taken decades earlier. The importance of revisionism lies in its successful attempt to focus the Party's attention upon these changes and consequently to produce policies relevant to them.

This change in policy and the context of political debate was important in itself; but just as integral to the modernisation of Labour was the reaffirmation by the Party of its fundamental attitude to itself and its role in the political process. Revisionists in general, and both Gaitskell and Wilson in particular, had helped in this process. They rooted the Party firmly in the ground of power rather than protest or affirmation. They were foremost in advocating that the prime function of political action was to gain power. This, together with the unquestioning acceptance of the parliamentary method, entailed steering a moderate course politically in order to gain the middle ground electorally. This attitude had far-reaching implications with regard to Party structure.

Revisionists were often seen as advocates of the devaluation of Annual Conference. Crossman expressed the commonly held view that:

> Broadly speaking, the right would like to see it [the Labour Party] follow the example of the German S.P.D., becoming an orthodox electoral machine, run by the politicians at Westminster and concerned solely to provide an alternative government.

This rather blunt interpretation of right-wing attitudes to the role of the Party and its internal decision-making process nevertheless contains elements of truth. Pressure for the devaluation of the Annual Conference has more often than not come from the revisionists and this culminated in Gaitskell's undoubted depreciation of the role of Conference in 1960. However, as the history of the period clearly illustrates, the question of intra-party sovereignty has often been used simply as a tool in the tactical battles between the various sections of the Party rather than as an issue of principle. Nevertheless, the Right has always been attracted to the idea of Labour as a political party in the traditional, constitutional sense rather than as a mass movement controlled and directed by the non-Parliamentarians of the Annual Conference. In short: sovereignty should reside at Westminster, not at the seaside. As a consequence of Gaitskell's Leadership, moreover, this argument was largely resolved. R. T. McKenzie points out: 'The great defence dispute of 1960–1 seems to have carried the parliamentary leadership further than it had gone before in insisting that, even in opposition, it cannot be subject to external direction.'[1]

The modernisation of Labour in readiness for the 1964 General Election was not a smooth operation. The new policies, the emergence of a changed context of political debate and the reaffirmation of parliamentarianism were no easy victories. The forces arraigned against the revisionist Right were considerable and we may ask how it was that they were overcome.

A paramount reason for the strength of revisionism in the Labour Party is its secure and permanent place in Labour history. It has as important a claim to Labour's heritage as

---

1. McKenzie, *British Political Parties*, 2nd (revised) ed., p. 625.

does the revolutionary socialist Left. But, unlike the Left, its loyalty to the Leadership of the Party was never in question. It remained faithful, if not to socialist principles as defined by the Left, then at least to the return of a Labour Government and the continuance of moderate, electorally-orientated Leadership. It was this loyalty that forged the alliance between the Gaitskellite revisionists and the trade union leaders and MPs. Revisionists were less restricted in their political scope than the right-wing trade unionists but an identity of interest grew up between them to ensure that Labour remained a powerful parliamentary force. The Left, on the other hand, was divided, confused and often ambiguous in its policy proposals while working within a parliamentary system that demanded responsiveness to the electorate. In fact, the more removed it became from the public the more integrated became its philosophy. Socialist abstractions never seemed relevant to the 'cut and thrust' of political life in the country; only in the partially empty committee rooms of the constituency parties did they have any meaning.

Therefore, as long as Labour remained a parliamentary force revisionism would inevitably play a more important role in the Party than would the Left.

Another factor that contributed to revisionist success was the virtual monopoly that it possessed in the field of detailed policy-thinking. The distrust of the revisionists for generalised dogma was a product of a training that many of them had acquired in detailed examination of political, social and economic issues. In contrast the 'Bevanite' Left and its heirs showed little or no interest in the complexities of taxation, welfare, defence or economic management, but rather were concerned with, and excited by, polemical discourses. The field was left to the Gaitskellites; consequently they became the sole politically-based experts upon a large range of subjects and thereby exerted an immense influence upon policy. Jay (taxation), Healey and Mayhew (defence) and Crosland (public ownership) are good examples of this process.

Revisionists also had the edge over the 'Bevanites' and the Left in terms of unity and leadership. The Labour Left was never united by an idea. There were deep ideological and philosophical divisions among them and although they would often form a common front to defend or advocate specifics their eclecticism would, in the end, always divide them; *Socialist Commentary*'s internal battles were nothing as compared with those of *Tribune*. With the revisionists it was the other way round. There was a unanimity of aims, attitudes and ultimates which provided a coherency that could transcend the particularised divisions that occurred from time to time and even surmount the dramatic cleavage of the Common Market debate.

Perhaps the greatest single factor, however, in the revisionists' post-war success was Hugh Gaitskell's Leadership. It was determined, and possessed certain well-defined political goals. The Left, on the other hand, was handicapped by Bevan's capitulation to Gaitskell in 1957 which left it leaderless in Parliament. Even before his desertion of the Left Bevan did not provide coherent leadership; he continually vacillated from one position to another and his credibility as a responsible leader was damaged by his two resignations and the confusion following them as to his motives for leaving. Bevan's failure was perhaps but an aspect of the general difficulty of left-wing leadership in Parliament. The maintenance of an integrated left-wing political posture among the pressures of parliamentary life is an almost impossible task. It was easier for Gaitskell, as it had always been part of his philosophy that Parliament, and the public opinion that it represented, would have to be catered for in policy-formation. This left him with fewer contradictions to resolve than Bevan, who, after all, was the self-styled protector of traditional socialism, a product for which there was much sales resistance among the general public in the fifties.

The defeat of the 'Bevanite' attempt to take over the Labour Party is considerable testimony to the influence of revisionism, but it would be a misreading of events to conclude that the period from 1951 to 1964 produced the type of change that overtook the Social Democratic Party (SPD) in the Federal Republic of Germany during the same period. The SPD underwent a significant political revolution in which not only was public ownership totally expunged from the Party platform but a decisive break was made with its traditional Marxist philosophical base. The British Labour Party, and indeed British Socialism, never owed as much to Marxism as did the SPD and therefore revisionism was accepted without the violent upheaval that it caused in its German sister party. Also, the Labour Party historically, unlike the SPD, has been moderate in its 'day to day' political demands. In 1945, with perhaps its most extremist policy programme, the Party was elected on a radical, but nevertheless empirical, programme of reform. A reading of *Let Us Face the Future*, the Labour Party's manifesto for the 1945 election, will confirm that all the nationalisation proposals outlined in the document were justified separately according to the conditions prevailing in each industry at the time and not by recourse to any socialist doctrine. When the Party left office in 1951 its policy was even more moderate in attitude and in many respects identical to that of the Conservatives. Indeed, at no time, save perhaps in 1960, during its thirteen years in opposition did the Party adopt an extremist position on any major political issue. The Leadership were anxious at all times to present to the electorate an image of the Party as the responsible alternative government of the nation. This moderate leadership was supported by the PLP and, again with only one major exception, by the Annual Conference of the Party.

Nevertheless, it is sometimes argued that the years in opposition saw Labour lapse into extremism and that it only achieved power again 'because the suppression of the extremists has brought it back once more, and unquestionably, into the mainstream of British politics'.[1] The extremists were certainly suppressed, but it is doubtful whether the Party ever left the 'mainstream' of British politics unless a narrow definition of 'mainstream', meaning loss of office, is adopted. The Party's vote at every General Election during its opposition years never fell below 43 per cent of the total voting electorate, and its representation in the House of Commons was always above 250. Labour's problem was not that it lapsed into extremism and left the 'mainstream' of British politics but that it lost the middle-ground electorally – a very different malaise.

1. *Political Quarterly* (Jul–Sep 1963) p. 371.

It lost office, and failed to regain it until 1964, not because it adopted extreme policies but because of incompetent economic management before 1951 and successful Conservative economic manipulation thereafter.

The history of the period 1951–64 is therefore the history of the successful attempt of the moderates to keep the Party a temperate, and thereby a viable, electoral force. In a sense it was an exercise in political education. Slowly but definitely the revisionists persuaded the bulk of the Party to adapt itself to the changing political, social and economic situation of post-war Britain. This process, though leaving intact the theoretical and abstract commitment to socialism in the form of Clause IV of the Party Constitution, resulted in a thorough-going restatement of Labour's basic political position: that of a parliamentary, reformist, social-democratic party. This process was often painful and has been the underlying cause of fundamentalist resentment and frustration.

This emphasis upon changed situations and the consequent need for the Party to adjust to them illustrates the point that revisionism was not a *status-quo* philosophy. On the contrary, in order to ensure that Labour remained a political force changes would constantly have to be made and a continuing critical faculty exercised over both policy and doctrine. This was what made revisionism so resented in the Party. In the name of modernisation and moderation it challenged many of the old, conservative, traditional precepts of socialism. It was not simply an organ of sterile moderation, as, to an extent, was Morrisonianism. Instead, it was continually questioning and probing old and accepted dogmas and, more important, it produced a new, and what it considered a relevant, practical political philosophy.

APPENDIX I

The Constitution of the Labour Party

Clause I. – NAME.

The Labour Party.

Clause II. – MEMBERSHIP

(1) There shall be two classes of members, namely:
(*a*) Affiliated Members.
(*b*) Individual Members.
(2) Affiliated Members shall consist of:
(*a*) Trade Unions affiliated to the Trades Union Congress or recognised by the General Council of the Trades Union Congress as *bona fide* Trade Unions.
(*b*) Co-operative Societies.
(*c*) Socialist Societies.
(*d*) Professional organisations which, in the opinion of the National Executive Committee, have interests consistent with those of other affiliated organisations.
(*e*) Constituency Labour Parties and Central Labour Parties in Divided Boroughs.
(*f*) County or Area Federations of Constituency Labour Parties, hereinafter referred to as Federations.
(3) Political organisations not affiliated to or associated under a National Agreement with the Party on 1 January 1946, having their own Programme, Principles and Policy for distinctive and separate propaganda, or possessing Branches in the Constituencies or engaged in the promotion of Parliamentary or Local Government Candidatures, or owing allegiance to

any political organisation situated abroad, shall be ineligible for affiliation to the Party.

(4) Individual Members shall be persons of not less than fifteen years of age who subscribe to the conditions of membership, provided they are not members of Political Parties or organisations ancillary or subsidiary thereto declared by the Annual Conference of the Labour Party (hereinafter referred to as 'the Party') or by the National Executive Committee in pursuance of Conference decisions to be ineligible for affiliation to the Party.

(5) British citizens temporarily resident abroad may become Individual Members, or retain such membership of the Party, by enrolment with the Head Office provided they accept the conditions of membership in Clause III.

Clause III. – CONDITIONS OF MEMBERSHIP

(1) Each affiliated organisation must:

(*a*) Accept the Programme, Principles and Policy of the Party.

(*b*) Agree to conform to the Constitution and Standing Orders of the Party.

(*c*) Submit its Political Rules to the National Executive Committee.

(2) Each Constituency Labour Party, Central Labour Party, and Federation must, in addition to the conditions mentioned in Section 1 of this Clause, adopt the Rules laid down by the Party Conference.

(3) Each Individual Member must:

(*a*) Accept and conform to the Constitution, Programme, Principles and Policy of the Party.

(*b*) If eligible, be a member of a Trade Union affiliated to the Trades Union Congress or recognised by the General Council of the Trades Union Congress as a *bona fide* Trade Union.

(*c*) Unless temporarily resident abroad, be a member of a Constituency Labour Party, either (*i*) where he or she resides, or (*ii*) where he or she is registered as a Parliamentary or Local Government elector.

Clause IV. – PARTY OBJECTS[1]

NATIONAL

(1) To organise and maintain in Parliament and in the country a Political Labour Party.

(2) To co-operate with the General Council of the Trades Union Congress, or other Kindred Organisations, in joint political or other action in harmony with the Party Constitution and Standing Orders.

(3) To give effect as far as may be practicable to the principles from time to time approved by the Party Conference.

(4) To secure for the workers by hand or by brain the full fruits of their industry and the most equitable distribution thereof that may be possible upon the basis of the common ownership of the means of production, distribution, and exchange, and the best obtainable system of popular administration and control of each industry or service.[2]

(5) Generally to promote the Political, Social and Economic Emancipation of the People, and more particularly of those who depend directly upon their own exertions by hand or by brain for the means of life.

INTER-COMMONWEALTH

(6) To co-operate with the Labour and Socialist organisations in the Commonwealth Overseas with a view to promoting the purposes of the Party, and to take common action for the promotion of a higher standard of social and economic life for the working population of the respective countries.

INTERNATIONAL

(7) To co-operate with the Labour and Socialist organisations in other countries and to support the United Nations Organisation and its various agencies and other international organisations for the promotion of peace, the adjustment and settlement of international disputes by conciliation or judicial arbitration, the establishment and defence of human rights, and the improvement of the social and economic standards and conditions of work of the people of the world.

1 See also Appendix II for an amplification of Party objects.
2 This sub-section is often referred to simply as Clause IV.

Clause V. – PARTY PROGRAMME

(1) The Party Conference shall decide from time to time what specific proposals of legislative, financial or administrative reform shall be included in the Party Programme. No proposal shall be included in the Party Programme unless it has been adopted by the Party Conference by a majority of not less than two-thirds of the votes recorded on a card vote.

(2) The National Executive Committee and the Parliamentary Committee of the Parliamentary Labour Party shall decide which items from the Party Programme shall be included in the Manifesto which shall be issued by the National Executive Committee prior to every General Election. The Joint Meeting of the two Committees shall also define the attitude of the Party to the principal issues raised by the Election which are not covered by the Manifesto.

Clause VI. – THE PARTY CONFERENCE

(1) The work of the Party shall be under the direction and control of the Party Conference, which shall itself be subject to the Constitution and Standing Orders of the Party. The Party Conference shall meet regularly once in every year and also at such other times as it may be convened by the National Executive Committee.

(2) The Party Conference shall be constituted as follows:

(*a*) Delegates duly appointed by each affiliated Trade Union or other organisations to the number of one delegate for each 5,000 members or part thereof on whom affiliation fees and by-election insurance premiums were paid for the year ending 31 December preceding the Conference.

(*b*) Delegates duly appointed by Constituency Labour Parties (or Trades Councils acting as such) to the number of one delegate for each 5,000 individual members or part thereof on whom affiliation fees and by-election insurance premiums were paid for the year ending 31 December preceding the Conference; where the individual and affiliated women's membership exceeds 2,500 an additional woman delegate may

K

be appointed; where the membership of Young Socialist Branches within a constituency is 200 or more an additional Young Socialist delegate may be appointed.

(c) Delegates duly appointed by Central Labour Parties or Trades Councils acting as such in Divided Boroughs not exceeding one for each Central Labour Party provided the affiliation fees and by-election insurance premiums have been paid for the year ending 31 December preceding the Conference.

(d) Delegates duly appointed by Federations not exceeding one for each Federation provided the affiliation fees have been paid for the year ending 31 December preceding the Conference.

(e) *Ex officio* Members of the Party Conference as follows:

(i) Members of the National Executive Committee.

(ii) Members of the Parliamentary Labour Party.

(iii) Parliamentary Labour Candidates whose candidatures have been duly endorsed by the National Executive Committee.

(iv) The Secretary of the Party.

Ex officio Members shall have no voting power.

(f) Any special Party Conference shall be called on the same basis of representation as that upon which the last Annual Party Conference was convened.

(3) In the event of a duly appointed delegate being elected as Treasurer or as a member of the National Executive Committee, the Affiliated Organisation responsible for his or her appointment as a delegate may claim authority at subsequent Party Conferences during his or her period of Office, to appoint a delegate additional to the number applicable to it under paras. (a), (b) and (c) of Section 2 of this Clause, provided the delegate elected as Treasurer or as a member of the National Executive Committee:

(i) Remains qualified to be appointed as a delegate under Clause VII; and

(ii) Continues to be duly appointed as a delegate by the Affiliated Organisation claiming authority to appoint an additional delegate within the provisions of this Section.

Clause VII. – APPOINTMENT OF DELEGATES TO THE PARTY CONFERENCE

(1) Every Delegate must be an individual member of the Labour Party as described in Clause II, Section 4, except persons resident in Northern Ireland who are duly appointed Delegates of affiliated trade unions and who individually accept and conform to the Constitution, Programme, Principles and Policy of the Party.

(2) Delegates must be *bona fide* members or paid permanent officials of the organisation appointing them, except in the case of Members of the Parliamentary Labour Party or duly-endorsed Parliamentary Labour Candidates appointed to represent Constituencies in accordance with Section 4 of this Clause.

(3) Delegates appointed by Federations or Central Labour Parties must be resident within the area of the organisation concerned or be registered therein as Parliamentary or Local Government electors.

(4) Members of the Parliamentary Labour Party and duly-endorsed Parliamentary Labour Candidates may be appointed as Delegates by Constituency Labour Parties responsible for their candidatures; otherwise, Delegates appointed by Constituency Labour Parties must be resident in the Constituency appointing them, or registered as Parliamentary or Local Government electors therein.

(5) No person shall act as a Delegate for more than one organisation.

(6) No person shall act as a Delegate who does not pay the political levy of his or her Trade Union.

(7) Members of Parliament not members of the Parliamentary Labour Party are ineligible to act as Delegates.

(8) The following are also ineligible to act as Delegates:

(*a*) Persons acting as candidates or supporting candidates in opposition to duly-endorsed Labour Candidates.

(*b*) Persons who are members of political parties or organisations ancillary or subsidiary thereto declared by the Annual Party Conference or by the National Executive Committee in pursuance of the Conference decisions to be ineligible for affiliation to the Labour Party.

Clause VIII. – THE NATIONAL EXECUTIVE COMMITTEE

(1) There shall be a National Executive Committee of the Party consisting of 25 members and a Treasurer, elected by the Party Conference at its regular Annual Meeting in such proportion and under such conditions as may be set out in the Standing Orders for the time being in force. The Leader and Deputy Leader of the Parliamentary Labour Party shall be *ex officio* members of the National Executive Committee. The National Executive Committee shall, subject to the control and directions of the Party Conference, be the Administrative Authority of the Party.

(2) The duties and powers of the National Executive Committee shall include the following:

(*a*) To ensure the establishment of, and to keep in active operation, a Constituency Labour Party in every Constituency, a Central Labour Party in every Divided Borough and a Federation in every suitable area, in accordance with the Rules laid down by the Party Conference for the purpose.

(*b*) To enforce the Constitution, Standing Orders, and Rules of the Party and to take any action it deems necessary for such purpose, whether by way of disaffiliation of an organisation or expulsion of an individual, or otherwise. Any such action shall be reported to the next Annual Conference of the Party.

(*c*) To confer with the Parliamentary Labour Party at the opening of each Parliamentary Session, and at any other time when it or the Parliamentary Party may desire a conference on any matters relating to the work and progress of the Party.

(*d*) To see that all its Officers and members conform to the Constitution, Rules and Standing Orders of the Party.

(*e*) To present to the Annual Party Conference a Report covering the work and progress of the Party during its period of office, together with a Financial Statement and Accounts duly audited. The Report, Financial Statement and Accounts shall be sent to affiliated organisations at least two clear weeks before the opening of the Annual Party Conference.

(*f*) To propose to the Annual Party Conference such

amendments to the Constitution, Rules and Standing Orders as may be deemed desirable and to submit to the Annual Party Conference or to any Special Party Conference, called in accordance with the Standing Orders, such resolutions and declarations affecting the Programme, Principles and Policy of the Party as in its view may be necessitated by political circumstances.

(g) To organise and maintain such fund or funds as may be thought necessary for any or all of the objects for which the Party exists, including a fund to finance Parliamentary by-elections and a fund established for the purpose of insuring against the forfeiture of Returning Officers' Deposits at every Parliamentary General Election.

(h) To secure advances from time to time or to raise loans, either on mortgage or otherwise and on such terms as it may deem expedient; to employ any part of the funds at its disposal in the purchase of any freehold or leasehold building or site and/or in the building, leasing holding or rental of any premises and in the fitting-up and maintenance thereof; and to invest any moneys not immediately required in such securities as it may deem proper and to realise or to vary such investments from time to time and to appoint Trustees and/or form a Society, Association, Company or Companies in accordance with the provisions of the Friendly Societies Acts or the Companies Acts for any or all of the above purposes and to define the powers of such Trustees, Society, Association, Company or Companies and the manner in which such powers shall be exercised.

(i) To sanction, where local circumstances render it necessary, modifications in the rules laid down by the Annual Party Conference for the various classes of Party Organisations in the Constituencies and Regions, provided that such modifications comply with the spirit and intention of the Annual Party Conference and do not alter the objects, basis or conditions of affiliated and individual membership, vary the procedure for the selection of Parliamentary Candidates (except as provided in the rules) or effect a change in the relationship of Central Labour Parties or Constituency Labour Parties with the Labour Party.

(3) The decision of the National Executive Committee, subject to any modification by the Party Conference, as to the meaning and effect of any rule or any part of this Constitution and Standing Orders, shall be final.

(4) The National Executive Committee shall have power to adjudicate in disputes that may arise between affiliated and other Party organisations, and in disputes which occur within the Party's Regional, Federation, or Constituency machinery, and its decisions shall be binding on all organisations concerned.

Clause IX. – PARLIAMENTARY CANDIDATURES

(1) The National Executive Committee shall co-operate with the Constituency Labour Party for each Constituency in selecting a Labour Candidate for any Parliamentary Election.

(2) The selection of Labour Candidates for Parliamentary Elections shall be made in accordance with the procedure laid down by the Annual Party Conference in the Rules which apply to Constituency and Central Labour Parties.

(3) The selection of Labour Candidates for Parliamentary Elections shall not be regarded as completed until the name of the person selected has been placed before a meeting of the National Executive Committee, and his or her selection has been duly endorsed.

(4) No Parliamentary candidature shall be endorsed until the National Executive Committee has received an undertaking by one of its affiliated organisations (or is otherwise satisfied) that the election expenses of the Candidate are guaranteed.

(5) Labour Candidates for Parliamentary Elections duly endorsed by the National Executive Committee shall appear before the electors under the designation of 'Labour Candidate' only. At any Parliamentary General Election they shall include in their Election Addresses and give prominence in their campaigns to the issues for that Election as defined by the National Executive Committee in its Manifesto.

(6) At a Parliamentary By-Election a duly-endorsed Labour Candidate shall submit his or her Election Address to the National Executive Committee for approval. The National

Executive Committee, whenever it considers it necessary shall give advice and guidance on any special issue to be raised, or in the conduct of the Campaign during such By-Election.

(7) No person may be selected as a Parliamentary Labour Candidate by a Constituency Labour Party, and no Candidate may be endorsed by the National Executive Committee, if the person concerned:

(a) is not an Individual Member of the Party and, if eligible, is not a member of a Trade Union affiliated to the Trades Union Congress or recognised by the General Council of the Trades Union Congress as a *bona fide* Trade Union; or

(b) is a member of a Political Party or organisation ancillary or subsidiary thereto declared by the Annual Party Conference or by the National Executive Committee in pursuance of Conference decisions to be ineligible for affiliation to the Labour Party; or

(c) does not accept and conform to the Constitution, Programme, Principles and Policy of the Party; or

(d) does not undertake to accept and act in harmony with the Standing Orders of the Parliamentary Labour Party.

(8) Any Candidate who, after election, fails to accept or act in harmony with the Standing Orders of the Parliamentary Labour Party shall be considered to have violated the terms of this Constitution.

Clause X. – AFFILIATION AND MEMBERSHIP FEES

(1) Each affiliated organisation (other than Federations, Constituency and Central Labour Parties) shall pay an affiliation fee of 1s. per member per annum to the Party.

(2) Each Constituency Labour Party shall pay an affiliation fee of 1s. per annum on each individual member attached to the Party directly or indirectly through its local Labour Parties, Polling District Committees, Ward Committees and Women's Sections, subject to a minimum payment of £50 per annum.

(3) Each Central Labour Party shall pay an affiliation fee at the rate of £5 per annum for each Constituency Labour Party within the Divided Borough.

(4) Each County Federation shall pay affiliation fees in accordance with the following scale:

						Per annum
Federations of 2, 3 or 4 Constituency or C.L.P.						£1 10s.
„	„	5 or 6	„	„	„	£2 5s.
„	„	7, 8 or 9	„	„	„	£3
„	„	10, 11, 12 or 13 „	„	„	£4 10s.
„	„	over 13	„	„	„	£6 15s.

(5) Each Individual Member of the Party shall pay a minimum membership fee of 1s. monthly to the Party to which he or she is attached in the manner laid down in Constituency and Local Labour Party Rules except Old Age Pensioners who have retired from work and they shall be allowed Individual Membership of the Party on the minimum payment of 1s. per annum. These contributions shall be entered on membership cards supplied by the National Executive Committee to Constituency Parties at 1s. per card, which sum shall include the affiliation fee payable by such organisation to the Party in respect of such members.

Clause XI. – PARTY CONFERENCE ARRANGEMENTS COMMITTEE

(1) There shall be appointed in accordance with the Standing Orders at each Annual Party Conference a Party Conference Arrangements Committee of Five Delegates for the Annual Party Conference in the year succeeding its appointment, or for any Party Conference called during the intervening period. A member of the Head Office staff shall act as Secretary to the Committee.

(2) The duties of the Party Conference Arrangements Committee shall be:

(a) To arrange the order of the Party Conference Agenda.

(b) To act as a Standing Orders Committee.

(c) To appoint Scrutineers and Tellers for the Annual Party Conference from among the Delegates whose names have been received at the Head Office of the Party two clear weeks prior to the opening of the Conference and submit them for approval to the Conference. In the case of a Special Party

Conference called under Clause VI, the National Executive Committee may appoint a date prior to which such names must be received.

Clause XII. – AUDITORS

There shall be appointed in accordance with the Standing Orders at each Annual Party Conference two Delegates to act as Auditors of the Party Accounts to be submitted at the Annual Party Conference next succeeding that at which they are appointed.

Clause XIII. – ALTERATION TO CONSTITUTION AND RULES

The existing Constitution and Rules or any part thereof, may be amended, rescinded, altered or additions made thereto, by Resolution, carried on a card vote at an Annual Party Conference (in manner provided in the Standing Orders appended hereto) held in every third year following the year 1956, unless the National Executive Committee advises that amendments shall be specially considered at any Annual Party Conference. Notice of Resolutions embodying any such proposals must be sent in writing to the Secretary at the Offices of the Party as provided in Standing Orders.

Clause XIV. – STANDING ORDERS

The Standing Orders of the Party Conference shall be considered for all purposes as if they form part of this Constitution and shall have effect accordingly. New Standing Orders may be made when required, or the existing Standing Orders amended, rescinded or altered by Resolution in the same manner as provided for alterations in the Constitution itself.

*

APPENDIX II

An Amplification of Labour's Aims

The following statement adopted in 1960 reaffirms, amplifies and clarifies Party Objects in the light of post-war developments and the historic achievements of the first majority Labour Government [i.e. the Constitution remained intact but the following was added].

The British Labour Party is a democratic socialist party. Its central ideal is the brotherhood of man. Its purpose is to make this ideal a reality everywhere.

Accordingly:

(a) It rejects discrimination on grounds of race, colour or creed and holds that men should accord to one another equal consideration and status in recognition of the fundamental dignity of Man.

(b) Believing that no nation, whatever its size or power, is justified in dictating to or ruling over other countries against their will, it stands for the right of all peoples to freedom, independence and self-government.

(c) Recognising that international anarchy and the struggle for power between nations must lead to universal destruction, it seeks to build a world order within which all will live in peace. To this end it is pledged to respect the United Nations Charter, to renounce the use of armed force except in self-defence and to work unceasingly for world disarmament, the abolition of all nuclear weapons and the peaceful settlement of international disputes.

(d) Rejecting the economic exploitation of one country by another, it affirms the duty of richer nations to assist

poorer nations and to do all in their power to abolish
poverty throughout the world.

(e) It stands for social justice, for a society in which the
claims of those in hardship or distress come first; where
the wealth produced by all is fairly shared among all;
where differences in rewards depend not upon birth or
inheritance but on the effort, skill and creative energy
contributed to the common good; and where equal
opportunities exist for all to live a full and varied
life.

(f) Regarding the pursuit of material wealth by and for
itself as empty and barren, it rejects the selfish, acquisitive doctrines of capitalism, and strives to create instead
a socialist community based on fellowship, co-operation
and service in which all can share fully in our cultural
heritage.

(g) Its aim is a classless society from which all class barriers
and false social values have been eliminated.

(h) It holds that to ensure full employment, rising production, stable prices and steadily advancing living standards the nation's economy should be planned and all
concentrations of power subordinated to the interests of
the community as a whole.

(i) It stands for democracy in industry, and for the right of
workers both in the public and private sectors to full
consultation in all the vital decisions of management,
especially those affecting conditions of work.

(j) It is convinced that these social and economic objectives
can be achieved only through an expansion of common
ownership substantial enough to give the community
power over the commanding heights of the economy.
Common ownership takes varying forms, including
state-owned industries and firms, producer and consumer co-operation, municipal ownership and public
participation in private concerns. Recognising that both
public and private enterprise have a place in the economy,
it believes that further extension of common ownership
should be decided from time to time in the light of these
objectives and according to circumstances, with due

regard for the views of the workers and consumers concerned.

(k) It stands for the happiness and freedom of the individual against the glorification of the state – for the protection of workers, consumers and all citizens against any exercise of arbitrary power, whether by the state, by private or by public authorities, and it will resist all forms of collective prejudice and intolerance.

(l) As a democratic Party believing that there is no true Socialism without political freedom, it seeks to obtain and to hold power only through free democratic institutions whose existence it has resolved always to strengthen and defend against all threats from any quarter.

At its meeting on 13 July 1960 the National Executive Committee passed the following:

The National Executive Committee resolves not to proceed with any amendment or addition to Clause IV of the Constitution, but declares that the statement which it adopted on 16 March is a valuable expression of the aims of the Labour Party in the second half of the twentieth century and commends it to the Conference accordingly.

Bibliography

PRIMARY SOURCES

A. *Interviews*

The following granted me formal interviews:

Dr Rita Hinden (Editor of *Socialist Commentary*) on 28 Feb, 12 and 19 Mar 1964 at *Socialist Commentary* offices.

Douglas Jay MP on 1 Oct 1964 at Battersea Labour Party offices.

Roy Jenkins MP on 12 Feb 1964 at the House of Commons.

William T. Rodgers MP on 21 Jan 1964 at the House of Commons.

Dick Taverne MP on 13 Apr 1965 at the House of Commons.

Brian Walden MP on 22 Mar 1965 at the House of Commons.

I have also had the benefit, while still an undergraduate, of informal talks regarding the subject with the *Rt Hon. Hugh Gaitskell* (Leader of the Labour Party).

B. *Unpublished Private Papers*

The Dalton Manuscript Diaries 1945–61 (deposited in the British Library of Political and Economic Science). Certain extracts are published in H. Dalton, *High Tide and After* (1962).

C. *Documents*

(*a*) *Hansard* (Parliamentary Debates)
(*b*) Labour Party
Policy Documents

Labour Believes in Britain (1949).
Labour and the New Society (1950).
Facing the Facts (1952).
Challenge to Britain (1953).
In Defence of Europe (1954).
Towards Equality: Labour's policy for social justice (1956).
Homes for the Future (1956).
Industry and Society (1957).
Public Enterprise: Labour's review of the nationalised industries (1957).

Disarmament and Nuclear War – The Next Step (1959).
Labour in the Sixties (1960).
Policy for Peace (1961).
Signposts for the Sixties (1961).
Labour and the Common Market (1962).
Labour and the Scientific Revolution (1963).
Manifestos
Let Us Face the Future (1945).
Forward with Labour (1955).
Britain Belongs to You! (1959).
Let's Go with Labour for the New Britain (1964).

Annual Conference *Reports*
Margate 1950, Scarborough 1951, Morecambe 1952, Margate
    1953, Scarborough 1954, Margate 1955, Blackpool 1956,
    Brighton 1957, Scarborough 1958, Blackpool 1959, Scar-
    borough 1960, Blackpool 1961, Brighton 1962, Scarborough
    1963, Brighton 1964.

Reports of the National Executive Committee
    1950–64. Incorporated in the Reports of Annual Conference.

National Executive Committee Pamphlets
Davies, E. *Problems of Public Ownership* (1952).
Healey, D. *Cards on the Table* (1947).
Labour's Aims (1960).

(*c*) Trade Union Congress

Annual Congress *Reports* 1950–64.
General Council *Reports* 1950–64 (incorporated in Annual Con-
    gress *Reports*).

(*d*) Individual Trade Unions

Amalgamated Engineering Union: *Amalgamated Engineering Union
    Journal* (monthly, 1945 to date).
National Union of General and Municipal Workers: *General and
    Municipal Workers Journal* 1945–58; and *Report of Congress*
    1958–64.
National Union of Mineworkers: *Information Bulletin* 1946–Jul/Aug
    1964 – ceased publication.
National Union of Railwaymen: *General Secretary's Report to the
    Annual General Meeting* 1945–64.
Transport and General Workers' Union: *Transport and General
    Workers' Record* 1945–64 (not published June 1957).

Union of Shop, Distributive and Allied Workers: *The Annual Report* 1957–64; and *Report of the Proceedings of the Annual Delegate Meeting* 1951–64.

D. *Private Newsletter*

Campaign. Issued by the Labour Manifesto Group to its key supporters. This was the publication of the Campaign for Democratic Socialism. First issued in January 1960. It ceased publication in September 1964.

E. *Social Surveys (Gallup Poll) Ltd*

Access was granted to certain published and unpublished material collected before 1960.
The Gallup Political Index 1960 ff.

F. *Major Works*

Bernstein, E. *The Suppositions of Socialism and Problems of Social Democracy* (Stuttgart, 1899).
— *Evolutionary Socialism: A Criticism and Affirmation* (1909).
Cripps, R. S. *Can Socialism Come by Constitutional Methods?* (1933).
— *Why This Socialism?* (1934).
— *The Struggle for Peace* (1936).
Crosland, C. A. R. *The Future of Socialism* (1956).
— *The Conservative Enemy* (1962).
Crossman, R. H. S. (ed.), *New Fabian Essays* (1952).
Dalton, H. *Inequality of Incomes in Modern Communities* (1920).
— *Practical Socialism for Britain* (1935).
Durbin, E. F. M. *The Politics of Democratic Socialism* (1940).
Fairlie, H. *The Life of Politics* (1968).
Gordon Walker, P. C. *Restatement of Liberty* (1951).
Jay, D. *The Socialist Case* (1937).
— *Socialism in the New Society* (1962).
Jenkins, R. *Pursuit of Progress* (1953).
Keynes, J. M. *The General Theory of Employment, Interest and Money* (1936).
Laski, H. J. *The State in Theory and Practice* (1936).
Powell, E. *A Nation Not Afraid: the thinking of Enoch Powell* (1965).
Socialist Union, *Socialism: A New Statement of Principles* (1952).
— *Socialism and Foreign Policy* (1953).
— *Twentieth-Century Socialism* (1956).

Stewart, M. *The British Approach to Politics*, 5th (revised) ed., (1965).
Strachey, J. *The Coming Struggle for Power* (1933).
— *The Nature of Capitalist Crisis* (1935).
— *Contemporary Capitalism* (1956).
— *End of Empire* (1959).
— *On the Prevention of War* (1962).
Tawney, R. H. *Equality* (1931).
— *The Acquisitive Society* (ed.) (1945).
— *The Attack, and Other Papers* (1953).
— *The Radical Tradition: twelve essays on politics, education and literature*
   (ed. Rita Hinden) (1964).

G. *Pamphlets*

(*a*) Fabian Tracts

Crosland, C. A. R. *Can Labour Win?* FT324 (1960).
Crossman, R. H. S. *Whither Socialism?* FT286 (1951).
— *Socialist Values in a Changing Civilisation* FT286 (1951).
— *Socialism and the New Despotism* FT298 (1956).
— *Labour in the Affluent Society* FT325 (1960).
Gaitskell, H. T. N. *Socialism and Nationalisation* FT300 (1956).
Healey, D. and Freeman, J. *Rearmament – How Far?* FT288 (1951).
Jay, D. *Beyond State Monopoly* FT320 (1959).
Jay, D. and Jenkins, R. *The Common Market Debate* FT341 (Fabian
   International Bureau, 1962).
Stewart, M. *Policy and Weapons in the Nuclear Age* FT296 (1955).
Strachey, J. *The Pursuit of Peace* FT329 (1960).

(*b*) Fabian Research Series

Albu, A. *Management in Transition* FRS No. 68 (1942).
Albu, A. and Hewett, N. *The Anatomy of Private Industry* FRS No. 145
   (1951).
Mikardo, I. *The Second Five Years* FRS No. 124 (1948).

(*c*) Other Pamphlets

Gaitskell, H. T. N. *The Challenge of Coexistence* (Harvard Lectures,
   1957).
— *Recent Developments in British Socialist Thinking* (1955).
Healey, D. *Neutralism* (1955).
Jay, D. *The Truth about the Common Market* (A Forward Britain
   Movement publication, 1962).

Keep Left (*New Statesman* publications, 1947).
Keeping Left (1950).
One Way Only (*Tribune* pamphlet, 1951).
Strachey, J. *Scrap ALL the H-Bombs* (1958).

H. *Articles*

Abrams, M. 'The Roots of Working Class Conservatism', in
    Encounter (May 1960).
— 'Why Labour Has Lost Elections', in *Socialist Commentary* (Jul
    1960).
Albu, A. 'Proposals for Industrial Reform', in *Socialist Commentary*
    (Sep 1952).
Balogh, T. 'Fabians at Sea', in *Tribune* (30 May 1952).
Bevan, A. 'The Fatuity of Coalition', in *Tribune* (13–26 Jun 1952).
Crick, B. 'Socialist Literature in the Fifties', in *Political Quarterly*
    (Jul–Sep 1960).
Crosland, C. A. R. 'Function of Public Enterprise', in *Socialist
    Commentary* (Feb 1950).
— 'Monopoly Legislation', in *Socialist Commentary* (Jan 1951).
— 'Thoughts on Nationalisation', in *Socialist Commentary* (Jan–Apr
    1956).
— 'British Labour's Crucial Meeting', in *New Leader* (3 Oct
    1960).
Epstein, L. 'Who Makes British Party Policy: British Labour
    1960–1961', in *Mid-West Journal of Political Science* (2 May
    1962).
Ewant, W., Anton, P. W., Best, A. A., and Thompson, J. 'Industrial
    Assurance', in *Socialist Commentary* (Feb 1950).
Fliess, W. 'Rearmament of Germany – Now or Later?', in *Socialist
    Commentary* (Mar 1951).
Healey, D. 'A Chance for Hungary's Socialists', in *Tribune* (14 Feb
    1951).
— 'Britain and Europe', in *Socialist Commentary* (May 1951).
— 'The Defence of Western Europe', in *Socialist Commentary* (Oct
    1951).
— 'When Shrimps Learn to Whistle', in *International Affairs* (Jan
    1956).
— 'Political Objections to British Entry into the Common Market',
    in *Observer* (25 May 1961).
Hindell, K. and Williams, P. 'Scarborough and Blackpool', in
    Political Quarterly (Jul–Sep 1962).

Jay, D. 'The Real Choice', in *New Statesman* (25 May 1962).

McCulloch, E. 'Workshop Representation', in *Socialist Commentary* (Aug 1951).

Robens, A. 'The Human Factor in Industry', in *Socialist Commentary* (Jul 1952).

Roper, J. 'Joint Consultation', in *Socialist Commentary* (Feb 1951).

Rose, R. 'Parties, Factions and Tendencies in Britain', in *Political Studies* (Feb 1964).

Rose, S. 'Back to Clause VIII', in *Socialist Commentary* (May 1960).

— 'Thoughts on the Constitution', in *Socialist Commentary* (Sep 1960).

Tawney, R. H. 'British Socialism Today', in *Socialist Commentary* (Jun 1952).

Turner, H. A. 'Is Joint Consultation Enough?', in *Socialist Commentary* (Jun 1952).

— 'Labour's Diminishing Vote', in *Guardian* (20 Oct 1959).

Younger, K. 'Germany and Western Defence', in *Socialist Commentary* (May 1952).

I. Editorials in Socialist Commentary

'French Working Class Unity' (Sep 1945).

'Britain and the Big Two' (Mar 1946).

'After the Moscow Conference' (May 1947).

'The Lessons of Czechoslovakia' (Apr 1948).

'The Atlantic Pact' (Mar 1949).

'For Better or for Worse' (Jan 1951).

'UNO and China' (Feb 1951).

'One Way Only' (Aug 1951).

'Defence of Western Europe' (Oct 1951).

'Europe Asks Why' (Jan 1952).

'Thoughts on Nationalisation' Symposium (Feb 1952).

'Militancy for What' (May 1952).

'A Socialist Foreign Policy' (Oct 1952).

'Uncle Sam' (Apr 1952).

'Working with the U.S.' (Feb 1954).

J. Broadsheets

A Manifesto Addressed to the Labour Movement (1960).

Counterblast – A Declaration for Labour Youth (1961).

SECONDARY SOURCES

A. *Autobiographies and Memoirs*

Attlee, C. R. *As It Happened* (1954).
Brockway, F. *Outside the Right* (1963).
Dalton, H. *High Tide and After* (1962).
Horner, A. *Incorrigible Rebel* (1960).
Lord Morrison of Lambeth, *Herbert Morrison, An Autobiography* (1960).
Shinwell, E. *Conflict without Malice* (1955).

B. *Biographies*

Foot, M. *Aneurin Bevan* (1962).
Jenkins, R. *Mr Attlee* (1948).
Krug, M. *Aneurin Bevan: Cautious Rebel* (New York, 1961).
Rodgers, W. T. (ed.), *Hugh Gaitskell: 1906–1963* (1964).

C. *Other Works*

(a) Books

Abrams, M. and Rose, R. *Must Labour Lose?* (1960).
Bagwell, P. S. *The Railwaymen* (1963).
Barry, E. *Nationalisation in British Politics* (1965).
Beer, S. H. *Modern British Politics* (1965).
Bevan, A. *In Place of Fear* (1952).
Burns, E. *Right-Wing Labour: Its Theory and Practice* (1961).
Butler, D. E. and Freeman, J. *British Political Facts 1900–1967* (1968).
Campbell, J. R. *Some Economic Illusions* (1959).
Caute, D. *The Left in Europe Since 1789* (1965).
Clegg, H. A. *General Union in a Changing Society* (1964).
Cole, G. D. H. *A Short History of the British Working-Class Movement*, vol. III (1948).
Donoughue, B. and Rodgers, W. T. *The People into Parliament* (1966).
Driver, C. P. *The Disarmers: a study in protest* (1964).
Epstein, L. *Britain – Uneasy Ally* (1953).
Harrison, M. *Trade Unions and the Labour Party Since 1945* (1960).
Healey, D. (ed.), *The Curtain Falls* (1951).
Hunter, L. *The Road to Brighton Pier* (1959).
Labedz, L. (ed.), *Revisionism: essays on the history of Marxist ideas* (1962).
McKenzie, R. T. *British Political Parties*, 2nd (revised) edition (1964).
Meehan, E. J. *The British Left Wing and Foreign Policy: a study of the influence of ideology* (New Brunswick, 1960).

Miliband, R. *Parliamentary Socialism: a study in the politics of Labour* (1961).
Mitchell, Joan. *Crisis in Britain, 1951* (1963).
Mulley, F. W. *The Politics of Western Defence* (1962).
Noel-Baker, P. *The Arms Race: a programme for world disarmament* (1958).
Page-Arnot, R. *The Miners* (1949).
Pritt, D. N. *The Labour Government, 1945–51* (1963).
Shinwell, E. *The Labour Story* (1963).
Sissons, M. and French, P. (eds), *Age of Austerity* (1963).
Trenaman, J. and McQuail, D. *Television and the Political Image: a study of the impact of television on the 1959 General Election* (1961).
Weiner, H. *British Labour and Public Ownership* (Washington, 1960).
Lord Windlesham. *Communication and the Political Process* (1966).

(b) Theses and Dissertations

Childs, D. H. 'The Development of Socialist Thought in the SPD 1945–58' (PhD thesis University of London, 1961: deposited in the British Library of Political and Economic Science).
Meehan, E. J. 'The British "Left" and Foreign Policy 1945–51' (PhD thesis: deposited in the British Library of Political and Economic Science).

D. *Periodicals and Journals*

American Political Science Review
Encounter
Forward
International Affairs
New Statesman
Political Studies
Political Quarterly
New Leader
Socialist Commentary
Spectator
Tribune
Amalgamated Engineering Union Journal
National Union of General and Municipal Workers' Journal
Transport and General Workers' Union Record

E. *Newspapers*

Daily Telegraph
Daily Herald
Manchester Guardian ✗
Observer ✗
News Chronicle ✗
The Times ✓
Sunday Times ✓

Index

Page numbers in italic refer to the main treatment of subject

Abrams, Mark, 144, 148 n. 1, 165
Abse, Leo, 229
Aero-engine industry, 46
Ainsley, J., 217 n. 1, 229
Aircraft industry, 46, 54, 108
Albu, Austen, 63, 65, 74, 149, 217 n. 1, 229
Amalgamated Engineering Union (AEU), 29, 110, 171, 172, 173, 193, 194, 199, 220, 222, 225
Annual Conference: power of, 11; composition of, 12; conflict with PLP, 152–4; sovereignty of, 249. *See also* Parliamentary Labour Party; National Executive Committee
Association of Supervisory Staffs, Executives and Technicians (ASSET), 230 n. 1
Attlee, Clement, 9, 11, 12, 14, 19, 22, 23, 40, 41, 127; attitude to Leadership, 10; attitude to Bevan, 28; support for New Fabian Essays, 67; on Socialist Union, 78; on German rearmament, 126; *New Statesman* article, 194

Barnett, Guy, 218, 229
Bartlett, C., 220
Beard, W. B., 220
Beer, Professor Samuel, 7
Bence, Cyril, 217 n. 1, 229
Bernstein, Eduard, 8, 81, 87, 145
Bevan, Aneurin, 4, 9, 21, 23, 28, 32, 36, 37, 46, 128, 135, 141, 155 n. 1, 163, 187, 193; attacks NUM leaders, 31; candidate for Treasurer, 39; defeated for Leadership, 41; criticises 'new thinkers', 61; on nudity, 182; on the Commonwealth and the bomb, 184–5
'Bevanism': the antecedents of, 19–21; in action, 21–3; end of, 23
Bevanites, the, 5, 19, 27, 35, 67, 77, 250; Attlee's attitude towards, 10; motion to abandon, 23
Bevin, Ernest, 1, 24, 25, 69, 112, 120; his anti-communism, 3; on German character, 130
Birch, A., 110, 129 n. 2, 220, 231
Blit, Lucjan, 68, 118
Blue Streak rocket, cancellation of, 179, 189–92
Blyton, W., 217 n. 1, 229
Bottomley, Arthur, 229
Bowman, Sir James, 29
Boyd, J. M., 219
Boyden, J., 217 n. 1
Braddock, Mrs E., 217 n. 1
Bradley, Tom, 218, 229
Bray, Jeremy, 218, 229
British rearmament, *see* Rearmament
Brown, George, 155 n. 1, 202, 203, 219, 229, 241, 242; on Clause IV, 168; on British bomb, 190; on over-reliance on nuclear weapons, 200; on NATO strategy, 204
Burnham, James, 83

Callaghan, James, 128, 219, 229, 230, 241, 242
Campaign, 212, 215, 217, 221, 223, 228

Campaign for Democratic Socialism (CDS), 76, 208, *209–36*; first stirrings, 209–12; the policy of, 212–16; support for, 216–25; success and importance of, 225–7; and the Common Market, 227–31

Campaign for Nuclear Disarmament (CND), 195, 211. *See also* Unilateralism

Capital-gains tax, *see* Taxation policy

Capitalism, transition from, 64; transfer of power within, 83–7; separation of ownership and control, 86–7. *See also* Socialism

Carron, William, 33, 110, 220, 222, 231

Casasola, R. W., 129, 132 n. 3

Castle, Mrs Barbara, 29, 149, 163

Cement industry, 45, 46, 48

Chapman, D., 217 n. 1, 229

Chemical industry, 52

Chester, Sir G., 29

Chetwynd, G., 217 n. 1, 229

Childs, David, 8

Christian Socialism, 91

Churchill, Winston, 130 n. 1, 178

'Classless society', 87, 88, 145, 164. *See also* Marxism

Clause IV, 1, 95, 142, 147, 148, 155, 156, 157, 208, 209, 215, 226, 245, 253; the debate on, *158–77*

Clause X, 169

Cole, G. D. H., 1, 62, 87, 93

'Committee of 12', 198, 199, 200

Common Market, the, 214, *227–36*, 238, 251; classification of 'pro' and 'anti' M.P.s, 229; arguments for and against British entry into, 231–6; Gaitskell's view, 235–6

Communists, British: infiltration into constituency parties, 38; CDS on, 213

Conscription, 20 n. 2, 30. *See also* Defence

Conservative Party, the, 1, 50, 189

Cooper, Jack, 25, 220, 230, 231

'Co-operation', *90–1*

Cotton industry, 46

Counterblast, 225

Cousins, Frank, 141 n. 2, 173, 199; on *Industry and Society*, 109; on NATO, 195, 198

Crawford, J., 220

Crick, Bernard, *97–8*

Cripps, Sir Stafford, 29, 66

Cronin, J., 217 n. 1, 229

Crosland, C. A. R., 8, 63, 82, 87, 88, 99, 100, 101, 102, 104, 112, 150 n. 1, 155, 159, 166, 209, 210, 217 n. 1, 229, 250; New Fabian Essay, 64–5; views on the transfer of economic power, 83–6; on equality, 89; on the co-operative ideal, 90; on comprehensive education, 91; on planning, 96; on capital-gains tax, 105–6; on party crisis, 156–7

Crossman, R. H. S., 20, 22, 62, 84, 87, 206, 212, 245; a revisionist approach, 63–4; on the threat of the 'managerial society', 85; on NATO, 198; on conscription, 201; on party sovereignty, 249

Dalton, Hugh, 40, 93, 101, 128, 155 n. 2; and Gaitskell, 36; on German rearmament, 127

Dalyell, Tam, 218, 229

Davies, Ernest, 60, 100

de Freitas, Sir G., 217 n. 1, 229

Deakin, Arthur, 10, 27, 28, 32, 50, 58, 173 n. 1; suspicion of communism, 26; impressed by Gaitskell, 38

Defence: 1952 statement on, 21–2; 1955 statement on, 134; hydrogen bomb and, 134–7; conscription, 136–7; Gaitskell–Healey draft on, 156, 198, 199, 200, 205, 206; the British bomb, *179–89*; NATO strategy, *199–206*; American bases in Britain, 205–6; the importance of, *206–8*. *See also* Nuclear weapons

Delargy, H., 227 n. 1
Diamond, J., 217 n. 1, 229
Dickson, H., 210 n. 2
Donnelly, Desmond, 129 n. 3, 217 n. 1, 229
Donoughue, Bernard, 218 n. 1
Douglas-Home, Sir Alec, 247
Douglass, H., 220
Dumont, A., 210 n. 2
Duncan, Sir Andrew, 47
Durbin, Evan, 8, 64, 87, 92, 93, 145

Ede, J. Chuter, 128
Eden, Sir Anthony, 136
Education policy, 63, 91
Edwards, Bob, 227 n. 1
Engineering industry, 53–4
'Equality', 87, 88; Jenkins's view of, 65, 88–9; Crossman's view of, 89; Crosland's view of, 89; Socialist Union's view of, 89; CDS and, 213; principle in relation to the Common Market, 232. *See also* Social justice
'Equality of opportunity', 65, 90
European Economic Community, *see* Common Market
European Free Trade Association, 230
European unity, 72. *See also* Common Market
Evans, Sir Lincoln, 29

Fabian Society, the, 53, 62, 81, 209
Fabianism, 65
Fienburgh, Wilfred, 51
Filson, Andrew, 67
Fitch, A., 217 n. 1, 229
Flanders, Allan, 68
Fletcher, Eric, 217 n. 1, 229
Fliess, Walter, 68
Foot, Sir Dingle, 229
Foot, Michael, 20, 22; attitude towards Parliament, 5; attitude towards Leadership, 154; on first use of nuclear weapons, 202

'Freedom', *91–3*
Freeman, John, 6, 21, 118 n. 4
Friends of Socialist Commentary, 68. See also *Socialist Commentary*

Gaitskell, Hugh, 7, 8, 15, 21, 23, 28, 60, 68, 93, 99, 100, 122, 123, 124, 132, 135, 141, 142, 146, 148, 159, 166, 170, 176, 177, 184, 185, 189, 191, 199, 201, 202, 203, 204, 205, 207, 222, 224, 226, 228, 229, 230, 248; early career in Government, 35–6; placings in Shadow Cabinet polls, 37; contests Treasurership, 38–40; Leader of Party, 41; on the separation of 'ownership' and 'control', 86–7; on public corporations as investment trusts, 102; on capital-gains tax, 105; on the balance of power, 119; on summitry, 136; on realignment of outlook, 143; Leadership of, *145–7*; his socialist priorities, *159–62*; and Douglas Jay, 164; and Clause IV, 166–7; setback on Clause IV, 171–2; on dependence on United States, 181; and the British bomb, 191–2; and neutralism, 193–6; victory in 1961, 208; CDS and, 214–16; on the Common Market, 234–6; political appeal of, *235–6*; his legacy to Labour, 237–40
Gaitskell–Healey draft, *see* Defence
Gallup Poll, 150, 164, 165
Gardner, Ben, 33
Gaullism, nuclear, 181
German rearmament, 24, 30, 113, 121, *125–34*, 178; *Socialist Commentary* and, 71; conditions for, 126; Attlee's attitude towards, 127; division in PLP on, 128–9; arguments for and against, 129–33
Ginsburg, D., 217 n. 1, 229
Godwin, Miss A., 220
Gooch, Edwin, 168

Gordon Walker, Patrick, 81, 97, 155, 184, 210, 219, 229, 230
Grant, A., 210 n. 2
Gray, Jack, 68
Green, G. F., 68
Greene, S., 220
Greenwood, Anthony, 168, 186
Greenwood, Arthur: death of, 37
Grey, C., 217 n. 1, 229
Griffiths, James, 22, 37, 73, 78, 120, 155 n. 1
Gunter, Ray, 229

Hannan, W., 217 n. 1, 229
Hayday, F., 220
Hayman, H., 217 n. 1, 229
Healey, Denis, 8, 63, 72, 112, 118, 120 nn. 2 and 3, 126, 130, 191, 201, 203, 204, 219, 229, 230, 250; New Fabian Essay, 65–6; attitude towards neutralism, 73, 196; on power politics, 113; on the United States, 116; on the Common Market, 233–4
Hinden, Dr Rita, 68, 71, 72, 80, 144 n. 2
Hockton, T. H., 210 n. 2
Horner, Arthur, 31
Horrabin, Frank, 68
Houghton, A. D., 229
Howell, Denis, 210, 218, 229
Hoy, J., 217 n. 1, 229
Hughes, H., 217 n. 1, 229

Image, see Party image
Immigration, 215
Independent Labour Party, 91
Industrial Assurance, nationalisation of, 45–6, 47, 48, 52–3
Industrial democracy, 59
Insurance, nationalisation of, 46
Irving, S., 217 n. 1, 229

Jay, Douglas, 87, 88, 103, 112, 155, 165, 167 n. 2, 169, 229, 250; on liberty, 92; on taxation, 105; on Labour's 'working class' image, 163; on nationalisation, 163–4; on the Common Market, 232–3
Jeger, George, 217 n. 1, 229
Jenkins, Roy, 8, 63, 81, 87, 112, 155, 217 n. 1, 229, 236; New Fabian Essay, 65; on equality, 88–9; on the mixed-economy, 95; on profits, 103; on 'ownership' and 'control', 104
Johnson, Carol, 229
Jones, D., 217 n. 1
Jones, Ernest, 31
Jones, S., 210 n. 2

Keep Left group, 4, 6, 47; the publication, 20, 46
Keeping Left, 20, 46, 101
Kennedy, J. F., 192 n. 2, 197
Keynes, J. M., 96
King, H., 217 n. 1, 229
Kissinger, Henry, 201
Korean War, 36, 49, 70, 117, 121, 122–3

Land, nationalisation of, 52, 108
Laski, Harold, 66
Lawther, Sir William, 25, 26, 31, 32, 38
Lee, Miss Jennie, 22
Lewis, W. A., 68
Liberal Party, the, 179
Liberty, see Freedom
Listowel, Lord, 219
Lloyd, Selwyn, 148
Lloyd George, Lady Megan, 217 n. 1, 229
Lohan, Emmeline, 68
Lowthian, G., 220

MacArthur, General Douglas, 123
Machine-tool industry, nationalisation of, 54, 57
McCann, J., 217 n. 1, 229
McCleavey, Frank, 168 n. 2
McDermot, Niall, 218

McKenzie, R. T., 249
Macmillan, Harold, 136, 192 n. 2, 238
McQuade, C., 210 n. 2
Madin, J., 68
Magee, B., 210 n. 2
Marquand, H., 229
Marshall Plan, 24, 30
Martin, A., 220
Marxism, attacked by: *Socialist Commentary*, 74; Socialist Union, 77; Crosland and Strachey, 82; Crossman, 85; Crick, 98; Healey, 113; CDS, 212–13; and the democratic process, 92; class view of, rejected, 145
Mason, Roy, 217 n. 1, 229
Matthews, D., 210 n. 2
Matthews, J. H., 210 n. 2
May, K., 210 n. 2
Mayhew, Christopher, 8, 112, 116, 217 n. 1, 250; on the unity of the West, 113
Meat Wholesaling industry, nationalisation of, 45
Mellish, R., 217 n. 1
Mendelson, John, 114
Mikardo, Ian, 20, 46, 63, 109, 110
Miliband, Dr Ralph, 7, 21
Millan, B., 217 n. 1
Miners, the, *see* National Union of Miners
Mining-machinery, nationalisation of, 57, 108
Mitchell, Joan, 122
Mixed-economy, 95. *See also* Public ownership; nationalisation; Jenkins, Roy
Morris, William, 90
Morrison, Herbert, 22, 35, 40, 49, 50, 51, 56, 123, 127, 130; political philosophy of, 41–2, 45; and the 'shopping-list', 43–5; reservations about Steel nationalisation, 47; on Germany, 130

Motor-car industry, nationalisation of, 54
Mulley, Fred, 68, 115, 217 n. 1, 229
Multi-lateralism, *182–5*. *See also* Defence; Nuclear weapons

Nabarro, Sir G., 245
National Executive Committee (NEC), 47, 48, 49, 50, 51, 107, 108, 143, 150, 156, 168, 170, 171, 172, 173, 175, 183, 215, 217, 222; responsibility and composition of, 13; union control of, 34; publishes *Labour Believes in Britain*, 45; publishes *Labour and the New Society*, 48; relationship to PLP, 152–4
National Health Service charges, 215
National Union of General and Municipal Workers (NUGMW), 24, 28, 29, 32, 33, 170, 172, 176, 193, 220; anti-communism of, 25–6; attitude towards the Common Market, 230
National Union of Mineworkers (NUM), 28, 29, 31, 33, 171, 172, 173, 176, 220
National Union of Railwaymen (NUR), 33, 171, 172, 173
National Union of Tailors and Garment Workers, 230 n. 1
National Union of Vehicle Builders, 176
Nationalisation: broad criteria for future, 44; proposals for in *Challenge to Britain*, 51–5; criticism of, 58–60, 100–1; *Socialist Commentary* and, 73–4; Gaitskell determined to erase image of, 147; proposals in 1959 election, 158; Clause IV dispute, *158–77. See also* Public ownership; 'Shopping-list'
Nelson, Leonard, 68
Neutralism: Mendelson's view of, 114; Healey's view of, 73, 196; as an issue, 192–9

New Fabian Essays, 62–8. *See also* Fabian Society; Crosland, C. A. R.; Healey, Denis; Jenkins, Roy
Nicholas, Harry, 107 n. 4, 168 n. 5
Noel-Baker, Francis, 65
Noel-Baker, Philip, 182, 217 n. 1
'Non-nuclear' Club, *see* Defence; Nuclear weapons
Norstadt, General, 201
North Atlantic Treaty Organisation (NATO), 24, 65, 113, 120, 136, 150, 179, 190, 193, 194, 196, 197, 198, 207, 214, 231, 248; *Socialist Commentary* and, 69–71; conventional aspect of, 134; strategy of, *199–205*. *See also* Defence; Nuclear weapons
Nuclear Gaullism, *see* Gaullism, nuclear
Nuclear weapons: Left's moral condemnation of, 114; Conservative Government's manufacture of, 134; testing of, 135–6; nuclear independence, 137; Gallup Poll on, 150; the British bomb, *179–89*; 'non-nuclear' club, *185–9*; over-reliance upon, *200–1*; the 'first use' of, *201–5*; difference between strategic and tactical, 202–3. *See also* Defence

O'Brien, Tom, 26, 220
O'Hagan, J., 220
Ollenhauer, Herr, 131
Owen, R., 210 n. 2

Padley, Walter, 91, 122, 170, 212, 222, 227 n. 1
Paget, Reginald, 51, 217 n. 1, 229
Pakenham, Frank, 62, 219
Parker, R., 210 n. 2
Parkin, Ben, 129, 131
Parliamentarianism, Strachey and, 65; Fabian essayists and, 66
Parliamentary Labour Party (PLP) 126, 128, 141, 216, 228, 230;

power of, 13–14; Gaitskell's strength in, 35–6; and the 'Movement' concept, 149–54; and the CDS, 218–19; ballot in, for Leader, 1963, 241–3
Party image, *143–9*, 164
Peart, F., 229
Phillips, Morgan, 143, 169 n. 1, 243
Pickstock, Frank, 210
Planning, *96–7*, *246–7*. *See also* Crosland, C. A. R.
Polaris, 206
Prentice, Reginald, 112, 130, 217 n. 1, 229
Price, F. L., 210 n. 2
Public ownership: Morrison and, 45; *Labour Believes in Britain*, 45–8; *Labour and the New Society*, 48–50; alternative methods of, 48, 101–4; and control, 95; rejection of as an 'end', 105–6; and Labour's image, 111; association of Labour with, 147–8; absence of, as an 'end' for Gaitskell, 161–2; and the mixed-economy, 169; Clause IV dispute, *158–77*. *See also* Nationalisation; 'Shopping-list'

Railwaymen, the, *see* National Union of Railwaymen
Ramsbottom, F. V. H., 210 n. 2
Rearmament, 30, *121–2*, 125; *Socialist Commentary* and, 71
Reynolds, G. W., 217 n. 1, 229
Road Haulage, nationalisation of, 46, 50, 53, 108, 111
Robens, Alfred, 69, 74, 210
Robinson, S., 220
Rodgers, G. R., 217 n. 1, 229
Rodgers, W. T., 209, 210, 211, 218, 229
Roper, J., 74
Rose, Dr Saul, 152
Russell, Bertrand, 184

Sandys, Duncan, 201

Saran, Mary, 68
Schuman Plan, 47, 72
Science and technology, 243, 244
Shanks, M., 210 n. 2
Shinwell, E., 29, 125 n. 2
Shipbuilding industry, nationalisation of, 46, 52, 54
'Shopping-list', 43-60
Smith, G. F., 220
Smith, R., 220
Social Democratic Party of West Germany (SPD), 131, 132
Social justice, 87, 88, 232. See also 'Equality'
Social welfare: Crosland's view of, 88; and the planned economy, 95-6; part of Labour's appeal in 1966, 246-7
Socialism: Morrison's view of, 45; Crosland's view of, 65; Tawney's view of, 74-5; Socialist Union's view of, 77; 'ends' of, 87-94; 'means' of achieving, 94-7; Gaitskell's brand of, 159-62; CDS's view of, 214-15
Socialist Campaign for Multilateral Disarmament, 182
Socialist Commentary, 9, 60, 62, 63, 68-76, 156; on nationalisation, 44, 58. See also Socialist Union; Friends of Socialist Commentary
'Socialist Foreign Policy', a: Healey on, 65-6; Socialist Commentary and, 72-3; Socialist Union and, 79; rejection by Revisionists, 112-21
Socialist International, 132
Socialist Union, 176-80, 213
Socialist Vanguard Group, 68
South-East Asia Treaty Organisation (SEATO), 9, 113
Soviet Union, the, 114, 115, 129, 130, 136, 178, 197, 231, 233; typical NEC attitude towards, 119-20; Bevan's view of, 120; CDS and, 213

Steel industry, 2, 46, 47, 48, 50, 53, 108, 111
Stewart, Michael, 114 n. 1, 229, 230; on disarmament, 181; on the Commonwealth and the bomb, 184-5; on neutralism, 196-7; attitude towards the Soviet Union, 197; on 'first use' of nuclear weapons, 202
Stokes, Richard, 51
Stonehouse, John, 153
Strachey, John, 63, 82, 87, 99, 112, 115, 159, 184, 191, 217 n. 1, 229; New Fabian Essay, 65; attitude towards parliamentarianism, 66; views on the transfer of economic power, 83-6; on the British bomb, 179; on multi-lateralism, 183; on balance of power, 197-8; on flexible response, 200-1; on 'first use' of nuclear weapons, 203
Strauss, George, 47, 217 n. 1, 229
Suez Crisis, 134
Sugar, nationalisation of, 45, 46, 48, 53
Sugar-refining, nationalisation of, 45
SPD, see Social-Democratic Party of West Germany

Tallon, W. M., 219
Tanner, Jack, 29, 33
Taverne, Richard, 210, 218, 229
Tawney, R. H., 74, 93
Taxation policy: Jay's contribution to, 88, 95; capital-gains tax, 105-6; and the Common Market, 232-3
Technology, see Science and technology
Thompson, A., 217 n. 1, 229
Thomson, G., 229
Tiffen, Jack, 141 n. 2
Titmuss, Professor Richard, 95
Tomney, F., 217 n. 1

Trade unions: the role of, *23–8*; unpopularity of, 145–6; Gallup Poll concerning, 165. *See also individual trade unions*

Trades Union Congress (TUC), 29, 205, 220

Transport and General Workers' Union (TGWU), 24, 28, 29, 31, 32, 33, 110, 171, 173, 194, 199, 205; anti-communism of, 26

Treasurership of the Labour Party, 29; contest for, *38–40*

Tribune, 9, 22, 52, 61, 70, 75, 79, 97, 110, 167, 169, 211, 225

'Triumvirate', the, *28–34*

Unilateralism, 30, 137. *See also* Campaign for Nuclear Disarmament

Union of Shop, Distributive and Allied Workers (USDAW), 110, 170, 173, 221, 222, 225, 231

United Nations, 71

United States, the, 114, 115, 121, 133, 136, 178, 181, 197, 231, 233; Healey and, 65; *Socialist Commentary* and, 69–70, 73; the Left and, 115–16; the Right and, 116–17; foreign policy of, denounced by the Left, 117; foreign policy of, supported by Revisionists, 117–19; Far Eastern policy of, and Labour, 122–5

U.S.S.R., *see* Soviet Union

Victory for Socialism (VFS), 210, 211

Walden, Brian, 210 n. 2

Walker, Miss H., 210 n. 2

Water, nationalisation of, 45–53

Waterhouse, R., 210 n. 2

Waterman, H. W., 210 n. 2

Watson, Sam, 26, 31, 32, 220, 231

Webb, Beatrice, 1

Webb, Sidney, 1

Webber, W. J. P., 220

Weber, Max, 97

Wells, Percy, 217 n. 1, 229

Wigg, George, 201, 245

Wilcock, C, 217 n. 1

Williams, Philip, 210

Williamson, Sir Thomas, 26, 38, 220; on 'factionalism', 27

Wilson, J. Harold, 14, 22, 23, 63, 154, 155 n. 1, 206, 212, 239, 248; resigns from the Government, 6, 21; and Bevan, 9; on common-ownership, 106; vindicated on re-armament, 125; moves motion on German rearmament, 128; on British bomb, 190; as Leader of the Party, *240–6*

Windlesham, Lord, 219, 220

Worswick, G. D. N., 68

Wright, L. T., 220

Wyatt, Woodrow, 169

Yates, Sir Tom, 220

Young, Michael, 43, 144 n. 2

Young Socialists, *see* Youth

Younger, Kenneth, 68, 72, 112, 126, 130

Youth: Labour's lack of appeal to, 146–7; Young Socialists, 225; a Declaration for Labour, 225